AF559885

CHILDREN WITH DISABILITIES

AWARENESS, ATTITUDE AND COMPETENCIES OF TEACHERS

CHILDREN WITH DISABILITIES

AWARENESS, ATTITUDE AND COMPETENCIES OF TEACHERS

By

Dr. G. Lokanadha Reddy

M.A., M.Ed., M.Phil., Ph.D.

Professor & Head

Department of Education

Periyar University

Salem–11

&

Dr. J. Sujathamalini

Lecturer

Avinashilingam Deemed University

Coimbatore

DISCOVERY PUBLISHING HOUSE

NEW DELHI-110002

Published by:

DISCOVERY PUBLISHING HOUSE PVT. LTD.
4383/4B, Ansari Road, Darya Ganj
New Delhi-110 002 (India)
Phone : +91-11-23279245; 23253475; 43596065
E-mail : discoverybooksindia@gmail.com
discoverypublishinghouse@gmail.com
namitwasan9@gmail.com
web : www.discoverypublishinggroup.com

First Published: **2006**
Reprinted: **2022**

ISBN: 978-81-8356-129-7

Children with Disabilities:
Awareness, Attitude and Competencies of Teachers

Printed at:
Infinity Imaging Systems
Delhi

Preface

Teachers play an important role in any educational system. He/she is an artist who moulds and shapes the physical, intellectual and moral powers of the children. The responsibility of the teacher working in special or integrated schools or normal schools is more when he/she is involved in dealing children with disabilities apart from normal children. In India, there are schools for special children like visually impaired, hearing impaired, mentally retarded, orthopaedically handicapped and also integrated schools for mainstreaming the disabled children. Apart from the above, in normal schools there are children with mild and moderate disabilities. These disabilities are unnoticed, unserved and ignored. Unless and untill such children's needs are met either in regular classroom or special classroom within the school, we cannot fulfil the aim of Universalization of Elementary Education and Equalisation of Educational Opportunity to All. To realise the goal of promoting equal educational opportunities, there is an urgent need to equip the existing and the would be teachers on different aspects of dealing children with disabilities. In fact, a teacher with good knowledge/awareness and attitude about the concept of disabilities, causes and characteristics, identification and assessment of children with disabilities, teaching and training methods, and guidance and counselling, will do better justice to the students with disabilities. For this, the teachers require specific competencies to perform diversified activities in various situations within and outside the school. The success of any teacher in the education of the disabled to a greater extent depends on the infrastructure facilities and the attitude of non-disabled peers towards their disabled peers.

The present investigation aimed to assess the awareness, attitude and competencies of special and normal school teachers in dealing children with disabilities. For this, the study developed rating scales to assess special and normal school teachers awareness and attitude towards children with disabilities and, competency assessment rating scale and checklist to assess the existing and required competencies of special and normal school teachers to deal children with disabilities. Similarly, it aimed to develop checklist to identify the infrastructure facilities available in special and normal schools for the disabled and peer attitude scale to assess the attitude of non-disabled peers towards their disabled peers. The focus of attention is also to find out the effect of independent variables of the teachers on their awareness, attitude and existing competencies. Further, the study aimed at predicting to what extent and how far the independent variables (gender, age, educational qualification, training in special education, years of experience, location of school, nature of school, category of school and type of school) influence the dependent variables (awareness, attitude and existing competencies). Attempts are also made to study the correlation between awareness and attitude, awareness and existing competencies and attitude and existing competencies. Likewise, the study attempted to estimate the dropout rate in special and normal schools keeping in mind the infrastructure facilities available in those schools.

The study covered two states i.e. Andhra Pradesh and Tamil Nadu. From each state two districts (Andhra Pradesh—Chittoor and Hyderabad districts; Tamil Nadu— Chennai and Madurai districts) are selected where all categories of special schools (VI, HI, MR and OH) are available. The total number of special schools covered in the two states is 84 and 76 normal schools in the same locality. All the teachers (Special schools— 660, Normal schools— 527) working in these schools are the sample of the study. Infrastructure facilities available in the schools are collected from the 160 schools heads. From each normal school, 5 students are randomly selected to know their attitude towards their disabled peers. Overall, 1187 teachers, 380 peers and 160 school heads formed the sample of the study.

The report is presented in five chapters. Chapter—I brings out the theoretical framework, need and importance, objectives, hypotheses, scope and limitations of the study. In chapter—II, review of literature is presented under the heads; studies on children with disabilities, teachers awareness about children with disabilities, teacher attitude towards children with disabilities and teacher competencies to deal children with disabilities. Chapter—III describes the development of the research tools, sampling, data collection and statistical techniques used in the study. Chapter—IV concerned with the data analysis, testing of hypotheses, presentation of the results and discussion in two parts. Part—I presents the descriptive analysis of special and normal school teachers awareness, attitude and competencies to deal children with disabilities. Part—II deals with differential analysis. In differential analysis, the difference between special and normal school teachers awareness, attitude and competencies; the effect of independent variables on the teachers awareness, attitude and competencies; the influence of independent variables on the dependent variable through stepwise multiple regression to predict to what extent and how far the independent variables are contributing to the dependent variables and; the relationship between awareness, attitude and competencies are presented. It also gives clear picture about the nature of infrastructure facilities available in special and normal schools with their corresponding percentage of dropout rate. This part also provides the attitude of non-disabled peers towards their disabled peers. In the last chapter, the summary of the investigation and its implications for policy formulation, planning and implementation are provided.

Any research work is an experience and joint venture of many research workers. This work is not far from this. I shall be failing in my duty, if I don't acknowledge their contribution and express my deep sense of gratitude and the word of thanks. First of all, I express my sense of gratitude to the Ministry of Social Justice and Empowerment, Government of India, New Delhi for providing adequate financial assistance to conduct this study. At the same time, with great reverence and respect.

I express my gratitude to Alagappa University Administration particularly, the Vice-chancellor and the Registrar for providing the adequate facilities and permitting me to carry out this scientific piece of work. I am also indebted to the Head of the Department of Education, Alagappa University for his support to carry out this work.

I fail in my duty if I don't acknowledge the contribution of Research Assistant Mrs. J. Sujathamalini and the Research Investigators Mr. K. Sundaram and Mr. D. Jawahar who worked in the project, without their assistance I might have not succeed in collecting, analysing and reporting the vast data for this study. I am also indebted to the special and normal school teachers and their school heads who served as the subjects of the study but for whose co-operation the investigation could not have been completed. Last but not least, I extend my thanks to Mr. A.M. Sivaraman, Sri Chandra Computers for his untiring work of entry of vast data, analysis and typing of this Project Report.

Dr. G. Lokanadha Reddy

Contents

Introduction

Concept, Meaning and Definition of Special Education

"Education is an allround drawing out of the best in child and man-body, mind and sprit."

—**Mahatma Gandhi**

Education promotes allround development of the child, which unites the soul, body and mind of an individual and helps in transmission of entire values. Education is increasingly being perceived as capable of modifying the economic scenario and transforming the dreams of millions of human beings for a better and higher quality of life into a reality. It is an effective system resulting in the development of learner's potentialities, competencies, interest, attitude and values. In the past, this potential educational right was denied for the disabled children. The National Policy on Education (1986) has made a significant contribution towards developing educational opportunity for the disabled children. The Programme of Action for implementation of the NPE, 1986 envisages education of a sizable number of the disabled in common with other children. The centrally sponsored scheme of Integrated Education for the Disabled (IED) children is geared to realise this objective.

Every individual is unique and hence 'special'. Education should bound to cater to the needs of all the individuals in compliance with the constitutional provision of equal opportunity. There are some individuals who by virtue of their physical and mental abilities require a more relevant or appropriate instruction than is usually available within formal and informal educational structures. A domain of education has been constructed to satisfy their learning requirements (Laura and Ashman, 1985). This domain is called 'Special Education'. Reddy et al. (2000) defined special education as 'specifically designed instruction that meets the unusual needs of special children. It requires special materials, teaching techniques or equipment and/or facilities. The prime aim of special education is drawing out and strengthening the special children's abilities. Related services like special transportation, psychological assessment, physical and occupational therapy, medical treatment and counselling also go hand in hand with special education.

Education of disabled children has basic concepts and goals in common with the education of all children. The children with visual impairment, hearing impairment, mental retardation and orthopaedically handicapped have feelings, emotions, drives and motives common to children in general. Along with those common characteristics there are some specific characteristics or handicap conditions that warrant special services in their educational programmes. It is obligatory to provide special services for exceptional children either in the regular classroom or special classes within the regular school and in special schools to strengthen their abilities and grow according to their potentialities. Such special services or special education may vary depending upon the type of disability.

Special Education for Different Categories of Children with Disabilities

Educational equality is not merely providing education in the same class with normal children, with same instruction. It demands to attend to the individual differences, needs, and the provision of special services to meet those needs. Teaching is not just confined to curriculum and instruction. It also involves managing the classroom, motivating the child to learn and meeting the needs of children.

There are children with mild and moderate degrees of visual impairment, hearing impairment, mental retardation and orthopaedic impairments, emotional or behaviour disorders apart from children with learning difficulties studying in schools. Some children are easily identified due to observable behaviour, but some need to be observed more carefully. As a teacher, one gets the opportunity to observe all the children in the initial grades in both academic and non-academic situations. This helps for early identification of children with disabilities. In turn, it facilitates to design individualised educational programmes to meet their learning requirements and adoption in the curriculum to provide learning experiences depending upon the degree of disability.

Special education helps to identify intra- and inter-individual differences. The general education principle is equally applicable to the area of special education. But something much more must be added to meet the needs of special children to compensate their disabilities. For example, Braille reading and writing for totally blind, large print materials and magnifying devices for low-vision children, hearing-aids for hearing impaired children, graded curriculum for mentally retarded and physical supportive services for orthopaedically handicapped help to compensate their disabilities and facilitate their learning to cope up with the normal children.

Peter Westwood (1998) proposes that effective teaching involves:

— the creation of a friendly, supportive learning environment,
— the presentation of the learning task in easy steps,
— resource materials at an appropriate readability level,
— direct teaching of task-approach strategies,
— clear modelling and demonstration by the teacher or other adult,
— provision for much guided practice with feedback,
— efficient use of available time,
— close monitoring of the child's progress,
— re-teaching particular skills wherever necessary,

— provision for successful independent practice and application and

— frequent revision of previously taught knowledge and skills.

To make the teaching effective a teacher has to perform diversified roles according to the needs of different categories of special children. Special education for different categories of children with disabilities can be explained as follows:

Visual Impairments

A child with seriously defective vision requires different techniques of instruction than the child who has normal vision. Teachers must adapt methods and materials in order to help the visually impaired to learn effectively.

Reddy and Sujathamalini (2000) pointed out that there are number of general factors that need to be considered when devising an appropriate teaching style for use to the child with a visual impairment. They are: (1) position, (2) presentation, (3) experiences, (4) expectations, (5) giving information and (6) speed of working.

Reddy and Rajaguru (1998) stated in his study that least restrictive environment facilitated the congenital blind children to have more divergent thinking ability. Reddy and Kusuma (2001) presented educational implications for various types of visual impairments such as—Albinism, aniridia, cataracts, coloboma, dislocation of lens, glaucoma, nystagmus, optic nerve atrophy, refractive errors, retinitus pigmentosa, retinoblastoma, retinopathy of prematurity and strabismus. Some of the educational implications are proper light arrangements, wearing glasses, magnifying devices and proper seating arrangements may help the child with aforesaid visual impairment.

The other groups who are partially sighted require large print or magnified print materials. Their visual acuity is very low (2/70 in the better eye). Their eyesight may be weak due to short-sightedness, long-sightedness, astigmatism, glaucoma or muscle detachment. The blind are those who need to be taught through braille or through aural methods. Their visual acuity may fall to 20/200. Such children must be prepared in pre-academic skills like braille reading, sensory training, auditory training and mobility training. Use of technological advance in teaching-learning process also plays a vital role in the education of the visually impaired.

Partially sighted children require better visual environment. Both lighting and decor need to be considered as these two factors are closely interrelated. As the colour of walls, floors and ceilings will greatly affect the amount of light arriving at a working surface, flexible and suitable lamp for better lighting should be used. Windows should be kept clean or covered with blinds to avoid glare from sunlight and shiny floors and work surface should be avoided as both should be of low reflectance. Blackboard with a matt surface is also required. Even without making any alterations to the lighting improving contrast can help a child with visual impairment to make more sense of the surrounding. Sensory training helps the visually impaired children to be independent in the society. To develop confidence in their surroundings it is necessary to create an environment within learning areas that does not present unexpected hazards or obstacles.

Hearing Impairment

Hearing impairment reduces or distorts our perception or knowledge of the world around us. A hearing impairment, whether permanent or fluctuating, adversely affects the child's performance in learning. 'Hearing impairment' as a generic term indicating a hearing disability which ranges in severity from mild to profound, includes the subsets of deaf and hard of hearing. A Deaf person is one whose hearing disability precludes successful processing of linguistic information through audition, with or without a hearing aid. A hard of hearing person is one who, generally, with the use of hearing aid, has residual hearing sufficient to enable successful processing of linguistic information through audition.

Educational programmes for hearing impaired children include oral approach and total communication approach. Oral approach includes auditory training and speech training. Total communication approach makes use of both oral approach and manual approach. Modifications of physical environment, instructional modifications, modifications of oral communication, modifications of written materials, peer tutoring and buddy system are some important techniques to teach speech and hearing impaired children in general education classroom. Use of residual hearing in teaching-learning process, use of microphones in teaching, avoiding external noises or disturbances within or outside the classroom, assisting through vision-based teaching to enhance better learning, use of centralised group hearing aid in the classroom, creating pleasant learning environment for hearing impaired children, modification of physical environment like changes in seating arrangements (placing students from background noise as open windows and doors, noisy hearing and cooling systems, making the child sit in the first row, turning the desks or chairs so that the child can face all other students and teachers) and use of overhead projector help hearing impaired children to note the points. Pictorial representation and graphics also help hearing impaired children's learning.

Reddy et al. (2004) presented various educational considerations for the children with hearing impairments. Use of hearing aids are discussed in detail for the effective use of residual hearing. The suggested teaching strategies for hearing impaired children by the authors are: use of curricular guide, developing unit plans, structuring the classroom, delivering instruction, teaching bottom-up skills, teaching study skills, helping the child to write, computer assisted learning, motivation, adapting Maslow's theory of needs, improving self concept and being efficient teacher. Importance of lip-reading, auditory training, and sign language are also stressed.

Mental Retardation

Children with mental retardation may be markedly different from the children in the next door in some ways, but also like them in others. Mental retardation refers to significantly sub-average general intellectual functioning resulting in or associated with impairments in adaptive behaviour and manifested during the developmental period. Mental retardation is classified into three groups, namely, educable, trainable and custodial.

Educational programme for mentally retarded children varies according to their degree of disability. The emphasis on academic skills will be more if the degree of retardation is less, whereas training in self help skills, community living and vocational training is the focus of the educational programmes for children with greater degree of retardation.

Reddy et al. (2004a) identified and listed out the causes and characteristics of mentally retarded. They grouped the causes under three categories—pre-natal, peri-natal and post-natal stages. Preventive measures such as nutritional diet during pregnancy, genetic counselling, avoiding X-rays during early pregnancy, avoiding improper intake of drugs, proper care during delivery and proper immunization were suggested. Basic academic skills and language development were suggested for educable mentally retarded. Self-help skills and vocational training were stressed in the education of trainable mentally retarded children. Education for severely or profound mentally retarded should be centered around self-help skills so as to make them independent as much as possible.

The concept individualisation of education is the appropriate theme, i.e. special method of instructing the educable mentally retarded. The basic principle of special education is learning by doing. Educable mentally retarded children learn better through experiences. In teaching mentally retarded, teachers should give due importance to the concept of maturation and readiness to learn. Teaching technique should include considerable amount of repetition so that they can retain the learned materials. Modular graded instruction with appropriate teacher support system in short duration will be very effective for retarded children. Educating trainable mentally retarded should centre upon self-care skills, and vocational training. Real life situations, experiences and group activities should be given to the mentally retarded children. Educational programmes for severe and profoundly retarded focus on preparing them to live as independently as possible. Family and community involvement also plays a vital role in the education of mentally retarded.

Orthopaedically Handicapped

Crippled children are those who have interference with the normal functioning of the bones, joints, muscles to such an extent that special arrangements are required to accommodate them in regular classes. Such children have problems like congenital anomalies such as dislocated hips or joints, clubbed foot, spinal bifida, poliomyelitis and tuberculosis of the bones or joints. If crippling conditions are so severe, then the children require assistance on either temporary or permanent basis. Children who are temporarily hospitalised can be integrated, but in the case of permanently hospitalised, hospital bound programmes are needed. Orthopaedically impaired children are easily identified as this disability is more visible than others like partially sighted, hearing impaired etc.

Modern technology has enabled the non-speaking to speak, the non-hearing to hear, and the non-seeing to see. This is achieved only if the professionals working for the disabled recognise the dramatic increase in the application of modern technology to adaptive assistive devices for the handicapped. Reddy et al. (1998) delineated the use of assistive technology for the children with learning disability. They presented the use of word processor, speech synthesiser, voice-input and word recognition programmes, talking story books, hand calculators, voice mail, listening to books on tape and hand held spelling devices are of much use for the children with learning disabilities.

Reddy (2003) also suggested some of the aids and devices that can be used to overcome visual and auditory difficulties. Some of them are: lamps with variable intensifiers, large type books, bolt line paper, talking calculators, optacon, electronic braille machines, reading machines, CCTV, view scan, travel devices, tape recorders and automatic page trainers. Adaptive-assistive devices may be beneficial to the disabled, but they should be provided with careful examination of their potential effect. It allows the physically disabled person to pursue activities necessary to sustain life. The dorsal feeding splints are structured to support the palm, wrist and forearm. Institutional relaxation chairs allow the person with no sitting balance and a severely involved trunk area to sit comfortably. Wheel chairs, hoists, canes, walkers and crutches help the physically handicapped to move either vertically or horizontally. Stair climbing wheel chairs provide better mobility than the standard wheel chairs.

The OH children are assisted with suitable prosthetic and orthotic devices so as to enable them to function as normal as possible. They are in need of physical environment modifications in classroom like seating arrangements, space to move around within classroom and easy transportation. These children do not have any learning problems whereas, they face problems in participation in regular classroom activities. The teacher should therefore be aware of the facilities to be provided to these children in classroom set up.

Thus, different categories of disabled children require different types of educational modifications. A teacher with multi-talents will provide well designed educational programme based on the nature, type and degree of disability to circumvent their disabilities and capitalise their abilities.

Need for Integration of Children with Disabilities in Normal Schools

Integration of disabled children with normal children is nothing but the provision of least restrictive environment for the disabled children. This approach helps the disabled children to grow and develop like normal children. It promotes healthy social relationships between normal and disabled children and provides equal educational opportunity. It enhance disabled children's growth and development on par with their normal peers. It gives a chance to participate in all academic and non-academic activities in society. Integration also leads to acceptance of disabled children by the society.

Promotion of positive attitude towards the disabled develops healthy social relationships among individuals. Integration helps to raise the disabled children's standard of living and prepares them to live independently. It reduces psychological problems of disabled children. Basic readiness skills are required to integrate disabled children more effectively. Special and regular school teachers require multi-talents and play diversified roles to handle these children. Special techniques are used only in the case of children with severe disabilities and for developing only the basic academic skills. The mildly disabled do not require such special skills and they need only modifications in the instruction. After learning special skills even the severely disabled children can be educated in regular schools with suitable assistive devices. A general teacher has to supervise and facilitate learning of these children in the normal classroom set up. Special educational needs of most of the children with disabilities can be met effectively in mainstream schools. Teacher has the responsibility for overall curricular experiences of these children. To fulfil this responsibility the teacher should possess better awareness about the concept, nature, type and educational requirements to deal children with disabilities. To understand the strengths and weaknesses, every teacher should possess positive attitude towards children with disabilities. Apart from awareness and attitude a teacher should exhibit specific competencies to plan educational programme for the children with disabilities. For better integration a teacher with better awareness, positive attitude and specific competencies can do better justice to the children with disabilities. Successful promotion of integration for the children with disabilities is achieved certainly if they possess the aforesaid components. Integration warrants whole school approach in which teacher plays a vital role.

The integration of students with special needs into regular classes must involve inclusive curricular rather than individual programming. The individualised education plan for the children with disabilities should indicate clearly not only what the students need to do which is different from the rest of the class, but also the areas of the curriculum where he or she can be counted in with the others. Campbell and Ramey (1994) and Wasik and Karweit (1994) suggest that early intervention in the pre-school period can have extremely beneficial outcomes in terms of higher success rates when the children begin formal schooling. The type of classroom learning environment created by the teacher and the instructional approach used, can both markedly influence the development of self-management and independence in children. The teacher should use cognitive and metacognitive strategies in their instruction to deal children with learning difficulties and behaviour disorders (Santhakumari, 2003; Shyamala, 2004 and Jayaprabha, 2003). Cognitive behaviour modification strategies are closely related to metacognitive training (Polloway and Patton, 1993). This strategy is very useful for decreasing undesirable behaviour and in increasing desirable behaviour among mentally retarded and emotionally disturbed children. A teacher should adopt the above strategies effectively to deal children with disabilities. A competent teacher with multi-talents use innovative strategies effectively to educate the children with diversified needs in integrated set up.

Role of Teachers in Dealing Children with Disabilities

According to Dr. Radhakrishnan, 'the teacher acts as the pivot for the transmission of intellectual traditions and technical skills from generation to generation and helps to keep the lamp of civilization burning'. The teacher is the centre point of any educational system. Teacher shapes and moulds the personality of the child. A teacher should realise that all children are special and that they have both strengths and weaknesses. To meet their learning requirements effectively the teacher should have a thorough understanding of the nature of disabilities/abilities and the academic and non-academic problems exhibited by them. To render their jobs effectively they should be familiar with the concept of disabilities, causes and characteristics, identification and assessment, teaching and training methods and guidance and counselling which are broadly classified under planning, teaching and guidance and counselling roles.

Planning Roles

A good teacher should possess knowledge about the nature and type of disabilities in children. This knowledge will promote better awareness on the concept of children with disabilities and develop positive attitude towards children with disabilities. Better awareness and right attitude evolve an inner urge to plan educational programme to meet the learning requirements of children with disabilities. Planning role starts from identification and assessment. To deal children with disabilities the foremost important competency is to identify and assess the level of disabilities in children. A teacher should know various assessment procedures to identify the disabilities. Assessment of young children is difficult. It is also difficult for teachers to distinguish between developmental delay and retardation.

Reddy and Kusuma (1995) listed out various causes for mental retardation, pre-natal causes like genetic irregularities, chromosomal defects, cretinism, microcephaly and macrocephaly were discussed. Problems during pregnancy, infections, Rh incompatibility, prolonged labour, forceps delivery, deprivation of oxygen, problems related to mother's small pelvis, severe jaundice in children immediately after birth, head injuries, brain tumors, infectious diseases, meningitis and encephalitis and lead located toys also result in mental retardation. Preventive measures such as good medical services, genetic counselling, conducting tests like amniocentesis, dietary treatment of PKU, proper maternal nutrition, proper vaccination, genetic counselling and community awareness were suggested to prevent mental retardation.

Reddy et al. (2004a) discussed in detail about the causes and characteristics of mental retardation and factors related to mental retardation in their book on *Mental Retardation : Education and Rehabilitation Services*. Identification and assessment procedures like testing general intelligence and adaptive behaviour were presented. Education for educable, trainable and severe or profound mentally retarded were discussed. Importance of basic academic skills were stressed in the education of educable apart from training in self help skills. Vocational training and self help skills were focussed in the education of trainable. On the other hand, self-care skills training was stressed in education of severely retarded.

Knowledge on the above aspects and observation and evaluation of intra individual strengths and weaknesses help the teacher to identify children with disabilities. A good teacher should possess the ability to administer formal and informal tests to assess the children with disabilities. Pitfalls in the educational programmes can be avoided if identification and assessment task is carried out properly. This is possible only if a teacher possesses better knowledge in these aspects. Planning individualised educational programme for each child is also an important task in planning. It also involves to set short-term goals and long-term goals and provision of least restrictive environment which pave a way for effective teaching-learning process.

Teaching Role

A teacher's major role in any educational system is teaching. A good teacher is able to provide appropriate placement services for the children with disabilities. It is important that the teachers require specific talents to develop individualised educational programme for the children with disabilities based on the degree of disability. A good teacher has the ability to use various strategies like cognitive, metacognitive and cognitive behaviour modification techniques to deal children with disabilities. Studies by Sathakumari (2003), Shyamala (2004) and Jayaprabha (2003) proved that effective use of above strategies are of much use in the education of children with disabilities.

Reddy and Shyamala (2003) stated that constructivism develops thinking skills, communication and social skills, encourages alternative method of assessment, helps students to transfer skills to the real world and promotes intrinsic motivation to learn. Thinking and constructivism are the big ideas in education.

The same authors (2004) also studied the thinking errors and antisocial behaviour of high school students. Constructive strategies such as co-operative learning, problem solving, role playing and through class discussions a teacher can help students to develop critical thinking skills to denounce thinking errors and thereby, antisocial behaviour.

Sivakami (2000) and Reddy and Sivakami (1999) discussed and used certain strategies to overcome learning disabilities in English. Such strategies are effectively used only by the teachers who are well trained and well informed about various instructional strategies.

They highlighted in their article about the concept of reading, difficulties, characteristics and identification and assessment of reading difficulties. Remedial measures have also been suggested to overcome reading difficulties. Remedial measures include overcoming auditory and visual problems by providing practice in pronunciation, listening, repetition, matching sounds, visual copying, visual discrimination, visual sequencing, visual rhymes, form perception, programmed series, and training in visual analysis and synthesis.

Reddy and Sujathamalini (2003) stressed the need to use strategies like crisis intervention, lifespan interview techniques, reality therapy, self-control curriculum and social learning therapy to develop social competence among disabled pupils.

A competent teacher should be able to sequence the instructional programme with appropriate duration. Communicative ability is an important skill that every teacher should possess. Hence, an effective communication helps in educating children with speech and language difficulties and communication difficulties. A good teacher prepares educational programmes based on the children's current performance level and degree of disability. This helps the children to achieve the set goal effectively. Considering the factors related to disabilities (Kusuma Harinath, 2000), the provision of assistive devices, materials and aids for the children with disabilities are to be carried out by a competent teacher. Effective teacher will make use of integrated therapy in teaching mentally retarded children. A teacher should be proficient in plus curriculum while handling children with visual impairment. A competent teacher is able to provide self-directed learning materials. A good teacher is able to provide peer tutoring, co-operative learning and group learning. An effective and talented teacher is always well informed about the technological advances available for the children with disabilities.

Reddy (2003) listed out some of the recent technological advances available for the children with disabilities. Non-optical aids such as book stands, felt tip pens, acetate placed over the printed page to darken the print, lamps with variable intensifiers, large type books, bolt line paper, page makers, braille writer, raised line drawing board, cubarith slate, abacus and raised line paper were useful for the children with visual impairments. Cassettes, tape recorders, talking books, talking calculators, reading machine, optacon, closed circuit television, view scan, computers, talking clocks, computers with voice input, automatic page turners, institutional relaxation chairs, travel devices like long canes, wheel chairs, walkers and crutches, hand cycles and artificial legs and hands are some of the devices used for different categories of children with disabilities. Appropriate technological devices, aids and supportive materials are presented to compensate the disabilities only if the teacher was competent enough to provide such facilities based on the specific requirements of the disability of that particular individual.

Reddy and Sujathamalini (2003) delineated the competencies to be developed during teacher preparation programmes to handle children with special needs. They classified the teacher competencies in three broad domains, namely, planning activities, interactive teaching activities and post-instructional activities. A teacher with these three competencies will be able to handle children with disabilities effectively.

Guidance and Counselling Role

If a teacher involves parents in the educational programmes, it will help the child to progress in a better way. Talking with parents reduces the anxieties and feelings of guilt experienced by almost all parents of children with disabilities. This, in turn, helps to alleviate negative feelings of the parents. Arrangements for parents' meetings and discussion by the teacher help parents to interact with other parents.

The importance of parent's counselling and methods of counselling were well defined by Reddy et al. (2004 and 2004a). Stages in parents' counselling—providing information regarding the condition of disabilities, developing right attitude towards their children, involving parents in the training were discussed. Different forms of counselling like individual, group, peer and community counselling play an important role to deal children with disabilities. Insight approach as well as client-centred approach was given in detail. The various reactions of parents towards their children's disabilities were also defined. A competent teacher should possess skills required by a counsellor, qualifications and do's and don'ts of a counsellor and interpersonal skills required for a counsellor.

A good teacher leads parents to know more about their children, appropriate child rearing practices, the way to assist in learning activities in the development of social and emotional maturity and use community resources.

An efficient and effective teacher should involve other professionals like psychologist, physiologist, occupationalist, speech therapist, paediatricians etc. for the betterment of children with disabilities. The integrated teamwork is adopted by a competent teacher to attain a greater success in the education of children with disabilities. These are some of the roles a teacher has to play effectively to deal children with disabilities.

Need for Identification of Awareness, Attitude and Competencies Required for Special and Normal School Teachers in Dealing Children with Disabilities

Meeting special educational needs in ordinary schools is much more than a process of opening school doors to admit children previously placed in special schools. The challenge of achieving full educational as well as social integration of children with disabilities within the society is achieved if the teachers possess better knowledge about disabilities, attitude towards children with disabilities and competencies to handle disabled children. The teacher should possess some specific competencies in assessment, planning individualised educational programme apart from guidance and counselling. A large number of studies have been quoted on different aspects of teacher behaviour, awareness, attitude and competencies in India and abroad.

In Indian context, studies have been conducted on teacher awareness (Dharmaraj, 2000; Sarojini, 2000; Selvakani, 2000; Sivakami, 2000; Nagomi Ruth, 2000 and Kusuma Harinath, 2000) and teacher competencies (Sujathamalini, 2002 and Jeevanantham, 2002). The role performance and problems faced by special education teachers were also identified by Reddy (2000). Sivakami (2000) and Santhakumari (2003) studied the effectiveness of instructional strategies like cognitive and metacognitive strategies to overcome learning difficulties in English. Jayaprabha (2003) and Shyamala (2004) used cognitive and metacognitive strategies to overcome behaviour difficulties in children and antisocial behaviour in students respectively. Kusuma Harinath (2000) studied the factors related to learning disabilities among students. Reddy and Ramar studied the effectiveness of multimedia based modular approach in teaching science and mathematics to slow learners (1999 and 1998) and low achievers (1995 and 1995a), teaching social science to low achievers (1994), slow learners (2000) and English to slow learners (1997). Reddy and Kanchanamala (2002) investigated the effectiveness of multimedia based modular approach in learning Botany by the slow learners. To find out the relative effectiveness of Tangible Materials (Braille) and Talking Books (Audio cassettes) in learning social science concepts by visually-impaired children in secondary schools, a study on divergent thinking, convergent thinking and mental ability of congenital blind children in secondary schools was carried out by Reddy et al. (2001) and Reddy and Rajaguru (1998). The self concept of blind and visually impaired children in Tamil Nadu was also studied by Reddy and Rajaguru (1995).

In abroad, Aker (1962), White (1950), Madry (1963) and Veri (1968) attempted to identify and list out the competencies for adult education workers in non-formal education. Brent and Margery (2003), Swartz (1995), Hoffman Barbara (1995) and Drury (1994) conducted a study on awareness of teachers towards children with disabilities. Likewise, Cook et al. (2000), Brownlee (2000), Treder David (2000), Praisner (2003), Westwood and Graham (2003), Susan Stainback and William Stainback (1982), Bill (1982) and Cornoldi (1998) studied the attitude of teachers towards children with disabilities and inclusion. Similarly, a good number of studies have been quoted on teacher competencies. Some of them are Blackhurst et al. (1977), Blanchett (2001), McNicholas and Jim (2001), Heller (1999), Knowlton et al. (1999), Kronick (1988), Spungin (1977) and Hudson et al. (1987).

From the above studies, it is evident that only limited number of studies have been conducted in India on teacher awareness, attitude and competencies to deal children with disabilities. In the Western world, the research in this area is far better than Indian scenario.

The success of integration programmes for children with special needs require careful planning, and organisation of physical as well as academic environment. The supportive system includes the involvement of the whole school in meeting the individual needs of children with disabilities. Here, once again the teacher's role is very important not only in teaching and learning but also in teaching and organising classroom activities, extending helping hands to his or her colleagues, providing intensive guidance and counselling to the parents and assisting the children to overcome learning as well as social deficiencies. To accomplish this task effectively a teacher whether he is working in normal school or special school or integrated school should possess thorough understanding about the concept and nature of disabilities with their causes and characteristics, identification and assessment, teaching and training methods and guidance and counselling to parents as well as children with disabilities. Such knowledge and understanding enable them to develop positive attitude towards children with disabilities which in turn leads to acquiring or developing better competencies to handle children with disabilities.

As already stated, the research done in special education particularly on teachers' awareness, attitude and competencies to deal children with disabilities is very limited in India and such studies are more warranted. Studies that focus their attention to assess the awareness, attitude and competencies of special school and normal school teachers will give a clear cut picture about the existing scenario and will pave way for better policy planning and organisation of training programmes for teachers working in special and normal schools. Further, it also gives an idea about the effect of independent variables on the teachers' awareness, attitude and competencies so as to plan for development of specific need-based and situation oriented training programmes.

Statement of the Problem

Keeping the above discussion in mind, the statement of the problem is as follows.

'Awareness, attitude and competencies required for special and normal school teachers in dealing children with disabilities.'

Operational Definitions of the Terms Used in the Study

Awareness

In the Hutchinson Encyclopedic Dictionary (1994) aware is explained as 'having knowledge or realisation.'

The New Roget's Thesaurus (1985) defines aware as 'appreciative, conscious, cognizant (knowledge).'

Oxford Advanced Learner's Dictionary (1996) defines aware as having knowledge of realising, be fully aware of.

Concise Oxford Dictionary (1990) also states that aware is conscious, not ignorant, having knowledge, well informed. Awareness is noun of aware.

In the present study, awareness is defined as having knowledge or being fully aware of or well informed about the concept of disabilities in children, causes and characteristics of children with disabilities, identification and assessment of children with disabilities, teaching and training methods, and guidance and counselling to the children as well as to the parents and community.

Attitude

Chamber's Concise Dictionary (1992) defines attitude as 'position expressing some thoughts or feelings'.

Laurouses Science and Technology Dictionary (1996) defines attitude as an inferred disposition to feel, think and act in certain ways which is used to explain the variation between individuals in their response to similar situation. Attitudes are assumed to represent the effect of past experience on behaviour, through their effects on the cognition, emotional and structuring of perception.

According to Encyclopedic Dictionary of Psychology and Education (1996), attitude is 'a learned disposition' to act in a consistent way towards particular persons, objects or conditions. Likewise, Oxford Advanced Learner's Dictionary (1996) defines attitude 'as a way of thinking about or behaving towards'. Similarly, the Hutchinson Encyclopaedic Dictionary (1994) defines attitude 'as a way of regarding, a disposition or reaction'.

In the present study, attitude refers to the special and normal school teachers' beliefs, feelings and behaviours towards the different aspects of children with disabilities.

Competencies

In Oxford Advanced Learner's Dictionary (1996) competence 'is being able to do'. It also defines competent 'as having the necessary ability, authority, skill, knowledge etc'.

The Hutchinson Encyclopedic Dictionary (1994) defines competency 'as being competent'. Similarly, Concise Oxford Dictionary (1990) state 'competence as ability, the states of being competent, competent as adequately qualified or capable, effective'.

In this study, competencies refer to the knowledge, attitude, skill and performance of special and normal school teachers in dealing children with disabilities.

Children

Encyclopaedic Dictionary of Psychology and Education (1996) defines children 'as young persons of either sex before puberty'.

In this study, children refer to the young persons from I to IV standard or at primary level.

Disabilities

Oxford Advanced Learner's Dictionary (1996) defines disability 'as the state of being disabled'.

Encyclopedic Dictionary of Psychology and Education (1996) explains disability 'as something that disables or disqualifies a person, a physical incapacity caused by injury, disease etc'. Similarly, Concise Oxford Dictionary (1990) explains disability 'as physical incapacity either congenital or caused by injury, disease etc'.

In this study, disabilities refer to physical and sensory impairments like visual impairment, hearing impairment, mental retardation and orthopaedically handicapped.

Objectives of the Study

1. To assess the awareness and attitude of special school teachers (VI, HI, MR and OH) working at primary level on different dimensions of children with disabilities.

2. To assess the awareness and attitude of primary school teachers working in normal schools towards different dimensions of children with disabilities.
3. To assess the extent of competencies possessed by the special school teachers and normal school teachers on different dimensions to deal children with disabilities.
4. To identify the competencies required for the teachers of special and normal schools on different dimensions to deal children with disabilities.
5. To find out the significant difference, if any, between the special school and normal school teachers' awareness on different dimensions (concept of disabilities in children, causes and characteristics of children with disabilities, identification and assessment of children with disabilities, teaching and training methods, and guidance & counselling) of children with disabilities.
6. To find out the significant difference, if any, between the special school and normal school teachers' attitude towards different dimensions of children with disabilities.
7. To find out the significant difference, if any, between the special school and normal school teachers' existing competencies on different dimensions to deal children with disabilities.
8. To find out the significant differences, if any, in the awareness of special school teachers on different dimensions of children with disabilities due to variation in their gender, age, educational qualification, training in special education, years of experience, location of school, nature of school, category of the school and type of school they are working.
9. To find out the significant differences, if any, in the awareness of normal school teachers on different dimensions of children with disabilities due to variation in their gender, age, educational qualification, training

in special education, years of experience, location of school, nature of school, category of the school and type of school they are working.

10. To find out the significant differences, if any, in the attitude of special school teachers on different dimensions of children with disabilities due to variation in their gender, age, educational qualification, training in special education, years of experience, location of school, nature of school, category of the school and type of school they are working.

11. To find out the significant differences, if any, in the attitude of normal school teachers on different dimensions of children with disabilities due to variation in their gender, age, educational qualification, training in special education, years of experience, location of school, nature of school, category of the school and type of school they are working.

12. To find out the significant differences, if any, in the existing competency of special school teachers, on different dimensions to deal children with disabilities due to variation in their gender, age, educational qualification, training in special education, years of experience, location of school, nature of school, category of the school and type of school they are working.

13. To find out the significant differences, if any, in the existing competency of normal school teachers on different dimensions to deal children with disabilities due to variation in their gender, age, educational qualification, training in special education, years of experience, location of school, nature of school, category of the school and type of school they are working.

14. To find out the relationship between:

    (a) Awareness and attitude of special school teachers towards children with disabilities.

    (b) Awareness and attitude of normal school teachers towards children with disabilities.

(c) Awareness and extent of competencies possessed by the special school teachers in dealing children with disabilities.

(d) Awareness and extent of competencies possessed by the normal school teachers in dealing children with disabilities.

(e) Attitude and extent of competencies possessed by the special school teachers in dealing children with disabilities.

(f) Attitude and extent of competencies possessed by the normal school teachers in dealing children with disabilities.

15. To study how far and to what extent the independent variables (gender, age, educational qualification, training in special education, years of experience, location of school, nature of school, category of the school and type of school) influence the dependent variables (awareness, attitude, and existing competencies) of special and normal school teachers in dealing children with disabilities.

16. To find out the infrastructure facilities available in special schools and normal schools for children with disabilities.

17. To find out the relationship between the infrastructure facilities and dropout rate in special and normal schools.

18. To study the attitude of non-disabled peers towards their disabled peers in special schools.

Assumptions of the Study

1. It is possible to develop a rating scale to measure the awareness of special and normal school teachers in dealing children with disabilities.

2. It is possible to develop a rating scale to measure the attitude of special and normal school teachers in dealing children with disabilities.

3. It is possible to develop a competency assessment rating scale to measure the existing competencies of special and normal school teachers in dealing children with disabilities.
4. It is possible to develop a checklist to identify the required competencies of special and normal school teachers in dealing children with disabilities.
5. It is possible to develop an attitude scale to assess the attitude of non-disabled peers towards children with disabilities.
6. It is possible to develop a checklist to identify the infrastructure facilities available in special and normal schools.

Hypotheses of the Study

1. There exists significant difference between the special and normal school teachers' awareness on different dimensions (concept of disabilities in children, causes characteristics of children with disabilities, identification and assessment of children with disabilities, teaching and training methods and guidance and counselling) of children with disabilities.
2. There exists significant difference between the special and normal school teachers' attitude towards different dimensions of children with disabilities.
3. There exists significant difference between the special and normal school teachers existing competencies on different dimensions to deal children with disabilities.
4. There exists significant difference in the special school teachers' awareness on different dimensions of children with disabilities due to variation in their gender, age, educational qualification, training in special education, years of experience, location of school, nature of school, category of school and type of school they are working.
5. There exists significant difference in the normal school teachers' awareness on different dimensions of children with disabilities due to variation in their gender, age,

educational qualification training in special education, years of experience, location of school, nature of school, category of school and type of school they are working.

6. There exists significant difference in the special school teachers' attitude towards different dimensions of children with disabilities due to variation in their gender, age, educational qualification training in special education, years of experience, location of school, nature of school, category of school and type of school they are working.

7. There exists significant difference in the normal school teachers' attitude towards different dimensions of children with disabilities due to variation in their gender, age, educational qualification training in special education, years of experience, location of school, nature of school, category of school and type of school they are working.

8. There exists significant difference in the existing competencies of special school teachers' on different dimensions to deal children with disabilities due to variation in their gender, age, educational qualification, training in special education, years of experience, location of school, nature of school, category of the school and type of school they are working.

9. There exists significant difference in the existing competencies of normal school teachers' on different dimensions to deal children with disabilities due to variation in their gender, age, educational qualification, training in special education, years of experience, location of school, nature of school, category of the school and type of school they are working.

10. There exists significant relationship between:

    (a) awareness and attitude of special school teachers towards children with disabilities.

    (b) awareness and attitude of normal school teachers towards children with disabilities.

(c) awareness and extent of competencies possessed by the special school teachers' in dealing children with disabilities.

(d) awareness and extent of competencies possessed by the normal school teachers' in dealing children with disabilities.

(e) attitude and extent of competencies possessed by the special teachers towards children with disabilities.

(f) attitude and extent of competencies possessed by the normal school teachers towards children with disabilities.

11. There exists positive relationship between infrastructure facilities and the dropout rate in special schools and normal schools.

Scope of the Study

In India, special education is a growing field. There are special schools for the children with disabilities and here and there, there are schools for integrated education. Some institutions are offering Master degree in special education, Bachelor degree in special education and Diploma in special education. Most of the existing schools are not fully equipped in terms of human resources as well as material resources to meet the heterogeneous group of children with disabilities. As the Indian Constitution says education is the basic fundamental right to receive, children with disabilities are entitled for equal educational opportunity in the regular schools. To provide this right in a fullfledged manner, trained teachers play a vital role. Identification and assessment procedures of children with disabilities are of paramount importance in educational system of children with disabilities. Teaching and training strategies and guidance and counselling activities help in the education of children with disabilities.

Teachers play a vital role in identification and assessment, planning and teaching and guidance and counselling activities for the children with disabilities. To perform the above said activities effectively, every teacher should possess specific competencies and perform various roles in complex situations. To acquire those specific competencies they should be aware of the concept, nature and type of disabilities in children and develop positive attitude towards children with disabilities.

The aim of the study is to develop a rating scale to measure the awareness of the special and normal school teachers in dealing children with disabilities. The study also focuses its attention to develop a rating scale to measure the attitude of special and normal school teachers in dealing children with disabilities. It also concentrates to list out the teacher competencies, assess the possessed and required competencies of special and normal school teachers. The study also aims at finding out the non-disabled peer attitude towards their disabled peers with the help of peer attitude scale. It also aims to study the infrastructure facilities available in special and normal schools for the education of children with disabilities, through the checklist. Further, the focus is on to how far and to what extent the independent variables (gender, age, educational qualification, training in special education, years of experience, location of school, nature of school, category of school and type of school) are contributing to dependent variable (awareness, attitude and existing competencies). It also finds out the relationship between awareness and attitude, awareness and existing competencies and attitude and existing competencies of special and normal school teachers to deal children with disabilities. The assessment of the infrastructure facilities available in the special and normal schools and dropout rate in the same schools are also made. Finally, the focus of attention is to study the effect of variation in independent variables on the teachers' awareness, attitude and existing competencies.

Need and Importance of the Study

Teacher is an artist who moulds and shapes physical, mental and moral powers of the mind. To accomplish their task effectively a teacher should be highly competent. In general, the teachers of children with disabilities should first obtain education and experience in teaching normal children and in addition, should become specialists in the area of special education. Special education, as it is a developing field of professional activity, warrants more competent teachers.

To become a competent teacher whether he/she is working in normal or special school or integrated school, one should possess thorough understanding about the various aspects of disabilities in children. Children with special needs are to be identified at an early stage for early intervention. This can be possible only if the teachers at primary level possess knowledge on the above said aspects. Teachers are the second parents and at early stage most of the children role model their teachers. The teachers are responsible for identification of children with disabilities in their classroom. For that, a teacher should exhibit better awareness about the concept of disabilities in children, causes and characteristics of children with disabilities, identification and assessment of children with disabilities, teaching and training methods and guidance and counselling to the children with disabilities as well as parents and community. As the children with disabilities need more care than the normal children, a teacher should have positive attitude towards these children.

A competent teacher has to exhibit various skills. The multiple skills that are to be exhibited by them require specific competencies. A teacher with kindness, patience and positive attitude will be an asset to the special education field. Intensive training and education help him/her to perform the diversified roles more effectively. As it is a growing field, the strong base should be laid down. As a first step, the present awareness, attitude and possessed competencies have to be assessed.

The research on special education is very scanty in India. Most of the researches available are from the western world. Jeevanantham (2002) studied the competencies of teachers at primary level. Reddy (1997, 2000 and 2000a) studied the teacher competencies and role performance of adult education, continuing education workers and special education teachers respectively. Santhakumari (2003), Jayaprabha (2003) and Shyamala (2004) conducted studies on instructional strategies like cognitive, metacognitive and cognitive behaviour modification. Kusuma Harinath (2000) studied certain factors related to learning disabilities in English. Sivakami (2000) studied the effectiveness of certain strategies to overcome learning disabilities in English. Geetha and Dash (2003) adapted physical education for hearing impaired children. Nagaraja (1996) studied the reading abilities in different groups of hearing impaired children.

Reddy et al. (2001) studied the relative effectiveness of tangible materials (Braille) and Talking books (audio cassettes) in learning social science concepts by the visually impaired children in secondary schools. An experimental study was conducted by Sujathamalini (2000) to develop daily living skills among intellectually disabled. Reddy and Kanchanamala (2002) found the effectiveness of multimedia based modular approach in learning Botany by the slow learners. Likewise, the effectiveness of multimedia based modular approach for slow learners and low achievers in teaching science, maths and social science was carried out by Reddy and Ramar (1999, 1998, 1995, 1995a, 1994 and 2000).

The above quoted studies are in general. On the other hand, Sujathamalini (2002) studied the competencies of primary school teachers to handle learning difficulties in children, Kusuma Harinath (2000), Dharmaraj (2000), Sarojini (2000), Nagomi Ruth (2000) and Selvakani (2000) conducted studies on teacher awareness. A close look at the studies reveals that there are very few researches available on children with disabilities in India and that too on teacher awareness, attitude and competencies, the studies are only handful in nature.

In foreign context, Brent et al. (2003), Swartz et al. (1995), Hoffman (1995), Logo-Delello (1998) conducted studies on awareness of teachers towards children with disabilities. Studies on teacher attitude towards children with disabilities were conducted by Cook (2000). Brownlee (2000), Treder (2000), Praisner (2003), Westwood (2003), Susan Stain Back (1982) and Cornoldi (1998). Likewise, Blanchett (2001), McNicholas, Jim (2001), Luckner (2001), Jairrels, Veda (1993), Heller (1999) and Knowlton (1999) studied the teacher competencies.

An analysis of the review of research presented in the second chapter clearly shows that there is a dearth of research in special education on teacher awareness, attitude and competencies to deal children with disabilities. Most of the research works are in general education and only a few are available in special education. The available studies too are done on various aspects of disabilities.

Specific studies on teacher awareness, attitude and competencies which help to develop need based training programmes are very scanty and such studies are the need of the hour.

The present study is an attempt to identify awareness, attitude and competencies of special and normal schools teachers to deal children with disabilities. Such a study facilitates to develop proper educational policies and programme planning for children with disabilities. The study also concentrates on studying the relationship between independent (gender, age, educational qualification, training in special education, years of experience, location of school, nature of school, category of the school and type of school) and dependent variables (awareness, attitude and existing competencies) paving way for organisation of awareness and sensitisation programmes apart from attitudinal building among the special and normal school teachers dealing children with disabilities. The study also aims to see how far and to what extent the independent variables influence the dependent variables, thereby paving way for taking care of these aspects while organising training programmes. Finally, the thrust is on studying the infrastructure facilities available for the education of children with disabilities in special and normal schools and the dropout rate existing in these schools, which in turn leads for provision of better facilities. On the whole, the present study gives better insight for policy planning, development and implementation of educational programmes for the disabled.

Limitations of the Study

1. Awareness, attitude and competencies of special and normal school teachers have been assessed based on the self-ratings of the teachers.
2. The study is confined to Madurai and Chennai districts of Tamilnadu and Chittoor and Hyderabad districts of Andhra Pradesh states only.
3. Rating scale is the only tool used to assess the awareness, attitude and the existing competencies of special and normal school teachers in dealing children with disabilities.

4. Required competencies of special and normal school teachers in dealing children with disabilities are assessed based on the questionnaire in the form of checklist.
5. The research tools used in the study are teacher made tests having reliability and validity.

The review of literature related to the present investigation is given in the succeeding chapter.

2

Review of Related Literature

Introduction

This chapter contains the review of related studies with regard to children with disabilities, awareness of teachers towards children with disabilities, teachers' attitude towards children with disabilities and teacher competencies to handle children with disabilities. Such a review will help the researcher to possess an indepth knowledge on the nature of the problem and the type of variables the researcher has to deal.

Many studies have been conducted on the different aspects of special education in foreign context. As this field is new in India and gaining momentum recently, there are only a few studies available in Indian context. The available studies in foreign as well as Indian contexts have been presented under the following headings:

- Studies on Children with Disabilities
- Studies on Awareness of Teachers towards Children with Disabilities
- Studies on Attitude of Teachers towards Children with Disabilities
- Studies on Competencies of Teachers Dealing Children with Disabilities
- An Overview of the Research Reviewed

Studies on Children with Disabilities

General studies on children with disabilities are reviewed and quoted under this heading. Studies on the abilities of disabled children, factors related, identification and assessment, academic performance, behaviour problems, social skills and personality of disabled children were presented under this heading.

Bindu Prasad (1992) identified problems of hearing-impaired children and suggested some solutions for them. The identified problems were limited facilities for diagnostic services, absence of adequate equipment and properly trained staff, poor awareness and inappropriate attitude among people regarding the need for early assessment, inadequate facilities for doing reliable hearing assessment and working out matching hearing aid and inadequate follow-up services. The child rejects the hearing aid because it does not function properly and child feels discomfort in using hearing aids. Parents also feel that hearing aid is expensive, the child may break it and at the same time parents are struggling to accept the fact that their child is hearing impaired. If the child is tested by other children, he/she becomes reluctant to use hearing aids. Bindu Prasad delineated the problem existing in educational services and she had also given some suggestions for improving. Provision and use of appropriate hearing aid and teaching methods to develop verbal communication skills. A teacher should not be wedded to one method against another. Depending upon the child's strength and weakness one should work out the method which would work best.

Divya Jindal (1996) stated that successful integration and inclusion of children with visual impairment depends on their active social interaction with peers, which is possible only when social skills are developed to an adequate level. However, due to various variables like lack of visual cues and imitation, opportunity, prompts and reinforcement, development of social skills is hampered. Through careful intervention on the part of teachers and researchers, these problems can be overcome.

Hampson and Duffy (1984) compared 8 congenital blind, 8 sighted, and 8 blind folded sighted female school students (mean age of 16 years) using a selected inference technique. Subjects categorised the words of sentences and corners of figures while responding either spatially (by typing), verbally, or while tapping. Spatial responding slowed response times more than tapping or verbal responding. No major differences were found between the response patterns of the three groups. It is argued that many imagery tasks involve a heavy dependence on spatial information processing, and to the extent that blind and sighted perform similarly in such situations, it follows that they are using similar spatial representations.

Kool (1981) explained about the memory of the blind. He used a sample of 378 blind matched with sighted blind folded subjects. Reproductions of movement were examined in relation to recall delays and also in relation to variety of activities using linear slide experimental approaches. Findings were revealed in the background of vocational, educational and other rehabilitation issues of the blind. He considered that the blind lack precision even when their task is pre-selected; it was therefore advised that blind people should not be given jobs in vocations where targets change frequently. Development of effective motor program was also recommended. Skill requiring dependence and integration of auditory and kinaesthetic modalities in the blind should be encouraged.

The research study conducted by Kool and Pathak (1985) revealed that in coding, storage and retrieval of distance, vision plays an important role. Results also demonstrated the condition in which the target point is selected by the subject himself and blind subjects failed to avail of this facility in coding, storing and retrieval.

Kundu et al. (1985) made an experimental study and compared muscular sensation of the visually impaired and sighted, using standard weight of 100 gms and series of nine comparable weights ranging from 92 gms to 108 gms and found that the blind were more sensitive in respect of muscular sensation as compared to the sighted.

Kusuma Harinath (2000) studied certain factors related to learning disabilities in English among school students. The objectives of the study were to develop diagnostic tests to identify reading, writing and spelling difficulties in English, to find out the intelligence of students with reading, writing and spelling difficulties; to study the personality characteristics of students with learning difficulties and; to study the awareness of teachers and parents about learning difficulties. The study revealed that (1) boys experienced more reading disabilities than girls, (2) age and class had no effect, (3) community influenced on their spelling difficulties, (4) parents educational qualifications influenced learning difficulties, (5) location of school influenced on the learning difficulties, (6) medium of instruction also influenced learning difficulties particularly spelling difficulties, (7) mass media had no influence, (8) parents income influenced learning difficulties but not writing difficulties etc. Thus this study delineates various factors related to learning difficulties in English among school students.

Mani (1993) studied the concept development of blind children. In his study, the concepts related to body awareness, object/situation characteristics time and distance, spatial skills-oriented concepts, measurement and environment had been considered as independent variables. The study yields a low cost assessment kit to assess concept development of visually impaired children as well as sighted children also.

Manju Pandey (1999) identified learning disabled children on the basis of academic disorders and to measure their level of intellectual development. This study was done on 100 learning disabled and 100 learning abled children of primary level. The results of the study indicated that the level of intellectual development plays an important role to determine the individual's learning ability/disability.

Mittal (1985) studied the personality factors of blind and sighted adolescents using Catell's 16 HPQ test. Significant differences were found between both the groups on factors BLOQ Q3 and Q4.

Moore, William (1991) made a survey to identify the children with hearing impairments. The study of 46 hearing-impaired 6 year old sought to determine the age and identification patterns of Oregon children with hearing impairments. Information is presented on parental observation of hearing behaviours during infancy; professionals contracted; average age to suspicion, confirmation, habilitation and amplification of hearing loss; and risk factors.

Nagaraja et al., (1996) conducted a study on speech reading abilities in different groups of hearing impaired (HI) children. This study evaluated the speech reading abilities of 60 hearing impaired children. Of them, 30 subjects belonged to oral group and 30 subjects to total communication group. As there were no standardized test for speech reading available, a test comprising of 10 word items and sentences hierarchically increasing in complexity was developed and used for the study. The influence of age, sex, hearing-aid usage, parental income and education on speech reading ability within oral, aural and total communication groups and between groups were also studied. The study indicated that oral aural group as a whole performed better than total communication group both for word and sentence level speech reading tasks. The study further indicated that hearing-aid users performed better on speech reading than hearing aid non-users. Female subjects of oral aural group did better on sentence level speech reading task than word level task. There seemed to be no significant difference in performance between different age children within oral aural and total communication groups. However, between the groups and within the same age, oral aural hearing impaired children performed better than total communication group children. Between grades and within a group there were not much of differences observed in speech reading. However, between grades of oral aural and total communication groups, oral aural hearing impaired performed better than total communication children on speech reading.

Pandey (1985) studied affectional deprivation, ego strength and adjustment pattern among visually handicapped children and their rehabilitation. Findings stated that the deprivation as felt by rural blind children was significantly more acute than that felt by urban blind children. Further, there was no significant difference in the pattern of affectional deprivation between congenitally blind children and postnatal blind children.

Prem Victor (1992) discussed early detection and early intervention of hearing handicapped children. Observation of a delay in the development of other modalities, which are dependent on hearing, is the common mode of detection. Opinions from family physician, child specialists, ENT specialist and Audiologist serve better in early detection. Early diagnosis is capable of assessing children from birth to teenage. Care must be taken to have a battery of-tests before taking any decision. Early detection, diagnosis and parent training are preparatory stages for the final act, which is early intervention. Intervention is the beginning, not the end. Early intervention can be provided in three areas

(i) amplification provision,

(ii) medical assistance, and

(iii) educational assistance.

Early diagnosis of a 'deaf' has a good possibility with proper assistance to move into the regular schools in class I. For children who come late, special schools are often required.

Premavathy Vijayan and Akkamadevi (2001) conducted a study on assessment and training of functional vision of the low vision children at the primary level. Fifty low vision children from primary level in integrated schools at Madurai and Coimbatore were selected, among whom 40 children (20 boys and 20 girls) were selected for giving functional vision training. It is also evident from the study that the instructional package prepared and used for functional vision training was found to be very effective. Therefore, the study revealed that there is a need for training to improve the functional vision of low-vision children.

Priti Rana and Sheela Sangwan (2000) assessed the memory of slow and average learners. 80 slow learners (IQ: 70-90) and 80 average learners (IQ: 90-110) and pre-school children (4 to 6 years old) constituted the sample. Stanford Binet Intelligence Scale was used to identify slow and average children whereas the memory of these children was assessed by a standardized cognitive test. Average learners were found to excel in memory than slow learners. Among the slow learners, girls performed better as compared to their counterparts. Whereas, average learner boys surpassed average learner girls only in object permanence and further this difference was non-significant. In all other sub-tests (object recalling, sequential memory and numerical memory) average learner girls were ahead of average learner boys although not significant.

Rajaguru (1996) conducted a study on divergent and convergent thinking of visually impaired children in secondary schools. The study aimed to develop tests to measure the divergent, convergent thinking and mental ability of visually impaired children. The findings of the study showed that 56 visually impaired children had got their convergent thinking score very close to the mean of the sample. Whereas 40 and 63 VI children got their convergent thinking score below average and above average respectively. Similarly, 68 VI children scored less than the mean score of the total sample distribution. 60 VI children scored higher than the mean of the distribution. More than 46.5 per cent of the visually impaired children (74) possessed low mental ability.

Reddy and Kusuma (1995) listed causes for mental retardation. Genetic irregularities, chromosomal defects, phenylketonuria, galactosemia, cretinism, microcephaly and macrocephly are the prenatal causes. Problems during pregnancy such as maternal diseases, diabetes mellitus or kidney diseases cause MR. Complication during pregnancy, drugs and exposure to large doses of radiation and poor maternal nutrition can also harm the foetus. Rh incompatibility, syphilis and measles can have disastrous consequences. Brain damage can be caused by prolonged or difficult labour, by difficult forceps manipulation and the problems related to mother's small pelvis. Cerebral palsy is due to anoxia, and excessive coiling of umbilical cord. Severe Jaundice in Children also causes mental retardation.

The problems after birth, i.e. head injuries, brain tumours, infectious diseases such as meningitis and encephalitis, hunger and malnutrition, some food additives, lead coated toys, whooping cough, chicken pox and measles cause mental retardation.

Preventive measures are good medical services, genetic counselling, conducting the tests like amniocentesis, dietary treatment of phenylketonuria, improvement in maternal nutrition, Vaccination against Rubella and against infectious diseases like diphtheria, tetanus, whooping cough, typhoid, measles and poliomyelitis, prevention of accidents and avoidance of smoking and consumption of alcohols.

Reddy and Rajaguru (1995) investigated the self concept of blind and visually impaired children in Tamilnadu. 80 visually impaired students studying in IX and X grade were selected for the study. Out of 80, 40 were totally blind and 40 belonged to the category of Low Vision. Children's self-concept scale and achievement test were administered. The results revealed that totally blind children have more self-concept than low vision children. Boys and Girls are alike in self-concept. Self-concept of VI children is positively correlated with their achievement. Further, the socio-economic status of VI children has least impact on their Self-concept.

Reddy (1997) studied personality correlates of coping behaviour in the physically handicapped students. 960 samples comprised the three categories of physically handicapped. Disabled Adjustment Inventory with 70 items was specially developed to find out coping problems in them. Dutt's Personality Inventory was employed to find out their personality correlates. The findings revealed that: (a) Insecurity and loneliness, depression, feelings of inferiority and emotional instability were the personality factors which registered negative responses from the subjects. (b) Loneliness, depression, guilt proneness and emotional instability revealed significant relationship with maladjustment in the subjects. (c) Visually handicapped were found to be the most problematic group, both in coping as well as in negative personality tendencies. (d) Boys and girls did not differ significantly on personality factors.

Reddy et al. (1999) discussed developmental disabilities in children. A disorder or disability that disrupts or changes the order of a child's developmental progress is known as developmental disability. The developmentally disabled children experience limitations in self-care, receptive and expressive language, learning, mobility, self-direction, and capacity of independent living. Chromosomal aberrations, neural tube defects, central nervous system damage during prenatal period and metabolic disorders cause developmental disabilities in children. Early intervention programmes that stimulate cognition, motor skills, language or socio-emotional development should be adopted to the children with developmental disabilities.

Sangeeta (1996) conducted a comparative study on learning aptitude of the congenitally and adventitiously visually impaired pupils. The study was conducted on 50 (25 congenitally and 25 adventitiously visually impaired) students ranging between 6 to 16 years of age and studying in the residential schools for the Blind in Haryana and Chandigarh. The findings revealed that the two groups did not differ significantly in their learning aptitudes. No significant differences were found between the congenitally and adventitiously visually impaired students in the time taken for test completion on BLAT, on any of the sub-tests of BLAT and the mean BLAT scores in three different age groups. (BLAT—Newland's Blind Learning Aptitude Test).

Sheela Sangwan et al. (2002) made a comparative study on the perceptual and conceptual abilities of 4-6 year-old slow and average learning children in Hisar city of Haryana state. The sample consisted of 160 pre-schoolers in which 80 were slow learners (IQ: 70-90) and 80 were average learners (IQ: 90-110). Standard-Binet Intelligence Scale was used to categorise the children according to their IQ level. The perceptual and conceptual abilities were assessed with the help of standardized cognitive test. The average learners were found to perform better than slow learners in both perceptual and conceptual abilities.

Sibnath Deb et al. (2002) identified the problems encountered by the visually handicapped in their daily social life and in the educational institution. Another objective was to compare the efficacy of the integrated education system with that of special education system. A total number of 101 visually handicapped children, 51 attending special education and 50 attending integrated education, aged between 10-19 years, were selected purposively from two pioneer residential schools for the blind population in Kolkata. Data were collected through face-to-face interview method using a semi-structured questionnaire. A comparative analysis of qualitative data to adjudge the efficacy of integrated education and special education revealed that integrated education in Narendrapur Blind Boys Academy is more effective in motivating the blind students to compete with sighted children and in helping them to develop a positive outlook towards their future, something which is almost absent among sightless children undergoing special education in Kolkatta blind school.

Sujata Satapathy and Sushila Singhal (2002) studied the academic performance of visually impaired and hearing impaired. Academic performance of 79 visually impaired, 80 hearing impaired and 111 non-impaired male and female adolescents in grade VIII to X following one curriculum was investigated. Final examination marks were considered as indicators of academic performance. Their age ranged from 13-21 years and majority of them were from the lower middle-class family background. Results revealed that the impaired groups performed significantly better than the non-impaired, while the visually impaired were the best performers. Adolescents in grade VIII and females performed significantly better than their respective counterparts in grade X males. Findings were discussed according to the impairment specific needs and problems, and education and examination system.

Vasuki and Mahima (2001) studied behaviour problems in intellectually disabled children. Case study method was followed in this study. The sample selected for the study was ten, out of them five were boys and five were girls. Behaviour Assessment Scale for Indian Children-Mental Retardation designed by National Institute for the Mentally Handicapped was used. The results revealed that profound intellectually disabled children had more behaviour problems than the other categories of children. It is also seen that the boys with intellectual disability had more problems than girls with intellectual disability.

Venkatesan and Hanumantha Rao (1996), attempted to profile commonly reported pre-natal, natal and post-natal factors from available case records of a clinical population of 1458 cases with mental retardation seen at the General services of Sweekar Rehabilitation Institute for Handicapped, Secundrabad, over the last one and half decades. The study reported 151 prenatal factors, 1146 natal factors and 813 post-natal factors in the sample. Among the pre-natal factors, attempted abortion, use of teratogenic drugs, maternal illhealth/illness and maternal hypertension/ pedaloedema were reported more frequently than maternal convulsions, anaemia, bleeding or falls/injury. In the natal factors there was a greater prevalence of absent birth cry followed by factors like delivery at home, low birth weight, delivery by caesarean section and so on. The analysis of pos-tnatal factors showed greater prevalence of convulsions followed by high-grade fever. Further, these trends were presented and discussed in the light of their relationship with specific socio-demographic variables and their implications to early intervention service programmers to be rendered for the prevention of mental retardation in the country.

Studies reviewed in this heading bring out the causes, factors related to disabilities, characteristics and problems faced by the disabled children (Bindu Prassad, 1992; Divya Jindal, 1996; Kundu et al., 1985; Pandey, 1985; Reddy and Kusuma, 1997; Sibnath Deb et al., 2002 and Vasuki and Mahima, 2001). Studies related to spatial abilities, perceptual abilities, conceptual abilities, sensory abilities, concept development, memory, divergent and convergent thinking evince the strengths and weaknesses of children with disabilities (Hampson & Duffy, 1984; Kool, 1981; Kool & Pathak, 1985; Mani, 1993; Moore, William, 1991; Nagaraja, et al., 1996; Priti Rana and Sheela Sangwan, 2000; Rajaguru, 1996 and Sheela Sangwan et al., 2002). Eventhough, the studies presented under this heading are not giving clear picture about the various aspects of disabilities, they provide an idea about the nature, causes, characteristics, identification and abilities of the children with disabilities apart from strengths and weaknesses of the disabled.

Studies on Awareness of Teachers Towards Children with Disabilities

There are special needs children who require special initiative on the part of teachers. The special and normal school teachers are able to meet the special learning needs of disabled children if they are willing and well-informed about the disabilities in children. Better awareness about the concept, causes, characteristics, teaching and learning methods helps to modify the learning environment and improve the quality of education. Here, an attempt is made to present the studies related to teacher awareness on different aspects of children with disabilities.

Brent et al. (2003) discussed the importance of teachers' self-awareness when they deal students with emotional and behaviours disorders. This article identified questions and strategies to help teachers become more self-aware regarding their interactions with students of behavioural and emotional disorders. The five key questions to increase teacher self-awareness are:

1. Am I taking proactive steps to identify and defuse my own emotional triggers?
2. Am I paying attention to what I need to pay attention to?
3. Am I using effective strategies to reduce burnout and nurture my own mental health?
4. Am I using an appropriate sense of humour to build relationships, diffuse conflict, engage learners and manage my own stress?
5. Do I regularly acknowledge significant ways are making difference in the lives of students.

They conducted that many teachers have not received adequate training to recognise how their own psychological histories and personalities affect their interactions with youth of emotional and behavioural disabilities. If teachers make conscious ongoing efforts to increase their own self awareness, they will likely enhance their effectiveness and their job satisfaction. They also stated that the overall attitude of the teacher and the classroom climate affect students much more than most other techniques or interactions.

Dharmaraj (2000) studied primary school teachers' awareness towards learning disabilities in mathematics at primary level. The objectives of the study were to develop rating scale to assess the awareness of primary school teachers on various aspects of learning disabilities in mathematics and to assess the awareness of primary school teachers towards learning disabilities in mathematics. The result of the study showed that teachers with higher educational qualification exhibited better awareness, i.e. post-graduate teachers possess better awareness than the secondary grade and graduate teachers on different aspects of learning disabilities in mathematics.

Drury (1994) conducted a survey to investigate teacher awareness of alternative assessment of students in Mathematics. The results confirmed that the teacher grade level groups had differing views of alternative assessment techniques, practices, and nomenclature. If more was known about the teachers' awareness of alternative assessment practices, this information would help to initiative, design and direct alternative assessment techniques, strategies and practices. The data on teacher awareness of alternative assessment could be used to: modify a course of study on assessment, develop objectives for an inservice or preserivce program, or improve national standards on assessment.

Hoffman and Barbara (1995) studied the teacher awareness of speech and language therapists, roles and services. A researcher—designed Likert Scale was administered to a sample of 67 anonymous regular education teachers. The survey provided statistical results regarding the teachers' ability to recognize students who have speech and language difficulties, teachers' knowledge of school-based speech and language services, and teachers' awareness of how to access the services for their students who need them.

Kusuma Harinath (2000) studied the awareness of teachers on learning difficulties/disabilities of children in English. The objectives of the study were to study the awareness of parents and teachers on different aspects of learning difficulties in English. 32 teachers teaching English subject for the children were selected for data collection. Awareness scale to teachers on learning difficulties/disabilities consisted of 46 students on various aspects of learning difficulties/disabilities namely—concept of learning difficulties, characteristics of learning difficulties in children, causes of learning difficulties and instructional strategies for learning difficulties in children. Out of 46 items, teachers exhibited high awareness on 17 items which are mostly falling under instructional strategies for learning difficulties in children. Moderate awareness and low awareness were exhibited in 16 and 13 items respectively.

Logo-Delello, Ellie (1998) investigated classroom dynamics and 13 young children at risk for the development of Serious Emotional Disturbances (SED) as compared to 13 typical peers.

Students at risk of SED were generally rejected by teachers, spend less time academically engaged, and received more negative or neutral non-academic teacher feedback.

Nagomi Ruth (2000) studied the awareness on learning disabilities among regular school teachers. Objectives of the study were

(i) to assess the knowledge among regular school teachers on learning disabilities,

(ii) to organise awareness programmes,

(iii) to give knowledge about identification and remediation for learning disabled, and

(iv) to evaluate the impact or effect of knowledge gained by regular school teachers.

The result of the study showed that the awareness programme was found to be effective.

Sarojini (2000) conducted a study on the awareness of primary school teachers towards learning disabilities in English at primary stage. The objectives of the study were: to develop awareness scale to assess the awareness of primary school teachers towards learning disabilities in English at primary stage and to assess the awareness of primary school teachers towards learning disabilities in English. The result showed that the primary school teachers exhibited low level of awareness and the study revealed the need to generate awareness among primary school teachers towards learning disabilities in English. The personal variables such as years of experience, type of school, locality of school also influenced awareness of primary school teachers towards learning disabilities in English at primary stage.

Selvakani (2000) conducted a study on creating awareness on integrated education of the disabled children to the regular teachers. The objectives of the study were: to find out the previous knowledge of the regular school teacher about disabled children, to prepare instructional materials on various concepts related to the education of disabled children, to organise an awareness programme for regular school teacher, to develop knowledge about the role of teachers to meet the special needs of the disabled children, and to evaluate the imparted knowledge gained by regular school teacher. The result revealed that the knowledge about the role of teachers to meet the special needs of the disabled children was improved by organising awareness programme and the developed awareness programme was found to be effective.

Swartz, Diana Denise (1995) studied teachers' awareness and willingness to report suspected child abuse. The purpose of this study was to determine what factors contribute to teachers' decisions to report suspected child abuse. Factors investigated in this research came from four main areas: teacher training, knowledge, severity of abuse, child behaviour, and family characteristics.

Subjects were elementary school teachers who completed a two-part questionnaire. Part-I consisted of questions designed to obtain information about experience and knowledge in the area of reporting child abuse and Part-II consisted of a set of three experimental vignettes. Vignettes were designed to manipulate five variables: gender, ethnicity, socio-economic status, behaviour, and severity of abuse. Respondents were asked to indicate whether they would report abuse for each vignette.

Data were analysed by using chi-square analysis and ANOVA. Results indicated that at least 3-4 hours of in-service training were needed before a relationship was shown to the probability of reporting abuse, and teachers' decisions to report abuse were affected by the socio-economic status of the child's family and the severity of abuse.

The studies reviewed (Kusuma Harinath, 2000 and Sarojini, 2000) reveal that teachers exhibited low and moderate awareness on concept, causes and characteristics of children with disabilities. The quoted studies also point out the dearth of such specific studies and highlight the need for research in identification of teachers' awareness on different aspects of disabilities in children.

Studies on Attitude of Teachers Towards Children with Disabilities

Teachers' attitude towards children with disabilities is a major and important aspect in the education of children with disabilities. Right type of teacher with right type of attitude can do better justice to the children with disabilities. Hence, research on teacher attitude paves way for better promotion of education to the children with disabilities. Studies on these aspects are presented under this heading.

Adams, Kimberly et al. (1998) studied the differences in parent and teacher trust levels. They suggested the implications for creating collaborative family school relationship. Parents (N=123) of regular and special education teachers and students (N=152) in three urban middle schools were surveyed regarding their attitudes about home-school collaboration. Findings indicated that parent trust was significantly higher than teacher trust. Implications for schools personnel working to build trust between families and schools were drawn.

Bearn et al. (1998) investigated how learning support was perceived by mainstream colleagues. Six British teachers were interviewed to investigate the commitment of mainstream subject teachers' to special needs pupils. Findings confirmed that territorial boundaries and other factors continue to inhibit support teaching and that teacher attitudes and possible antipathy remain stubborn stumbling blocks to the implementation of whole-school policies.

Bill et al. (1982) studied the elementary teachers' attitudes toward mainstreaming educable mentally retarded students. This study examined elementary teacher attitudes towards mainstreaming EMR children on the basis of teacher age, academic training and teaching experience with mainstreamed EMR children. Multivariate analysis of variance revealed no significant overall differences in teachers. A consistent pattern, however, of positive attitudes toward mainstreaming was clearly evident.

Bowers et al. (1998) conducted a study on the code in action: Some school perceptions of its user-friendliness. A British study investigated the attitudes of 160 centrally employed local educational agencies, 290 educators, and 296 parents towards the Special Education Needs (SEN) Code of Practice. Results found that overall the code had been well received by its users, however, there were identifiable areas that would need some modification.

Brownlee et al. (2000) studied the Opportunities for authentic experience and reflection: A teaching programme, designed to change attitudes towards disability for pre-service teachers. Eleven pre-service Australian teachers were interviewed concerning their beliefs and attitudes about students with disabilities, both before and after meeting and interacting with a teaching assistant severely disabled by cerebral palsy. Findings were reported concerning students' perceptions of the teaching assistant, effectiveness of the current teacher education programme and effectiveness of the interview process.

Butera Gretchen et al. (1998) conducted a statewide study of FAPE and school discipline policies. Telephone interviews with 141 randomly selected special education co-ordinators, principals and special and general education teachers analysed issues related to special education including a Free and Appropriate Public Education (FAPE), Individualised Education Programme (IEPs) and school discipline procedures. Respondents found IEPs too cumbersome and reported they did not always review IEPs prior to discipline decisions.

Cook and Bryan et al. (2000) conducted a study on teachers' attitude towards their included students with disabilities. Seventy general education elementary teachers nominated students corresponding with the attitudinal categories of attachment, concern, indifference and rejection. Analysis indicated that students with disabilities were significantly under represented in the attachment category and significantly over represented in the concern and rejection categories.

Cornoldi and Cesare et al. (1998) surveyed teacher attitudes in Italy after twenty years of inclusion. A survey of 523 teachers in Italy was conducted 20 years after nationwide inclusion of students with disabilities in neighbourhood schools and general education classrooms. Overall, support for the inclusion concept was found but teachers responded less positively on practical items addressing their satisfaction with tune, training personal assistance, and resources provided for inclusion efforts.

De Bettencourt and Laurie (1999) examined general educators' attitudes toward students with mild disabilities and their use of instructional strategies. The study examined the frequency of use of several instructional strategies by 59 general educators at the middle school level with time spent collaborating with special educators and course work taken in specialised techniques. Attitude towards the inclusion of students with mild disabilities was also examined. Number of instructional strategies used correlated with course work and collaboration time.

Guido (1990) studied educators attitude towards the inclusion of severely/profoundly disabled students in regular classrooms. The purpose of the study was to investigate the relationship between professional educators' attitude and integration of severely/profoundly disabled students in regular classroom. The present research showed that increased specific special education knowledge and experience is a key factor in more favourite attitude towards case of placement of severely/profoundly disabled students in regular educational classrooms. Formatting opportunities for regular/special educators to take advantage of specialised course appears to support integration efforts for more severely disabled students in regular classes.

Harris, Mary (1998) conducted an explanatory study on the knowledge, attitudes and concerns about portfolio assessment: A survey of 209 educators taking graduate classes in general and special education examined their knowledge, attitudes, and concern about portfolio assessments. The survey found that the respondents had some knowledge of and positive attitude towards portfolios. They viewed inadequate training and support and lack of time to design and implement portfolio assessment as major concerns.

Hoffman et al. (1997) analysed inclusion in New Jersey school districts. This study was concerned with general education teachers' experiences and perceptions about inclusion and supports these teachers received from their administration in order to implement inclusion in their classes. The study also focused on general education teachers' attitude about inclusion and their perceptions of possible effects, if any, students with moderate to severe disabilities had on general education teachers. To accomplish this task, a qualitative study was conducted. Standardized open-ended interviews were conducted with 22 general education teachers and five Directors of special services about (a) school operation, (b) teacher preparation (c) implementation and d) evaluation. A follow-up survey was mailed to 40 teachers (including the 22 interviewed teachers). The purpose of the survey was to gain a broader sample.

In this study, teachers shared common experiences regarding the placement of students with moderate to severe disabilities in general education classes. Teachers reported that the integration of students with moderate to severe disabilities in their classes had a positive impact on students with disabilities, as well as on non-handicapped classmates. Teachers discussed the positive aspects of inclusion for students with moderate to severe disabilities. According to the teachers, most of the inclusion students had positive experiences in regular education classrooms and had a chance to be with positive role models.

The teachers who volunteered to have inclusion students in their classes were willing to take a risk and were willing to accept the challenge of having these students in their classes. The positive reactions experienced by these teachers appeared to be due to their own initiatives and willingness to integrate students with moderate to severe disabilities in their classes. On the other hand, teachers who were assigned by the administration to have inclusion students in their classrooms were not sure of their capabilities and they felt they did not have the knowledge, skills, and training needed to teach students with moderate to severe disabilities. Teachers reported that support from the administration and special education teachers, initial and ongoing training and additional planning time were essential elements for inclusion.

Jena (2000) investigated the priorities of training and attitude of special educators towards people with mental handicap. Qualified special educators (N-26) attending a refresher course, were studied through a priority rating and attitude questionnaire. Most of the special educators indicated early intervention as the most preferred area of training in special education. They agreed that people with mental handicap are burden for the family and do not contribute to the society but in spite of that, parents can love them. They strongly felt that people with mental handicap should be prevented from having sex and children.

Kusuma Harinath (2000) made a study to identify the teachers' attitude towards learning difficulties/disabilities of children in English. He developed an attitude scale and the same was administered to the sample of 32 teachers teaching English subject to the children. The result showed that in 19 statements the teachers exhibited high attitude, in 16 and 13 statements they possessed moderate and low attitude towards learning difficulties/disabilities in children.

Lombard, Richard et al. (1998) conducted a "Survey on school-to-work and technical preparation: Teacher attitudes and practices regarding the inclusion of students with disabilities". This survey of secondary-school-to-work and technical preparation teachers from 45 states concerning inclusion of students' with disabilities found that the 169 respondents did not feel prepared to meet the needs of their students with disabilities, had received little or no in-service training regarding inclusive practices, and had not participated in developing individual education programs for students with disabilities.

Meltzer, Lynn et al. (1998) investigated the perceptions of academic strategies and competence in students with learning disabilities. The study involved 308 students with learning disabilities (LD), 355 typical students, and 57 teachers, found that students with LD rated themselves lower than average achievers in nine academic and organizational domains. While they considered themselves competent in five areas, teachers rated them as weak in all areas.

Poon-McBrayer and Kim Forg (1998) conducted a "study on integrating students with disabilities in Hong Kong: classroom teachers' attitudes and beliefs". This study surveyed 58 classroom teachers' views and attitudes toward integrating students with disabilities in Hong Kong. Results indicated that the availability of necessary resources, training of teachers, and the suitability of instruction and services were prime concerns and priorities for respondents. Recommendations on how to promote integration considering these concerns were offered.

Praisner (2003) surveyed 408 elementary school principals to investigate relationships regarding attitude towards inclusion of students with disabilities, variables such as training and experience and placement perceptions. Result showed that about/ in 5 principals' attitude towards inclusion were positive while most were uncertain. Positive experiences with students with disabilities and exposure to special education concepts were associated with a more positive attitude toward inclusion. And also the principals with more positive attitudes and/or experiences were more likely to place students in less restrictive settings. Differences in placement and experiences were found between disability categories. Results stressed the importance of inclusionary practices that give principals positive experiences with students of all types of disabilities as well as provided principals with more specific training.

Reiter, Shunit et al. (1998) studied Isreli elementary school students' and teachers' attitudes towards mainstreaming children with disabilities. This study examined attitudes of Isreli elementary school students (n=2845) and their teachers (n=145) towards children with disabilities and mainstreaming. Findings indicated that students displayed a custodial, patronizing attitude, while the teachers' approach was of a more medical and diagnostic in nature. Previous contacts of children with disabilities correlated with positive students' attitude.

Rita (1994) studied the attitude of case managers towards the employability of a person with several disabilities. Research objectives were

(a) to observe the direction and strength of the attitudes

(b) to examine the relationship between attitude and a numb er of subject characteristics, self perceptions, and experiences as well as relationships between attitude and the reported characteristics of subject case management clients

(c) to compare developmental services case managers' attitudes with those of other professionals.

The analysis yielded two sets of significant results. The first set revealed strong inter-relationships between positive attitude towards CE case manager age and case managers' perception of their client's desire for CE and client's success in CE. The second set of results related positive attitudes with subject hours to face to face contact with persons who have severe disabilities, number of trainings on CE attended, self-assessment of success as a case manager, and not having a school aged case load.

Roush and Jackson's (1991) nationwide survey examined the attitudes and options of 203 professionals regarding parent-professional involvement in the planning and implementation of goals and services for hearing-impaired infants, toddlers and their families, as required under Public Law 99-457, the Education of the Handicapped Act Amendments (1986). Respondents stressed the value of family-centred intervention.

Schunm and Vaughn (1992) surveyed general educators at the elementary middle and secondary school levels to determine their attitudes about planning as well as their planning practices for students with disabilities. Some of the findings from their study included the following:

(i) Planning practices differ across grade levels. Middle and secondary school teachers frequently responded that mainstreamed students with disabilities should be prepared to cope with the demands of the general curriculum. To illustrate this finding, Schunm and Vaughn include a representative comment from a teacher expressing this belief. "There is absolutely no time for mainstreamed students'. They adopt to the programme, the programme does not adopt to them".

(ii) Many teachers feel under prepared by their teacher education programme to work effectively with mainstreamed students.

(iii) Overall, teachers are willing to have students in their classrooms "as long as they do not exhibit emotional and behaviour problems".

Susan Stainback and William Stainback (1982) studied the influence of attitudes of regular class teachers about the education of severely retarded students. Data from an investigation on ways of influencing the attitudes of regular class-teachers towards integration of severally retarded students into regular schools indicated that the attitude of prospective regular class teachers could be significantly influenced by the method used to present introductory information about severally retarded students and their education in a survey course on exceptional students. The results were discussed in the light of past research findings related to influencing teachers' attitude about integrating mildly handicapped students into regular school programmes and activities.

Taplin, Margaret and White, Marian (1998) studied parents' and teachers' perception of gifted provision. Seventy-one parents of gifted children completed a questionnaire concerning their perceptions of the current services provided their children and the parents' preferences. 61 teachers completed a parallel questionnaire. Results indicated that both groups preferred services with enabled students to stay in the regular classroom and that this preference was linked to concerns about social development.

Tobin (1972) conducted a study on 'the attitudes of non-specialist teachers towards visually handicapped pupils'. In a large sample of teachers and trainee teachers studying postgraduate and educational degree courses at Birmingham University, the majority were somewhat daunted by the prospect of including visually handicapped pupils in their classes and rated them low in terms of pupils whom they would feel confident to accept in their classes. These negative views must be faced and teachers must be given the information, training and support to overcome them. It would be interesting to see the results of such a study undertaken more recently, as since that date special education modules have been incorporated into initial teacher training.

Treder and David (2000) studied the relationship between teacher effectiveness and teacher attitude towards issues related to inclusion. The study re-examined the results of a study, which indicated that more effective teachers were less willing to include students with special needs in their classrooms.

Trzcinka and Sheila Marie (1996) conducted a study on curriculum and teachers' attitudes: the impact of the change process in special education. This research was conducted in a large metropolitan city with eighty-seven schools, three of which housed classes for trainable mentally retarded children aged six to thirteen. One additional school prepared students aged thirteen to twenty-one for the mainly non-competitive labour force. A descriptive case study recorded the impact of the change variables of teacher participation and the consultancy feedback on curriculum and teachers' attitude change. The sample from the population of teachers included twenty predominately veteran teachers responsible for teaching trainable mentally retarded children. Internal and external consultants, versed in organisational developmental and staff development in the areas of community based instruction, behaviour modification, peer mediation and systematic instruction, provided a series of staff development and curriculum development sessions for the participants. Communications were enhanced by task force meetings that brought representatives from each content area session together with consultants and administrators to discuss concerns at next steps.

Data sources included observation, audiotapes and transcriptions, interviews and questionnaire and document searches.

Through naturalistic inquiry and the field study approach, an extensive mandated change process documented a participatory staff development and curriculum development process in an otherwise traditionally top-down system. The analysis enhanced the research on the role of teacher participation, the co-ordination of consultants' feedback and the significance of a catalytic building administrator. This study suggested that participatory decision-making is effective. The ramifications of a co-ordinated, administratively and financially supported staff development and curriculum development change process influenced not only teachers' attitudes but also student achievement, parental appreciation, and community involvement.

Westwood and Graham (2003) conducted comparative study on "inclusion of students with special needs: benefits and obstacle perceived by teachers in New South Australia". This study showed the views of primary teachers from South Australia and New South

Wales on selected aspects of inclusive education. The structured questionnaire was sent to a representative sample of schools listed in the disadvantaged schools and country area programs in both states. Major findings indicated that approximately one-third of teachers in both South Australia and New South Wales reported definite benefits associated with having students with disabilities enrolled in their classrooms. Specific problems to implement inclusive practice included class size, lack of appropriate, teaching resources, behaviour problems exhibited by some student and lack of appropriate professional training in inclusive methods.

To sum up, the quoted studies under this head promote better insight about the teacher's attitude towards children with disabilities apart from inclusion and mainstreaming the children with disabilities. The studies gives an indepth analysis of disabilities in children and the effect of inclusion (Adams, Kimberly, 1998; Bearn et al., 1998; Bowers, 1998; Brownlee et al., 2000, Butera Gretchen et al., 1998; Cornoldi & Cesare et al., 1998; Cook & Bryan et al., 2000; Hoffman et al., 1997; Lombard & Richard, 1998 and Poon-McBrayer & Kim Forg, 1998). Overall, better teacher attitude towards children with disabilities develops a will, interest and positive views about children with disabilities. But most of the studies quoted are in the Western context and the studies in Indian sub continent are limited suggesting the need for such research.

Studies on Competencies of Teachers Dealing Children with Disabilities

Competency is the knowledge, attitude and skill to do particular job. A teacher should be able to guide and direct their students. Only competent teachers facilitate the way for better integration of children with disabilities. A teacher should possess certain specific competencies to realise the strengths and weaknesses of children with disabilities and to teach them effectively. Studies on teacher competencies to deal children with disabilities are given under this heading.

In 1918, the American Association of Instructors of Blind (AAIB) identified a list of goals which would help to make the education of visually handicapped pupils more effective. The list included:

1. The adoption of a uniform type for the blind of the English speaking world.
2. The gradual elimination of pupils of very low mental ability from our schools.
3. The introduction of sight saving classes for the partially blind in institutions for the blind and in public schools.
4. The regular and scientific training of girls in home making.
5. The systematic physical training given to our pupils in the gymnasium, the swimming pool and on the athletic field, the holding of competitive athletic meets which has done much to promote self-confidence and school pride.
6. The education of the blind with the seeing in high schools and universities, as well as in special classes for the blind in public schools.
7. The introduction of new courses of study which are more elastic and which give equal opportunity for the development of the bright as well as the dull child.
8. The establishment of separate kindergartens for the young blind.
9. Greater attention to vocational work, especially for those of lower mentality (Abel, 1967, p. 107).

Aker (1962) in his study identified 23 behaviours which were judged to be adequate criteria for determining the achievement of educational objectives. They are:

— helps people to control and adjust to change rather than maintain the status quo.

— intelligently observes and listens to what is being said or done and uses this information guiding his respondents.

— selects and uses teaching method, materials and resources that are appropriate in terms of what is to be learned and in terms of the needs and abilities of the individual learner.

— helps his client to acquire the ability for critical thinking.

— provides an atmosphere where adults are free to search through trial-and-error without fear of instructional or interpersonal threat.

— Identifies potential leaders and helps them to develop their potentials and capacities.

— make use of existing values, beliefs, customs and attitudes as a starting point for educational objectives.

— is actively involved in continuing study that will increase his professional competence.

— understands the role of adult education in society and is aware of the factors and forces that give rise to this function.

— actively shares, participates and learns with the learners in learning experience.

— helps adults to actively set their goals and provides a variety means and opportunities for intensive self-evaluation.

— identifies and interprets trends that have implications for adult education.

— has clearly defined his unique role as an adult educator and understands his responsibility for performing it.

— arranges learning experiences so that learners can integrate theory and practice.

— is effective in building teaching team among lay leaders and group members.

— uses the process of appraisal to evaluate programmes and to help clarify and change objectives.

— is creative and imaginative in developing new programmes and experiments that are necessary for the expansion of adult education.

— make use of the contributions of all group members through the utilization of individual talents and abilities.

— works with schools, teachers, parents and pre-adults so as to assist them in developing motivation, attitudes, understanding and skills necessary for lifelong learning.
— objectively presents contrasting points of view.
— assumes the initiatives in developing a strong rational perception of importance and essentiality of continuing education.
— recognises when the communication process is not functioning adequately or when it breaks down.
— identifies, critically evaluates and discuss scholarly works by investigators in adult education and related fields.

Akkammadevi and Nagarani (2003) developed improvised aids to enhance tactual discrimination ability of visually impaired children. The data was collected from the resource teachers, special teachers and visually impaired children from special school for the blind and integrated schools in I and II standards, at Madurai and Palayamkottai. Experimental method was used in the study, with 12 groups of improvised aids which were prepared by the investigator to improve the tactual discrimination ability of the visually impaired children. The result showed that improvised aids prepared by the investigator were effective to enhance tactual discrimination ability of visually impaired children.

Anita Jukla (1998) examined the role of regular school teacher and special teacher in mainstream schools in the existing system and to delineate needs that call for their empowerment in successful mainstreaming of visually impaired children. In-depth interviews were carried out with 15 persons involved with visually impaired children for a number of years. It was found through qualitative analysis that both the regular and special teachers had to assume great responsibility for providing quality education to children with visual impairments.

Annakodi (2003) studied the techniques of teaching self help skills to intellectually disabled children. Thirty intellectually disabled children, 15 boys and 15 girls of moderate trainable category between the age group of 10 to 15 years from two different special schools were selected as sample for the study. Prompting, imitation and shaping technique was used to teach six self help skills such as fine motor, meal time activity, dressing, grooming, receptive and expressive language. Prompting technique was more effective in teaching self help skills among children with intellectual disability.

Barber (1960), Bourgeault (1960), Enright (1953), Fortner (1945), Gilmore (1956), Grant (1966), Heimbuch (1962), Irwin (1961), Johnson (1961), Meyer (1925), Paterson (1913) and Root (1960) listed out the competencies that are necessary for resource teachers of visually handicapped students. They are:

1. Knowledge of communication skills and utilisation of devices.
2. Understanding the educational implications of eye conditions.
3. Skills in curriculum development and adaptation.
4. Skill in public education.
5. Skill in guidance and counselling.
6. Skill in orientation and mobility.
7. Knowledge of how to utilize and develop local, state and national resources.
8. Ability to do teacher consultation.
9. Understanding the sociological and the psychological needs of children.
10. Skill in paper and record keeping.
11. Knowledge and procurement of educational equipment.
12. Knowledge of child growth and development.
13. Background in general education.
14. Ability to develop and provide supplementary devices, e.g. readers, tutors, class activities etc.
15. Skill in classroom observation.

Bessant-Byrd (1981) proposed that people preparing to teach minority students in special education programmes should be able to:

- demonstrate knowledge of the role of a value system and evaluate its influence on behaviour.
- demonstrate knowledge of the philosophy of various cultures and exhibit an interest in expanding that knowledge.
- use relevant information and materials characteristics of both traditional and contemporary lifestyles of various cultures.
- understand different patterns of human growth and development within and between cultures.
- recognise potential cultural and linguistic biases in the composition, administration, and interpretation of existing assessment instruments and,
- demonstrate the ability to provide of flexible learning environment which meets individual needs of learners from various culture groups.

Blanchett (2001) studied the importance of teacher transition competencies as rated by special educators. Seventy-four special educators who were involved in transition-related activities rated the importance of 30 transition-related teacher competencies. All competencies were identified by the majority of respondents as important competencies related to teaching money management skills and involving parents received the highest ratings.

Cowasji (1983) studied the effectiveness of the orientation programmes for teachers working in the integrated education for the disabled children. The study aimed to find out the present position of available resources, system of working and implementation of institutional plans in the schools selected for orientation by SIERT, Udaipur. The study revealed that the teachers found the orientation programme to be helpful in raising their standard and useful.

Geetha and Dash (2003) studied the outcomes of adapted physical education on the physical fitness of hearing impaired children. In this study, 15 integrated and special schools in Coimbatore city were selected. Adapted physical education training programmes were adopted for a period of six weeks to the randomly selected 15 children with hearing impairment in the age range 10-15 years. The developed adapted physical education training programme showed significant improvement in the physical fitness of the selected sample with disabilities.

Gold Hammer, Rader and Reuschelin (1977) surveyed fourteen colleges and universities that were conducting programmes to prepare regular classroom teachers to mainstream mildly handicapped students. This research yielded a list of some 464 competencies clustered into thirteen areas: nature of mainstreaming, nature of the handicap, attitudes, resources, teaching techniques, learning environment, learning styles, classroom management, curriculum, communication, assessing student needs, evaluating student progress and administration.

Heller, Kathryn Wolff (1999) conducted a study on a national perspective of competencies for teachers of individuals with physical and health disabilities. The study involved 59 teachers instructing students with physical and health disabilities, 26 universities, 36 local school system directors, and 29 state departments of education and found over 40 per cent of the teachers did not feel well trained in half of the competencies.

Jairrels, Veda (1993) conducted a study on the multicultural competence of special education teachers. The purpose of this study was to investigate special education teachers' perceptions of multicultural competence as it pertains to cultural diversity. Specifically, the issue of multi-cultural competence as related to race, religion, ethnicity, socio-economic status and gender was examined. 94 African-American special education teachers and 133 Caucasian special education teachers rated their degree of competence for 36 skills using a 5 point Likert-type scale. There was a significant difference between African-American special education teachers and Caucasian special education teachers in their perceptions of multicultural competence. African-American special education teachers had higher levels of perceived competence than Caucasian special education teachers. There were no other significant difference found on the basis of gender, years of teaching experience, years of teaching in special education, school level, the classification of student taught, and certification levels. This might indicate that multicultural education in teacher education institutions has not changed over years. The result of this study can be used to assist school administrators and teacher educators in the design of in service training programmes and college curricula that would incorporate multicultural education.

Jangira (1992) discussed about the education of children with mental retardation in natural setting. Steps in achieving education in natural setting were (i) having faith and educate public opinion, (ii) provide home-based early intervention programmes to prepare these children for education, (iii) prepare teachers in general schools to meet diverse educational needs in the classroom, (iv) have functional assessment rather than clinical assessment, (v) provide curriculum and teaching flexibility, (vi) provide alternative clearing material to schools to meet special needs and (vii) encourage the use of other people support in the classroom.

Jayaprabha (2003) studied the metacognitive and cognitive strategies to overcome behaviour difficulties. The objectives of the study were (i) to identify children with behaviour difficulties (conduct disorder socialised aggression, attention problems, motor over activity, anxiety disorder and psychotic disorder), (ii) to develop and implement metacognitive and cognitive strategies to overcome the above said behaviour difficulties. Metacognitive strategies such as underlining, outlining, note taking, summarizing and self-questioning and cognitive strategies such as modelling, overt external guidance, overt self-guidance, faded self-guidance and covert self-guidance were given through the following steps:

1. Narrative descriptions
2. Pictorial representation
3. Role play and
4. Interactions with the non-problematic peer with guided questions.

The results of the study showed that the behaviour difficulties in children were curtailed to a greater extent by the implementation of aforesaid metacognitive and cognitive strategies inside and outside the classroom.

Jeevanantham (2002) studied the competencies of teachers. The objective of the study was to find out the significant differences, if any, in the competencies (planning, instruction, preparation of instructional materials, defining learning objectives and providing learning activities) possessed by the secondary grade teachers and B.T. assistants. Four point rating scale was used to observe classroom instruction and for perusing the teacher records. The constructed tools consisted of (a) planning instruction competency, (b) preparation of instructional materials, (c) defining the learning objectives and (d) providing learning activities. The study found the competencies of Secondary grade teachers and B.T. Assistants to be very low in (i) planning instructions, (ii) defining the learning objectives, (iii) providing learning activities and (iv) preparing instructional materials.

Knowlton and Marie (1999) studied the competencies required for Braille teachers. A survey of 51 teachers licensed to teach children with visual disabilities in Minnesota found they had high abilities for using references when transcribing Braille, producing Braille with Braille writers, interlining braille, and using software for braille transcription, low abilities for writing with slate and stylus and that few had braille transcribers certification.

Luckner and John (1991) studied "the competencies needed for teaching hearing-impaired students: a comparison of elementary and secondary school teacher perceptions". Elementary and secondary teachers (N=285) of hearing-impaired students were surveyed to compare perceptions of competencies needed to work with hearing-impaired students. Results suggested that teachers at both levels believed some skills to be fundamental for all teachers of the hearing impaired regardless of students' age level, though there were some important differences.

Luckner and John et al. (2001) conducted a study to identify the essential competencies for teaching students with hearing loss and additional disabilities. In a survey of 233 educators working with students who are deaf or hard of hearing with additional disabilities, educators identified 67 specific competencies needed for working with this diverse population of students. A list of the specific competencies and a rationale for providing more in-depth training for teachers was provided by them.

Madry (1963) distributed a questionnaire which contained 77 statements of functions, 33 competency statements and questions about problem areas. Competencies which were rated highest were basic understanding of programmes organisation and administration, ability to establish wholesome relationships, and executive and supervisory ability. The major functions reported by respondents included: (1) Organisation and structure, (2) programme purpose, (3) programme planning and development, (4) instructional services and materials, (5) student personal service, (6) staff personnel, (7) facilities and business management, (8) school community relations and promotion, (9) community services, (10) programme evaluation and (11) research.

McNicholas and Jim (2001) studied the assessment of pupils with profound and multiple learning difficulties. The study involved 114 educators of students with profound and multiple learning difficulties. Interviews with 20 head teachers and observation in four British schools found students' assessment was largely informal; individualised education programmes were often lacking in detail; and about one-third of teachers has no special education qualifications.

Merry (1933) surveyed the basic qualification of experienced educators of the blind. They were:

1. four year high school course;
2. three or four years of normal training, special training for non-academic courses;
3. a course in the history of education for the Blind; and
4. in psychological and educational problems in blindness;
5. curriculum adaptation and development;
6. assessment and evaluation; and

7. knowledge of role and ability to work with other specialists, agencies, and appropriate organisations (Mackie & Dunn, 1955, pp. 76-77).

Premila Bala Sundaram (1992) explained dramatic play for mentally handicapped children. Situations can be created where only sounds are used. Mime is actually a highly sophisticated acting technique. Gestures can be introduced through mime. Drama work encourages children to work in pairs or worth an adult.

Ramar (1999) studied the effectiveness of multimedia based modular approach with special reference to slow learners. The study aimed to develop multimedia based modules for English, Maths, Science and Social Science subjects of standard VIII and to find out the effectiveness of the developed multimedia based modules. The study result showed that there was significant difference between the pre-test and post-test scores of experimental group slow learners when the subjects were taught through multimedia based modular approach. The findings of the study found the multimedia based modular approach to be more effective for slow learners.

Redden and Blackhurst (1978) reported research directed at identifying competencies of elementary teachers who were mainstreaming handicapped students. Using a research procedure known as the critical incident technique (Flangan, 1962), 828 specific incidents in which teachers had been either effective or ineffective in their mainstreaming efforts were collected from 184 elementary teachers. After eliminating redundancies, some 271 different tasks were identified that seemed to be important. These tasks were clustered into thirty-one competency statements, which were subsequently grouped into six areas of teachers' functioning-developing orientation strategies for mainstream entry, assessing needs and goal setting, use of resources, implementing teaching strategies and utilization of resources, facilitating learning and evaluating learning.

Reddy and Ramar (1994) studied effectiveness of multimedia based modular approach in teaching social science to low achievers. The objectives of the study were (i) to develop multimedia based modules for social science in standard VIII and (ii) to measure the effectiveness of multimedia based modular approach with special reference to low achievers. Two matched groups of low achievers were constituted for the purpose of experiment and a normal group was also formed in order to assess how far this multimedia based modular approach enabled the low achievers to cope with normal children. The control group and the normal group were taught through traditional lecture method while the experimental group was taught through multimedia-based modular approach. The obtained results showed that the multimedia based modular approach was more effective than the traditional lecture method in teaching of social science and it enabled the low achievers to cope up with normal students to a greater extent.

Reddy and Ramar (1995a) made a study on the effectiveness of multimedia based modular approach in teaching mathematics to low achievers. The objectives were (i) to develop multimedia based modules, (ii) to measure the effectiveness of multimedia based modules. 50 low achieving students of VIII std. were selected. Two matched groups-control and experimental groups of low achievers and normal group were selected. Control group and normal group were taught through traditional lecture method. But the experimental group was taught through multimedia based modules. The results showed that multimedia based modular approach was more effective than the traditional lecture method in teaching of mathematics of std. VIII to low achievers.

The same authors (1995) conducted an experimental study with the objective to develop multimedia based modules for science subject on VIII standard and to measure the effectiveness of multimedia based modular approach with special reference to low achievers. Two matched groups of low achievers and a normal group comprising average and above average students formed the sample for the study. The control and normal group were taught through traditional lecture method while the experimental group was taught through multimedia based modular approach. The media method was more effective than the traditional lecture method in teaching of science and it enabled the low achievers to cope up with normal students to a greater extent.

Reddy and Ramar (1999) investigated the effectiveness of multimedia instructional strategy in teaching science to slow learners. The study was undertaken with two objectives in view (i) to develop multimedia packages for class VIII science subject, and (ii) to measure the effectiveness of multimedia instructional strategy with special reference to slow learners. Two matched groups of slow learners were formed for the purpose of this experiment and a normal group comprising average and above average students was also formed in order to assess how far multimedia instructional strategy enabled the slow learners to cope with normal students. The control group and the normal group were taught through traditional lecture method while the experimental group was taught through multimedia instructional strategy. The obtained results showed that the multimedia instructional strategy was more effective than the traditional lecture method in teaching science and it enabled the slow learners to cope with normal students to a considerable extent.

Reddy and Ramar (1997) conducted a study to find out the effectiveness of multimedia based modular approach in teaching English to slow learners. The objectives of the study were (i) to develop multimedia based modules for VIII standard English subject, and (ii) to measure the effectiveness of multimedia based modular approach with special reference to slow learners. Two matched groups of slow learners were constituted for the purpose of this experiment and a normal group comprising average and above average students was also framed in order to assess how far multimedia based modular approach enables the slow learners to cope with normal students. The control group and the normal group were taught through traditional lecture method while the experimental group was taught through multimedia based modular approach. The obtained results showed that the multimedia based modular approach was more effective than the traditional lecture method in teaching English and it enabled the slow learners to cope with normal students.

Reddy and Ramar (1998) studied the effects of Video instruction on achievement of slow learners in Mathematics. Video instructional programmes in mathematics were developed for the slow learners. 50 slow learners of VII std were divided into two groups, namely, control and experimental group. Normal group was also selected to assess the extent to which the video instructional method enabled the slow learners to cope with normal students. After statistical treatment of the data, the superiority of video instruction over the traditional lecture method in helping the slow learners of standard VIII to learn mathematics was inferred.

Reddy and Ramar (1999) investigated the effectiveness of computer-assisted instruction in teaching science to slow learners. The objectives of the study were (i) to develop software for computer assisted instruction to teach science subject to slow learners and (ii) to measure the effectiveness of computer assisted instructions with special reference to slow learners. Two matched groups of slow learners and normal group of average and above average students formed the sample for the study. The control and normal group were taught through traditional lecture method. Experimental group was taught through computer-assisted instruction. The obtained results showed that the computer-assisted instruction was more effective than the traditional lecture method in teaching science and it enabled the slow learners to cope with normal students to a considerable extent.

Reddy (2000) studied the role performance of special education teachers. In this study, the role performance of teachers dealing visually impaired, hearing impaired, mentally retarded and orthopaedically handicapped was studied. He also investigated the problems faced by these teachers in organisation, teaching and providing guidance and counselling. Role performance scale and problem checklist were developed and used in this study for data collection. The result of the study showed that the performance of special school teachers in guidance and counselling was low when compared with organisation and teaching roles. The study also revealed the dearth of infrastructure facilities in special schools.

Reddy et al. (2000) found the impact of modular approach on the achievement of slow learners in social science. The study was undertaken with two objectives (i) to develop modules in social science for class VIII in order to teach slow learners, and (ii) to measure the effectiveness of modular approach with special reference to slow learners. Two matched groups of slow learners were constructed for the purpose of this experiment and a normal group comprising average and above average students was also formed in order to assess how far modular approach enabled the slow learners to cope with normal students. The control group and the normal group were taught through traditional lecture method while the experimental group was taught through modular approach. The obtained results showed that the modular approach was more effective than the traditional lecture method in teaching social science and it enabled the slow learners to cope with normal students.

Reddy et al. (2001) studied the relative effectiveness of tangible materials (Braille) and talking books (Audio cassettes) in learning social science concepts by the visually impaired children in secondary schools. 54 visually impaired children were selected from 6 integrated educational programme of Coimbatore district of Tamilnadu state. These 54 children were divided into two equated groups. One group was treated with tangible material and the other with talking books for a period of 3 months. The result revealed that both the educational media was effective in learning social science concepts by the VIC but the talking books were slightly more advantageous than the braille media. The learning achievement of different group of VI children exposed to braille and VI children exposed to audio cassette was similar. On the other hand, the talking books facilitated the learning achievement of born blind children than the braille media. From the results of the study, it is stressed that the VI children should be facilitated and motivated to use more talking books, keeping the advantage of their low cost preparation compared to braille materials.

Reddy and Kanchanamala (2002) investigated the effectiveness of multimedia based modular approach in learning Botany by the slow learners. 60 slow learning students of XI std. were selected. They were put into two groups, namely, an experimental group and control group. Normal group of 30 above average was also selected. The 60 slow learning students were divided into two equated groups of 30 students each. The experimental group slow learners were taught through multimedia based modular approach. Control group slow learners and normal group were taught through traditional lecture method. The results of the study proved that multimedia based modular approach was more effective than lecture method in teaching Botany to slow learners.

Reddy and Shyamala (2003) quoted that 'constructivism develops thinking skills, communication and social skills, encourages alternative methods of assessment, helps students transfer skills to the real world and promotes intrinsic motivation to learn. Thinking and constructivism are the big ideas in education. Their implications for how teachers teach, and learn to teach are enormous. Rather than receiving 'knowledge' from experts in training sessions, teachers and administrators will have to collaborate with peers, researchers and their own students to make sense of thinking and constructivism. Only then we can transform our nation through education, into a thoughtful, critical, scientific community, imbued with the passion for truth and for total human welfare'.

Reddy and Shyamala (2004) studied the thinking errors and antisocial behaviours of high school students. A sample of 50 students with antisocial behaviour were rated by the teachers by using rating scales to assess antisocial behaviour and thinking errors. The results revealed that students belonging to SC/ST communities with birth order later than second, hailing from rural areas, living in the joint family system, and staying with both parents and guardians exhibited more thinking errors. No significant difference had been observed in the thinking errors of students with antisocial behaviour due to variations in their background factors. Further, there was a significant positive correlation between the thinking errors and the antisocial behaviour of high school students. They came to the conclusion that by the use of constructive strategies such as co-operative training, problem-solving, role playing, and class discussions, teachers can help students develop critical thinking skills to denounce thinking errors and thereby antisocial behaviours.

Reddy and Sujathamalini (2003) presented instructional paradigms to promote learning among the learning disabled students. Reductionism and constructivism were the two general instructional paradigms that promote learning using an information processing approach. Behaviour approaches are based on reductionism. Cognitive behaviour modification is an example of a reductionism approach for cognitive training. Constructivist approach is based on the premise that the student is a naturally active learner who constructs new personalised knowledge through linking prior knowledge and new knowledge. There is one more approach which moves towards combining or integrating paradigms to teach. Integration or combination of paradigms to meet the needs of diverse learners was stressed.

Reddy and Sujathamalini (2003) discussed strategies for development of social competence among the disabled pupils. They explained that the psycho-educational perspective is the foundation for crisis intervention and lifespan interview techniques, reality therapy, the self-control curriculum, and social learning therapy helps students to develop positive feelings and internal control over their behaviour. Further, cognitive behaviour modification is also very useful in developing social competence among the disabled.

The same authors (2003) delineated the various inputs that are required for the people's committee and voluntary organisations to overcome learning disabilities/difficulties in adults such as knowledge about the concept of LD, characteristics of LDs, various instructional strategies and materials, ability to use instructional strategies and materials and ability to use the strengths and weakness of LD adults. Multi-sensory learning techniques are stressed by the authors for handling adults with LD.

The same authors (2004) stressed that intervention programme has to maximise the mentally retarded individuals skills and abilities so that he can become as independent as possible. They suggested that rehabilitation psychology must consider the etiology of mental deficiencies, the nature of mental deficiencies with characteristics, preventive and curative measures, training and intervention strategies for effective integration of these individuals in larger society.

Santhakumari (2003) studied the effectiveness of metacognitive strategies in overcoming language learning difficulties among higher secondary students. The objectives of the study were to find out the students with language learning difficulties, develop metacognitive strategies, implementation of the strategies and to find out the effectiveness of metacognitive strategies to overcome language learning difficulties. The metacognitive strategies developed by the investigator were: (i) task orientation, (ii) task planning, (iii) self monitoring, (iv) self-regulation and (v) self-evaluation. The results of the study revealed that the developed metacognitive strategies were effective in overcoming language learning difficulties among higher secondary students.

Sass-Lehrer and Marilyn (1986, 1986a) assessed competencies for effective teaching of hearing impaired students. Supervisors (N=150) of programmes for the hearing impaired rated a set of 40 competencies for teachers of elementary level, hearing impaired students. Seven of ten competencies identified as critical to teaching effectiveness reflected the broad area of instruction and international planning skills, almost half of which related to assessment.

Sharma et al. (1992) conducted an experimental study to assess the effectiveness of adapted instructional material in science on hearing impaired from IED and special schools. This study sensitised teachers to device better teaching methodologies for IED class I-VII std. The result of study evinced that the performance of the hearing impaired from IED and special schools on post-test was better than on the pre-test. But the performance of classes II and IV std of special schools was better than the students of class II and IV std studying in IED setting, both on pre-test and post-test. Further, it was also found that the performance of the hearing impaired was better on the post-test than on the pre-test.

Shyamala (2004) investigated the effectiveness of certain strategies in overcoming antisocial behaviour among high school students. The objectives of the study were to identify students with various antisocial behaviours such as attention deficit hyperactivity disorder (ADHD), oppositional defiant disorder (ODD) and conduct disorder (CD) and, to develop and implementation of comprehensive intervention strategy to overcome antisocial behaviour among high school students. Comprehensive intervention strategy included cognitive-behavioural strategies. These strategies were implemented at three levels: (a) Individual level, (b) Parental level, and (c) Peer group level.

In Parental level- (i) introducing systematic monitoring, reward and discipline systems, (ii) prompting parents to communicate effectively with each other about adolescent problems, (iii) solving problems arising out of day-to-day conflicts and (iv) developing social support networks with friends, extended family and so forth. At peer level—to decrease the student's involvement with delinquent and drug using peers and increasing his or her association with prosocial peers (e.g. through youth clubs, organised athletics and after school activities. At school level—Anger management and inter-personal skills development by use of role play and involving the students in creative activities such as music, drama, arts and craft, sports and games. Self-control and self-analysis were given due importance through activities such as yoga, meditation and modelling. Individual counselling session was also conducted which helped the students with anti-social behaviour to identify their thinking errors and also found means and ends to find measures to rectify them by orientation and imitation techniques. The results of the study showed that developed comprehensive intervention strategy was more effective in overcoming antisocial behaviours such as ADHD, ODD and CD among high school students.

Sujathamalini (1997) conducted an experimental study on developing daily living skills among intellectually disabled. The study revealed that modelling, shaping, promoting, reinforcement and fading techniques were very useful in developing daily living skills among intellectually disabled.

Sujathamalini (2002) studied the competencies required for primary school teachers to handle learning difficulties in children. The study aimed to list out the competencies and measured existing and required competencies of primary school teachers to handle learning difficulties in children. The result of the study shows that the teachers exhibited low level of competency in causes and characteristics and identification and assessment of children with learning difficulties. Whereas, teachers exhibited moderate level of competency in teaching and guidance aspects. High level of competencies were found in some of the competency statements. More than 75 per cent of teachers had the need to enrich their competency level and this result showed that there is a need to organise competency based teacher training programmes for the teachers to handle learning difficulties in children.

Wallace and Teri et al. (2001) conducted a study on knowledge and skills for teachers supervising the work of paraprofessionals. The study involving 92 administrators, 266 teachers, and 211 paraprofessionals identified competencies needed by the teachers to supervise or direct the work of paraprofessionals in educational settings. Results indicated that participants considered the competencies very important but the competencies were not observed as frequently as their perceived importance.

White (1950) developed the following list of competencies which are appropriate for adult educators.

1. To gain a better understanding of the basic needs which cause adults to participate in educational programmes.
2. To gain a clear insight into the changing interests of adults in vocations, religion, family, leisure time activities, health and other areas of life.
3. To increase ability to apply psychological principles to the selection of objectives. To acquire techniques for relating the programmes more closely to the general needs of the community.
4. To acquire techniques for relating programmes more closely to the needs and interests in adults.
5. To acquire techniques for relating programmes more closely to the needs of the community.
6. To become more skilful in recognising community needs and resources that are important to adult education programmes.

7. To develop a better understanding of the kinds of educational methods most suitable for mature persons.
8. To develop a better understanding of the kinds of educational materials most suitable for mature persons.
9. To become familiar with procedures for 'keeping up' with new developments and material for adult education programmes.

Adult educators who have doctorates were surveyed by Veri (1968) to assess their reaction to 60 learning total programmes which would provide graduates with necessary competencies. The following list of 19 programme areas resulted from this survey. They were: (1) history and philosophy of adult education; (2) designing and evaluating adult education programmes; (3) psychology of adult education; (4) sociology of adult education; (5) social change; (6) special problems; (7) motivation; (8) organisation and administration of adult education; (9) methods and media in adult education; (10) educational psychology; (11) cultural change; (12) fundamental research techniques; (13) utilisation and evaluation of audio-visual aids; (14) public relations; (15) personnel administration; (16) internship in adult education to determine research needs and design a research project; (17) budget development and control in education (18) public speaking; and (19) community planning and organisation.

Vinita Krishna (1992) dealt with instructional strategies for teaching the mentally handicapped. Instructional strategies such as-motivation, shaping, prompting, fading, chaining were suggested for teaching mentally retarded.

To conclude, a wholistic view on competencies of teachers to handle children with disabilities were seen through the quoted studies. Studies that are conducted directly on competencies of teachers have listed out the important competencies required for a teacher (Abel, 1967; Barber et al. 1960; Gold Hammer, Rader and Recuschelin, 1977, Redden and Blackhurst, 1978). Some researchers carried out their studies to find out the effectiveness of certain instructional strategies in dealing children with disabilities which a competent teacher should use in their teaching-learning process (Akkammadevi, 2003; Jayaprabha, 2003; Reddy and

Kanchanamala, 2002; Reddy and Shyamala, 2004; Reddy and Ramar, 1999; 1998; 1997; 1994, 1995, 1995a, 1995b, Santhakumari, 2003; Sharma et al., 1992; and Shyamala, 2004). Instructional strategies used in the above quoted studies are of much use in educating the children with disabilities. A teacher should possess the abilities or competency to adopt those instructional strategies effectively to deal children with disabilities. The study conducted by Reddy (2000) clearly indicated the special education teachers' low performance in guidance and counselling activities and poor infrastructure facility available in special schools.

An Overview of Research Reviewed

A close look at the studies quoted above clearly reveals the work that has been carried out on various aspects of disabilities in children. Studies under general heading covers the causes of disabilities, characteristics and abilities of disabled children, behaviour problems, academic performance, and on identification and assessment (Divya Jindal, 1996; Hampson and Duffy, 1984; Kundu et al., 1985; Mani, 1993; Manju Pandey, 1999; Pandey, 1985; Reddy and Kusuma, 1995; Rajaguru, 1996; Reddy, 1997; Sheela Sangwan, 2002; Sibnath Deb et al., 2002 and Vasuki and Mahima, 2001).

Awareness about disabilities in children gives a clear picture about the teacher's lack of knowledge on various aspects of disabilities in children (Brent, 2003; Dharmaraj, 2000; Drury, 1994; Hoffman, 1995, Lago-Delello, 1998; Nagomi Ruth, 2000; Sarojini, 2000; Selvakani, 2000 and Swartz, 1995).

Right type of teacher with right attitude can do better justice to the children with disabilities. Any educational system is successful if the teacher has right attitude towards teaching. Teachers pre-conceived beliefs and opinions about the children counts. Knowing its importance, there are research works attempted on teacher attitude in general. Some studies have also been carried out on teacher attitude towards children with disabilities. Adams and Kimberly (1998), Bearn et al. (1998), Brownlee et al. (2000), De Bettem Court Laurie (1999), Hoffman (1997), Kusuma Harinath (2000), Lombard and Richard et al. (1998), Meltzer and Lynn et al. (1998), Poon McBrayer and Kim Forg (1998) and Praisner (2003) studied the teacher's attitude towards children with disabilities: These studies give insight about teacher's positive and negative attitude towards children with disabilities.

An efficient teacher with specific competencies can handle children with disabilities more effectively. Every special and normal school teacher needs certain specific competencies to know the nature and type of disabilities in children. The teacher should be prepared to recognise the problem or a condition and cause for it. Identification and assessment ability is a must for a teacher as they are with the children and considered as a second parent. Proficient in teaching strategies and methods is an important task of a teacher. Use of innovative teaching strategies to compensate the disabilities in children is one of the competencies a teacher should possess. Studies conducted by Abel (1967), Barber et al. (1960), Bessant-Byrd (1981), Blanchett (2001), Heller and Kathryn Wolff (1999), Jairrels and Veda (1993), Jeevanantham (2002), Luckner and John (1991), Redden and Blackhurst (1978), and Sass-Lehrer Marilyn (1986), give a better insight to know the competencies required by the teacher to handle children with disabilities, effectively.

Further, the studies conducted to find out the effectiveness of certain instructional strategies to overcome different disabilities give an idea that the teacher should use such strategies to handle children with disabilities (Akkammadevi, 2003; Annakodi, 2003; Jayaprabha, 2003; Reddy and Ramar, 1995, 1995a, 1995b, 1997, 1998 and 1999; Reddy and Kanchanamala, 2002; Santhakumari, 2003; Sharma et al., 1992 and Shyamala, 2004). The instructional strategies used by these researchers are found to be effective for the children with disabilities. So, it is evident that every teacher must be able to adapt such strategies in their teaching process for children with disabilities.

The above review clearly indicates that the researches conducted are more in western world than in India. Further, studies on teachers awareness, attitude, competencies and infrastructure facilities available in special and normal schools are very limited in Indian situation. Indepth studies which focus their attention on identifying the awareness, attitude and competencies required for special and normal school teachers; the attitude of peers towards their disabled peers; the infrastructure facilities available in the special and normal schools for meeting the needs of disabled children; and the relationship between infrastructure facilities and drop out rate are the need of the hour to get clear picture about the ways and means of developing appropriate policies and programmes to the children with disabilities in an integrated set-up. The present study is an attempt in this direction and the methodology used in the study is presented in the succeeding chapter.

3

Methodology

Introduction

Methodology layout helps the investigator to proceed with the proposed research in a systematic way. It helps to select or construct suitable tools for data collection. This chapter contains the lay out description of the methodology followed to study the awareness, attitude and competencies required for special and normal school teachers in dealing children with disabilities. The methodology followed in this study such as construction of research tools, reliability of the tools, sampling procedures, methods of data collection and statistical techniques used are discussed here under.

Construction of Research Tools

The result of any scientific investigation depends upon the tools used in the study. To arrive at logical conclusions, the reliable and valid tools play a vital role. There are so many standard tools available which may vary in design, administration and interpretation. Depending on the nature of study, a researcher can make use of standardised tools or they can develop their own tools. Considering the nature and purpose of the study, the researcher selected rating scale to measure the awareness, attitude and competencies required for special and normal school teachers dealing children with disabilities.

Researchers like Dharmaraj (2000), Sarojini (2000), Kusuma Harinath (2000) and Hoffman (1995) developed their own rating scales to assess the teacher awareness. Bearn (1998), Brownlee

(2000), Hoffman (1997), Taplin (1998), Tobin (1972) and West Wood (2003) used interview technique questionnaire and rating scale to investigate teacher perception and attitude. Kusuma Harinath (2000) used rating scale. Hoffman et al. (1997) used open ended interviews to study the teacher attitude towards learning disabilities and inclusion respectively. Blanchett (2001), Jairrels, Veda (1993), Jeevanantham (2002), Sass Lehrer, Marilyn (1986) and Sujathamalini (2002) used rating scales to study the teacher competencies. Critical incident technique was used by Redden and Blackhurst (1978). Considering the previous researches, the investigator developed Awareness Rating Scale and Attitude Scale to assess the awareness and attitude of special and normal school teachers towards children with disabilities. A competency Assessment Rating Scale was prepared to assess the existing competencies of special and normal school teachers to deal children with disabilities. To assess the required competencies, a checklist was prepared. Peer Attitude Scale was developed to identify the attitude of normal children towards their disabled peers. For identifying the infrastructure facilities available for the education of disabled children in special and normal schools, a checklist was developed.

Development of Research Tools

The objectives of the study were to assess the awareness, attitude, existing and required competencies of special and normal school teachers to deal children with disabilities. To achieve these objectives, the researcher developed the following tools:

1. Rating Scale to assess the Awareness of Special and Normal school Teachers towards various aspects of children with disabilities.

2. Attitude Scale to assess the Attitude of Special and Normal School Teachers towards various aspects of children with disabilities.

3. Competency Assessment Rating Scale to assess the Existing Competencies of Special and Normal School Teachers in dealing children with disabilities.

4. Checklist to identify the Required Competencies of Special and Normal School Teachers to deal children with disabilities.
5. Peer Attitude Scale to identify the Attitude of Normal School Children towards their disabled peers.
6. Checklist to identify the infrastructure facilities available for disabled children in special and normal schools.

Rating Scale to Assess the Awareness of Special and Normal School Teachers Towards Various Aspects of Children with Disabilities

To develop rating scale to assess the awareness of special and normal school teachers towards various aspects of children with disabilities, the investigator had to construct awareness statements on the concept of disabilities in children, causes and characteristics, identification and assessment, teaching and training methods and guidance and counselling to the children with disabilities as well as their parents and community. To prepare these statements, a thorough and indepth study of relevant literature, consultation with educationists, discussions with special education experts, professionals etc., were made by the researcher. A draft pool of awareness statements was thus prepared. The statements were presented in a clear and concise form for better understanding. Care was taken to avoid ambiguity and repetition in the statements.

Thus the drafted statements were given to a panel of experts who are familiar with the education of disabled, with a request to review and restructure or reword the items, if necessary. They were also requested to arrange the items under different areas (dimensions) such as concept of disabilities, causes and characteristics, identification and assessment, teaching and training methods and guidance and counselling. Based on their comments, the items were restructured and reworded and certain items were deleted and added. At this stage, there were 48 awareness statements falling under different awareness dimension. The number of statements falling under each awareness dimensions has been given in Table 3.1.

Table 3.1:

Awareness Area/Dimension	Number of Statements
Concept of disabilities in children	7
Causes and characteristics of children with disabilities	10
Identification and assessment of children with disabilities	7
Teaching and training methods	16
Guidance and counselling	8
Total	48

Against each statement, 3 gradations were given, namely, 'aware to greater extent'. 'aware to certain extent' and 'not aware', having the scores 3, 2 and 1 respectively.

For positive statements, the scoring was 3, 2, and 1 and for negative statements the scoring was in reverse order. To know the personal information about the teachers, such as gender, age, educational qualification, training in special education, years of experience, location of school, nature of school, category of school and type of school have been included in the Part-I of the rating scale.

Using this awareness rating scale, teacher's self ratings were derived to assess the awareness of special and normal school teachers on different dimensions of children with disabilities.

Attitude Scale to Assess the Attitude of Special and Normal School Teachers Towards Children with Disabilities

To assess the attitude of the special and normal school teachers towards children with disabilities, an attitude scale was developed by the investigator. The attitude scale consisted of the same statements as in awareness scale. The only difference was that the statements had been structured to assess the attitude component of that particular aspect. In developing the attitude scale, the procedure followed for the development of awareness scale was adopted and finally the attitude scale too consisted of 48 statements falling under the five attitudinal dimensions. The number of statements under each dimension was same as in the awareness scale.

Against each statement, 5 gradations were given, namely, 'strongly agree', 'agree', 'agree to certain extent', 'disagree' and 'strongly disagree' with scores 5, 4, 3, 2 and 1 respectively for positive statements and 1, 2, 3, 4 and 5 for negative statements.

Competency Assessment Rating Scale and Checklist to Assess the Existing and Required Competencies of Special and Normal School Teachers in Dealing Children with Disabilities

One of the major objectives of the study was to assess the existing and required competencies of special and normal school teachers to deal children with disabilities. For this, the researcher had developed the competency assessment scale. In developing this scale, the investigator transformed the awareness statements into competency statements. The concept of the awareness, attitude and competency statements was the same but they measured the different aspects, namely, awareness, attitude and competency of the teachers. Thus the developed statements were given to a panel of experts with a request to point out ambiguity, inaccuracies and repetitiveness, if any. Based on their comments, the statements were restructured to suit the needs of the study. At this stage, there were 48 competency statements falling under 5 competency areas as in the case of awareness and attitude.

Against each competency statement, three ratings were given, namely, 'competency to greater extent', 'competency to certain extent' and 'no competency', having scores 3, 2 and 1 respectively.

To identify the required competencies of special and normal school teachers in dealing children with disabilities the same competency statements were used. But rating was given in the form of 'Yes' or 'No' type. The scoring was '1' for 'Yes' and 'Zero' for 'No'.

Peer Attitude Scale to Identify the Attitude of Normal School Children Towards Their Disabled Peers

Peer attitude statements were drafted in consultation with experts, educationists and professionals. The statements were prepared with utmost care to avoid ambiguity, repetitions and inaccuracies. At the end, 16 attitude statements were constructed in a clear and concise form. Against each peer attitude statement, the option 'Yes' and 'No' were given. The normal school children were asked to say 'Yes' if they possess positive attitude on that particular statement and say 'No' if they have negative attitude. The scoring for 'Yes' was 1 and Zero for 'No'.

Checklist to Identify the Infrastructure Facilities Available for Disabled Children in Special and Normal Schools

A checklist was developed to identify the infrastructure facilities available in special and normal schools for the education of disabled children. Against each infrastructure facility, 'Yes' or 'No' was given. The school heads were requested to put tick mark on 'Yes' if the particular infrastructure facility is available or otherwise put tick mark on 'No'. The infrastructure facilities checklist consisted of 22 statements

Reliability of the Tools Used in the Study

There are four methods of establishing the reliability of a test. They are: (a) Test-retest method, (b) Alternate or Parallel forms, (c) Split-half method, (d) Rational equivalence method. Out of these four methods, split-half method is regarded as the best method. In this method, the data for calculating reliability can be obtained in one single occasion. So variations brought about by differences between the two testing situations are eliminated.

In the present study, split-half method was administered to establish the reliability of the rating scales and checklists. In this method, the tool was divided into two equivalent 'halves' and the correlation was found for these half-tests by using Karl Pearson's Correlation Coefficient formula.

$$r = \frac{N\Sigma xy - \Sigma x \Sigma y}{\sqrt{(N\Sigma x^2 - (\Sigma x)^2)(N\Sigma y^2 - (\Sigma y)^2)}}$$

r = Correlation co-efficient

x = Score obtained in one half of the test

y = Score obtained in another half of the test

Σx = Sum of obtained x values

Σy = Sum of obtained y values

Σx^2 = Sum of squared x values

$\Sigma y2$ = Sum of squared y values

$(\Sigma x)^2$ = Squared value of the sum of obtained x values

$(\Sigma y)^2$ = Squared value of the sum of obtained y values

N = Number of cases

From the reliability of the half test, the self correlation of the whole test is then estimated by using Spearman Brown Prophecy formula.

$$r_{11} = \frac{2r_{1/2}\ 1/11}{1 + r_{1/2}\ 1/11}$$

r_{11} = Reliability co-efficient of the whole test

$r_{1/2}$ = Reliability co-efficient of the half test found experimentally

The reliability values for (a) Awareness rating scale, (b) Attitude scale, (c) Competency assessment rating scale, (d) Checklist to assess the required competencies of special and normal school teachers to deal children with disabilities, (e) Peer attitude scale and (f) Checklist to identify the infrastructure facilities in special and normal schools for the disabled children were established by administering the same on a random sample of 7 per cent of total sample of the study i.e. 83 teachers for awareness scale, attitude scale, competency assessment scale and checklist to identify the required competencies; 28 peers for peer attitude scale and; 12 school heads for infrastructure facilities checklist. The obtained reliability values for the tools used in the study are presented here under.

(a) Awareness Rating Scale

$r_{1/2}$ = Half test reliability = 0.61

r_{11} = Whole test reliability = 0.76

(b) Attitude Scale

$r_{1/2}$ =Half test reliability = 0.76

r_{11} = Whole test reliability = 0.86

(c) Competency Assessment Rating Scale

$r_{1/2}$ = Half test reliability = 0.84

r_{11} = Whole test reliability = 0.91

(d) Checklist to identify the required competencies

$r_{1/2}$ = Half test reliability = 0.84

r_{11} = Whole test reliability = 0.92

(e) Peer Attitude Scale

$r_{1/2}$ = Half test reliability = 0.73

r_{11} = Whole test reliability = 0.84

(f) Checklist to identify the infrastructure facilities

$r_{1/2}$ = Half test reliability = 0.48

r_{11} = Whole test reliability = 0.65

The r-values of half test and the whole test with respect to each tool used in the study were high and hence the research tools used in the study were highly reliable.

Validity of the Tools Used in the Study

Validity is the quality of the research tool or procedure that measures what it purports to measure. A tool is said to be valid if it possesses content validity, face validity and intrinsic validity.

Content Validity

The content validity shows the adequacy of the content of a test. The tools used in the current study possessed content validity. The items in the tools were based on the relevant literature, and consultation with experts in the related field. Their valid suggestions were taken into account while constructing each scale and checklist used in the study and hence the tools used possessed content validity.

Face Validity

It refers to the way the test appears to those it is meant, to experts and educationists. That is, the test items should be related to the variable being measured. Based on the experts' consultation and opinion, it can be said that the tools used in the study possessed face validity.

Intrinsic Validity

Intrinsic validity shows how well the obtained scores measure the test's true score component. The square root of reliability is the intrinsic validity. The obtained intrinsic validity of the Awareness Rating Scale (0.87), Attitude Scale (0.93), Competency Assessment Rating Scale (0.95), Checklist to identify the Required Competency (0.96), Peer Attitude Scale (0.81) and Checklist to identify the Infrastructure Facilities in special and normal school (0.92) were high and hence the tools used in the study possessed intrinsic validity.

Sample of the Study

The area of the study comprised both Andhra Pradesh and Tamilnadu states in south India. For the purpose of the study, the investigator selected randomly two districts in each state where all categories of special schools (VI, HI, MR and OH) are existing. In Andhra Pradesh, Hyderabad and Chittoor districts were selected as the study area. In Tamil Nadu, Chennai and Madurai districts were selected. The selected districts have all the four categories of special schools.

In 1995, the National Information Centre on Disability and Rehabilitation, Ministry of Welfare, Govt. of India had prepared a Directory Compiling the list of institutions working for the disabled. According to this Directory, there are 31 institutions for VI, 46 institutions for HI, 63 institutions for MR and 37 institutions for OH functioning in the selected four districts.

Out of these 177 institutions, 84 institutions are running schools for different categories of disabled children. There are 660 teachers working in 84 special schools. All the 660 teachers working in these schools form the sample of the study.

The number of schools and teachers working in each category of disability in the selected four districts of AP and Tamilnadu states are presented in Table 3.2.

Table 3.2: Number of Schools and Teachers Working in Different Category of Special Schools

	Schools for VI	No. of Teachers	Schools for HI	No. of Teachers	Schools for MR	No. of Teachers	Schools for OH	No. of Teachers	Total Number of Schools	Total Number of Teachers
Madurai	2	16	–	–	3	23	–	1	5	40
Chennai	4	47	7	88	21	167	7	50	39	352
Chittoor	1	8	2	26	2	12	–	–	5	46
Hyderabad	2	24	17	99	14	91	3	8	35	222
Total	**9**	**95**	**26**	**213**	**40**	**293**	**10**	**59**	**84**	**660**

Note: 1. The total number of special schools together are 84 only.

2. One school is working for both HI and MR and hence this school is added to MR totalling 40 schools.

The normal schools located in the area where the special schools are functioning also formed the sample of the study. There were 76 primary schools existing for normal children in the special schools localities. All the 527 teachers working in those schools formed the sample of the study. Thus the study covered 84 special schools with 660 teachers and 76 Normal primary schools with 527 teachers in the four districts of the Andhra Pradesh and Tamil Nadu states in South India.

To know the attitude of non-disabled peers towards children with disabilities, 5 non-disabled children from each primary school were selected randomly by using simple random sampling technique. Thus the total number of non-disabled children covered in the study was 380.

All the school heads of special and normal schools (160) were also selected to rate the infrastructure checklist.

Overall, 1187 teachers, 380 peers and 160 school heads formed the sample for the study.

Data Collection

The research investigators of the project personally visited the schools and got permission from the school heads to collect data from their teachers. Good rapport was established with the heads and teachers of special and normal schools before administering the tools. The developed awareness rating scale was administered to the special and normal school teachers to know their awareness on various aspects of children with disabilities. Teachers were instructed to go through each statement and asked to rate their awareness on the gradations against each statement. The special and normal school teachers were asked to provide their personal information in Part-I of the awareness rating scale.

Attitude scale was administered to both special and normal school teachers to know their attitude towards children with disabilities. While administering the attitude scale, instructions were given to rate their attitude on the gradations given in the scale.

Likewise, competency assessment rating scale was administered to the special and normal school teachers to measure their existing competencies to deal children with disabilities. To identify the required competencies of special and normal school teachers, the developed checklist was administered. Teachers were directed to go through the instructions before rating their existing and required competencies against each statement.

Peer attitude scale was administered to the non-disabled peers studying in normal schools to assess the peer attitude towards their disabled peers. To fill up the peer attitude scale, each attitude statement was explained by the Research investigators to the sample pupils in normal schools. Their responses were then noted down.

Checklist to identify the infrastructure facilities in special and normal schools was given to the heads of special and normal schools. In the same checklist, heads were requested to mention the dropout rate. The filled in scales and checklists were collected and scored.

Scoring Procedure

For the purpose of statistical analysis, the collected data need to be quantified. To quantify the data, the following scoring procedure was adopted. In the awareness rating scale, against each item three responses were given. For positive statements the scoring was 3, 2, and 1 for 'awareness to greater extent', 'awareness to certain extent' and 'not aware' respectively and for negative statements the scoring was in reverse order. Similarly, to quantify the attitude scale, 5 gradations, namely, 'strongly agree', 'agree', 'agree to certain extent', 'disagree' and 'strongly disagree' were offered the scores 5, 4, 3, 2 and 1 respectively for positive statements and 1, 2, 3, 4, and 5 for negative statements.

To quantify competency assessment rating scale, the scores 3, 2 and 1 were given for 'competency to greater extent', 'competency to certain extent' and 'no competency' respectively.

Similarly, to score the required competencies through the checklist, for each competency statement 'one' mark was given for 'yes' and 'zero' for No. Likewise, for checklist to identify the infrastructure facilities, one mark was given for the availability of each infrastructure facility i.e. for 'Yes' and '0' for non-availability of the facility.

For peer attitude scale 'one' for 'Yes' (i.e. for positive attitude) and '0' for 'No' (i.e. for negative attitude) were given.

Statistical Techniques Used in the Study

The collected data were analysed by using appropriate statistical techniques such as percentage, mean, SD, t-test, F-test, Stepwise multiple regression, correlation etc., with the help of computer.

To assess the awareness, attitude and existing competencies of special and normal school teachers, mean and standard deviations were computed. By using mean $\pm$ 1SD, the level of awareness, level of attitude and the level of existing competencies of primary school teachers had been divided into three groups—low, moderate and high. To find out the required competencies of special and normal school teachers, the number of teachers requiring and not requiring each competency and the corresponding percentage was computed for each competency statement.

To find out the significant differences between special and normal school teachers' awareness, attitude and existing competencies in dealing children with disabilities, t-test had been worked out. To study the effect of gender, age, educational qualifications of teachers, training in special education, years of experience, location of school, nature of school, category of school and type of school they are working, mean and standard deviations had been calculated. Based on mean and standard deviation, t-test and F-test had been worked out, accordingly. Whenever two groups were involved in a variable, t-test had been used to know the significant difference between the groups. When more than two groups were involved in a variable, F-test was used to know the significant difference among these groups.

Similarly, to find out the influence of independent variables (gender, age, educational qualification, training in special education, years of experience, location of school, nature of school, category of school and type of school they are working) on the dependent variables (awareness, attitude and existing competencies), stepwise multiple regression analysis was carried out. This analysis is very useful to predict as to what extent and to how far the independent variables influence the awareness, attitude, existing and required competencies of special and normal school teachers to deal children with disabilities.

Correlations were computed to find out the relationship between awareness and attitude; awareness and existing competencies; attitude and existing competencies of special and normal school teachers.

To identify the non-disabled peer attitude towards their disabled peers, number and percentage of pupils having positive and negative attitude were calculated.

To find out the infrastructure facilities available in special and normal schools for the disabled children, number and percentage were computed. Likewise, mean and standard deviation were calculated for each school. Based on mean $\pm$ 1SD, the schools were grouped in to good facility schools, moderate facility schools and poor facility schools. This was done to know the dropout rate in good, moderate and poor facility schools.

The obtained results are presented in detail and discussed in the succeeding chapter.

Results and Discussion

Introduction

This chapter deals with the analysis and interpretation of the data collected from the sample of the study. It is presented in two parts.

Part-I deals with the descriptive analysis. In this part, the description of the sample with their background characteristics are explained as a first step. The data obtained through the awareness rating scale were analysed. Mean and SD were computed. Based on the mean $\pm$1SD, the obtained mean scores are grouped under three categories namely—low, moderate, and high to indicate the level of awareness of special and normal school teachers on various aspects of disabilities in children. Similarly, mean and SD were calculated for attitude scale. By using mean $\pm$1SD, the mean scores obtained from the attitude scale were grouped under three categories—low, moderate and high level of attitude.

Likewise, to assess the existing competencies of special and normal school teachers, mean and SD were computed. Based on mean $\pm$1SD, the special and normal school teachers' level of competencies were grouped as low, moderate and high. The number as well as percentage of special and normal school teachers requiring each competency aspect has been calculated to know the required competencies of special and normal school teachers.

Part-II deals with the differential analysis. To find out the significant difference between the special and normal school teachers' awareness, attitude and existing competencies in dealing children with disabilities, mean and SD were calculated. Based on mean and SD, t-test was worked out.

One of the major objectives of the study was to find out the significant differences, if any, in the awareness, attitude and existing competencies of special and normal school teachers dealing children with disabilities due to variations in their personal variables such as gender, age, educational qualification, training in special education, years of experience, location of school, nature of school, category of school and type of school. For this, mean and SD of each group in a variable with respect to awareness, attitude and competencies were calculated. Based on mean and SD, t-test/F-test was worked out to know the significant difference between/among the groups. Whenever, two groups were involved in a variable, t-test was applied and in case of more than two groups F-test was applied to know the significant differences between/among these groups.

Correlation studies were made to find out the relationship between awareness and attitude, between awareness and existing competencies and between attitude and existing competencies of special and normal school teachers to deal children with disabilities. For this, Karl Pearson correlation coefficient was used.

One of the major objectives of the study was to know how far and to what extent the independent variables (gender, age, educational qualification, training in special education, years of experience, location of school, nature of school, category of school and type of school) are influencing the dependent variables (awareness, attitude and existing competencies). For this, stepwise multiple regression was calculated. This analysis predicted the contribution of independent variables to the dependent variable.

To identify the infrastructure facilities available in special and normal schools for the children with disabilities, number and percentage of availability and non-availability of each infrastructure facility was calculated. Likewise, mean and SD were calculated. By using mean $\pm$1SD, the schools were grouped into three categories namely, schools with good facility, schools with moderate facility and schools with poor facility. The mean dropout rate was also computed in the above three types of school.

The attitude of the peer towards their disabled peers was analysed based on their responses 'Yes or No'. These responses were converted into percentages. Based on this, the number and percentage of peers with positive and negative attitude were worked out.

PART-I: DESCRIPTIVE ANALYSIS

Descriptive Analysis of the Awareness, Attitude and Existing Competencies of Special and Normal School Teachers in Dealing Children with Disabilities

The major objective of the study was to assess the awareness, attitude, existing and required competencies of special and normal school teachers in dealing children with disabilities. Mean and SD were calculated with respect to awareness, attitude and existing competencies. By using mean $\pm$1SD, the level of awareness, attitude and existing competencies of special and normal school teachers were divided into three categories—low, moderate and high. To identify the required competencies of special and normal school teachers, number and percentage was calculated. The obtained results were presented in the form of tables and discussed here under.

Background Characteristics of the Sample

The area of the study was the Chitoor and Hyderabad districts of Andhra Pradesh State and Madurai and Chennai districts of Tamilnadu State. There were 10 special schools in Chitoor, 65 in Hyderabad, 11 in Madurai and 91 in Chennai functioning for the different categories of children with disabilities. Out of these, 5 schools from Chittor, 35 from Hyderabad, 5 from Madurai and 39 from Chennai totalling 84 special schools were selected as the sample of the study. The normal schools were selected in the localities where the special schools are functioning. Altogether, there were 84 special schools and 76 normal schools. All the teachers working in these schools were selected as the sample. The selected sample were analysed with their background characteristics. Table 4.1 shows the characteristics of the sample.

Table 4.1: Background Characteristics of the Sample

Personal Variables	*Special Schools (N = 660)*	*Normal Schools (N = 527)*
(1)	*(2)*	*(3)*
Gender		
Men	206	265
Women	454	262
Age		
20-30 years	241	221
31-40 years	306	219
41-50 years	80	68
51 & above	33	19
Educational Qualification		
Teacher Training	217	255
Graduate with B.Ed.	325	168
Graduate with B.Ed. & M.Ed.	66	66
Postgraduate with B.Ed.	35	22
Postgraduate with B.Ed. & M.Ed.	17	16
Training in Special Education		
One month training by RCI	109	95
Diploma in Special Education	441	45
B.Ed. in Special Education	49	33
M.Ed. in Special Education	6	76
Others Specify	55	278
Years of Experience		
1-5 years	291	187
6-10 years	222	166
11-15 years	78	49
15-20 years	36	58
21 & above	33	67
Location of School		
Rural	44	11
Urban	616	516
Nature of School		
Government School	39	438
Private/Voluntary Organisation	621	89

(Contd...)

(1)	(2)	(3)
Category of School		
Special School	660	
Normal School	–	527
Type of School		
VI	95	
HI	213	
MR	293	
OH	59	

Out of 660 special school teachers, 206 were men and 454 were women teachers. In normal schools, out of 527, 265 were men and 262 were women teachers. With respect to their age, 241 special school teachers and 221 normal school teachers were under 20-30 years of age group, 306 special school teachers and 219 normal school teachers were between 31-40 years age group, 80 and 68 special and normal school teachers were 41-50 years of age, 33 and 19 special and normal school teachers were falling under 51 years and above age group. Under educational qualifications, 217 special school teachers and 255 normal school teachers were with teacher training, 325 special school teachers and 168 normal school teachers were possessing graduation with B.Ed., 66 special and 66 normal school teachers were having graduation with B.Ed. and M.Ed., 35 special school teachers and 22 normal school teachers were with postgraduation with B.Ed. and 17 and 16 special and normal school teachers are having postgraduation with B.Ed. and M.Ed. qualification. One month training by RCI was received by 109 special school teachers and 95 normal school teachers. 441 special school teachers and 45 normal school teachers were with Diploma in special education. 29 and 33 special and normal school teachers were with B.Ed. in special education. M.Ed. in special education is the qualification by 6 special school and 76 normal school teachers. 55 special school teachers and 278 normal school teachers had other training. With reference to years of experience, 291 special school and 187 normal school teachers with 1-5 years, 222 special school and 166 normal school teachers with 6-10 years, 78 special school and 49 normal school teachers with 11- 15 years,

36 special school and 58 normal school teachers with 15-20 years, 33 special school and 67 normal school teachers were with 21 years and above years of experience. 44 teachers in special school and 11 normal school teachers were from rural and the remaining 616 and 516 special and normal school teachers were working in urban schools. 39 special school teachers and 438 normal school teachers were from government schools. But the rest 621 and 89 were working in the schools run by the private/voluntary sector. Overall, 660 special school teachers and 527 normal school teachers formed the sample for the study. Among 660 special schoo' teachers, 95 of them were working in the schools for VI, 213 in schools for HI, 293 in schools for MR and 59 in schools for OH children.

Awareness of Special and Normal School Teachers on Various Aspects of Children with Disabilities

The teacher is playing a vital role in any educational system. The National Policy on Education (1986) emphasises the teacher's accountability to the pupils, their parents, the community and to their own profession. At primary level, the teachers play an important role. Teacher has the responsibility for overall curricular experiences of children irrespective of their disabilities. To cater to the needs of children with different disabilities a teacher should be aware of different categories of disabled children, difficulties of disabled children in communication, language, perceptual and social development, able to understand that disabled children are differently abled and finding ways and means to adopt instructional materials to the needs of these children. Table 4.2 presents the mean awareness score and level of awareness of different categories of special school teachers, special school teachers together and normal school teachers, on different dimensions of children with disabilities.

Table 4.2: Mean scores and level of awareness of special and normal school teachers on each aspects of children with disabilities

Sl. No.	Awareness Statements	Special School Teachers								Special School Teachers together (N = 660)		Normal School Teachers (N = 527)	
		VI (N = 95)		HI (N = 213)		MR (N = 293)		OH (N = 59)					
		Mean Score	Level of Awareness	Mean Score	Level of Awareness	Mean Score	Level of Awareness	Mean Score	Level of Awareness	Mean Score	Level of Awareness	Mean Score	Level of Awareness
(1)	(2)	(3)	(4)	(5)	(6)	(7)	(8)	(9)	(10)	(11)	(12)	(13)	(14)
I.	Concept of Disabilities												
1.	Children with visual, hearing motor difficulties and mental retardation come under the category of disabled children.	2.84	H	2.75	H	2.68	H	2.73	H	2.75	H	2.19	M
2.	Children with disabilities do not differ significantly with other children in learning.	1.74	L	1.73	L	1.86	L	1.54	L	1.71	L	2.23	L
3.	Children with disabilities have difficulty in communication, language, perceptual and social development.	2.47	H	2.44	H	2.44	H	2.41	H	2.44	H	1.90	M

(*Contd...*)

(1)	(2)	(3)	(4)	(5)	(6)	(7)	(8)	(9)	(10)	(11)	(12)	(13)	(14)
4.	Children with disabilities do not have special abilities and they exhibit only disabilities.	1.76	L	1.89	M	1.78	L	1.71	L	1.78	L	2.07	M
5.	The disabled children learning needs and learning styles are same as normal children and they need not require special attention in regular classrooms.	1.57	L	1.78	L	1.77	L	1.71	L	1.70	L	2.16	M
6.	Children with physical disabilities may not possess equal intelligent quotient (IO) as per with the average children.	1.72	L	1.62	L	1.76	L	1.69	L	1.69	L	2.22	M
7.	Slow learners and children with learning difficulties are not the part and parcel of children with disabilities.	1.55	L	1.85	L	1.80	L	1.78	L	1.74	L	2.22	M
II.	**Causes and Characteristics of Children with Disabilities**												
8.	Disabilities in children are the result of hereditary and environmental factors.	2.52	H	2.58	H	2.44	H	2.34	M	2.47	H	2.04	M
9.	Exposure of women to hazardous environment in pre- and perinatal period leads to disabilities in children.	2.54	H	2.63	H	2.50	H	2.49	H	2.54	H	1.91	M

(Contd...)

(1)	(2)	(3)	(4)	(5)	(6)	(7)	(8)	(9)	(10)	(11)	(12)	(13)	(14)
10.	Children's exposure to lead coated toys, infectious diseases, and physical abnormalities leads to disabilities in children.	2.29	M	2.31	M	2.38	M	2.37	M	2.33	M	1.84	L
11.	Mental retardation is the result of brain injuries and accidents in early years.	2.15	M	2.28	M	2.22	M	2.42	H	2.36	M	1.83	L
12.	Faulty child bearing and rearing practices, and teaching-learning practices may have their own effect on language learning disabilities in children.	2.47	H	2.55	H	2.42	H	2.44	H	2.47	H	1.87	M
13.	Children with disabilities exhibit, perceptual, motor co-ordination, cognitive and metacognitive as well as social skills deficits.	2.39	M	2.53	H	2.47	H	2.56	H	2.48	H	1.90	L
14.	Children with disabilities exhibit hypo - and hyperactivity.	2.32	M	2.24	M	2.23	M	2.58	H	2.34	M	2.00	M
15.	Children with visual impairment will not exhibit stereotype behaviours.	1.65	L	1.92	M	1.90	M	1.78	L	1.81	L	2.14	M

(Contd...)

(1)	(2)	(3)	(4)	(5)	(6)	(7)	(8)	(9)	(10)	(11)	(12)	(13)	(14)
16.	Children with disabilities exhibit psychological problems such as inferiority complex, stress, strain, low span of attention and emotional instability etc.	2.35	M	2.32	M	2.31	M	2.42	H	2.35	M	2.08	M
17.	Children with disabilities possess better abstract thinking than the normal	1.63	L	1.71	L	1.82	L	1.69	L	1.71	L	2.15	M
III.	**Identification and Assessment of Children with Disabilities**												
18.	Direct observation and academic records may serve as primary tools for identification of children with disabilities.	2.38	M	2.41	H	2.40	M	2.54	H	2.43	H	1.93	M
19.	Informal tests (classroom tests such as oral, reading, writing, dictation etc.) may not help to identify children with learning difficulties.	1.72	L	1.75	L	1.76	L	1.92	M	1.78	L	2.14	M
20.	Intelligence tests are the basis for identification of mental retardation and giftedness in children	2.52	H	2.35	M	2.51	H	2.46	H	2.46	H	1.83	L

(Contd...)

(1)	(2)	(3)	(4)	(5)	(6)	(7)	(8)	(9)	(10)	(11)	(12)	(13)	(14)
21.	Classroom observation, visual screening and opthalmological tests are the procedure to identify the children with visual impairment.	2.57	H	2.42	H	2.41	H	2.46	H	2.47	H	1.90	M
22.	Observation and hearing tests are essential to identify children with hearing impairment.	2.29	M	2.38	M	2.37	M	2.32	M	2.34	M	1.94	M
23.	Language assessment tests (reading, writing and spelling) are not essential to identify children with language learning difficulties.	1.65	L	1.95	M	1.74	6	1.71	L	1.76	L	2.10	M
24.	Assessment of adaptive behaviour may not help to identify social skill deficits in children with disabilities.	1.60	L	1.96	M	1.72	L	1.42	L	1.67	L	2.16	M
IV.	**Teaching and Training Methods**												
25.	Appropriate placement services benefit children with disabilities.	2.38	M	2.39	M	2.39	M	2.41	H	2.39	M	1.84	L

(Contd...)

(1)	(2)	(3)	(4)	(5)	(6)	(7)	(8)	(9)	(10)	(11)	(12)	(13)	(14)
26.	Individualised Education programme should not be developed based on the degree of disability.	1.84	L	1.91	M	1.86	M	1.61	L	1.81	L	2.27	M
27.	Current performance ability of children with disabilities will account in providing teaching and training programme.	2.50	H	2.39	M	2.40	M	2.47	H	2.44	H	2.04	M
28.	Long-term and short-term goals setting is not necessary to educate children with disabilities.	1.79	L	1.89	M	1.89	M	1.64	L	1.80	L	2.28	M
29.	Self directed learning materials enhance gifted children's learning.	2.57	H	2.36	M	2.36	M	2.47	H	2.44	H	1.81	L
30.	Mentally retarded and slow learners may not learn effectively when a task or activity is broken down into smaller sequential steps with short duration.	2.23	M	2.05	M	2.26	M	2.46	H	2.25	M	1.88	M
31.	Integrated therapy (speech, physical, occupation therapy, etc.) is a must in the educational programme for the mentally retarded children.	2.44	H	2.31	M	2.41	H	2.47	H	2.40	M	1.98	M

(Contd...)

(1)	(2)	(3)	(4)	(5)	(6)	(7)	(8)	(9)	(10)	(11)	(12)	(13)	(14)
32.	Peer tutoring, group learning and multi-sensory approaches facilitate learning in children with learning difficulties and slow learners.	2.37	M	2.35	M	2.33	M	2.47	M	2.38	M	1.90	M
33.	Low vision children need not require large print materials, magnifying devices and corrective lenses in learning.	1.32	L	2.00	M	1.94	M	1.71	L	1.86	M	2.20	M
34.	Totally blind children are able to learn with the help of plus curriculum (Braille-reading) and writing, orientation and mobility and sensory training).	2.51	H	2.39	M	2.43	H	2.24	M	2.42	H	1.84	L
35.	Talking books or audiotapes helps the blind children in learning.	2.52	H	2.52	H	2.43	H	2.24	M	2.43	H	1.84	L
36.	Hearing-impaired children learn better through total communication approach.	2.52	H	2.66	H	2.41	H	2.19	M	2.45	H	1.89	M
37.	Through hearing aids residual hearing can be used for learning in HI children.	2.47	H	2.60	H	2.41	H	2.27	M	2.44	H	1.91	M
38.	Group hearing aids will facilitate teaching learning process in the classroom set-up for the hearing-impaired children.	2.47	H	2.50	H	2.43	H	2.27	M	2.42	H	1.84	L

(Contd...)

(1)	(2)	(3)	(4)	(5)	(6)	(7)	(8)	(9)	(10)	(11)	(12)	(13)	(14)
39.	Closed Circuit Television (CCTV) helps hearing-impaired children in learning.	2.43	H	2.42	H	2.27	M	2.22	M	2.33	M	1.88	M
40.	Orthotic devices helps orthopaedically handicapped children to function in a better way.	2.48	H	2.41	H	2.45	H	2.49	H	2.46	H	1.86	M
V.	**Guidance and Counselling**												
41.	Guidance and counselling by a teacher promotes self-confidence among children with disabilities.	2.56	H	2.55	H	2.50	H	2.49	H	2.52	H	1.94	M
42.	Proper guidance about prenatal, perinatal and postnatal problems by a teacher to the parents and community helps in prevention of disabilities in children.	2.49	H	2.60	H	2.44	H	2.41	H	2.49	H	1.95	M
43.	Peer group guidance and counselling by the teacher develops positive attitude towards children with disabilities.	2.53	H	2.60	H	2.52	H	2.61	H	2.57	H	1.92	M

(Contd...)

(1)	(2)	(3)	(4)	(5)	(6)	(7)	(8)	(9)	(10)	(11)	(12)	(13)	(14)
44.	Parents counselling helps them to understand different aspects of difficulties faced by the children with disabilities.	2.48	H	2.62	H	2.51	H	2.37	M	2.50	H	1.95	M
45.	Involving parents in planning development and organisation of educational programmes for children with disabilities leads for better understanding of their children's ability.	2.60	H	2.51	H	2.50	H	2.54	H	2.54	H	1.87	M
46.	Community counselling facilitates development of positive attitude towards children with disabilities.	2.51	H	2.56	H	2.41	H	2.42	H	2.48	H	1.90	M
47.	PTA meetings, discussions and group work may not give a chance to know the progress of the children with disabilities.	1.73	L	1.92	M	1.89	M	1.88	M	1.86	M	2.15	M

(Contd...)

(1)	(2)	(3)	(4)	(5)	(6)	(7)	(8)	(9)	(10)	(11)	(12)	(13)	(14)
48.	Directing parents to the specialist (Audiologist, speech therapist, ophthalmologists, physiologist, psychologist and occupational therapist) will be useful for the children with disabilities.	2.48	H	2.68	H	2.49	H	2.46	H	2.53	H	1.89	M

Note:

Level of Awareness

Low : Value from 1.85 and below.

Moderate : Values from 1.86 to 2.40.

High : Values from 2.41 and above.

In the present study, the teachers working in the schools for VI, HI, MR, OH and special school teachers together demonstrated high level of awareness about different categories of disabled children (s. no. 1) whereas moderate level of awareness was exhibited by the normal school teachers on the same aspect. The mean score 2.84 for teachers working in schools of VI showed their better awareness followed by the teachers working in schools for HI (2.75), OH (2.73), and MR (2.68). Similarly, the special school teachers showed high level awareness (VI-2.47, HI and MR-2.44, OH-2.41 and special schools teachers together-2.44) on the awareness aspect (s. no. 3). For the same aspect the normal school teachers' awareness was moderate (1.90). The special school teacher awareness was low for s. no. of awareness aspect 2, (VI-1.74, HI-1.73, MR-1.86, OH-1.54 and special school teachers together-1.71), s. no. 4 (VI-1.76, MR-1.78, OH-1.71 and special school teachers together-1.78), s. no. 5 (VI-1.57, HI-1.78, MR-1.77, OH-1.71 and special school teachers together-1.70), s. no. 6 (VI-1.72, HI-1.62, MR-1.76, OH-1.69 and special school teachers together-1.69) and s. no. 7 (VI-1.55, HI-1.85, MR-1.80, OH-1.78 and special school teachers together-1.74). On the otherhand, the normal school teachers possessed moderate level of awareness on s. no. 2 (2.23), 4 (2.07), 5 (2.16), 6 (2.22) and 7 (2.22).

It means, the special school teachers possessed better awareness on different disabilities in children and the disabled children's difficulty in communication language, perceptual and social development. Their awareness was at low level on the aspects—"children with disabilities do not significantly differ with other children in learning", "disabled children do not, have special abilities and they exhibit only disabilities", "the learning needs and styles of disabled children are same as normal children and they need not require special attention in regular classrooms", "the intelligent quotient of children with physical disabilities is as par with the average children" and "slow learners and children with learning disabilities are part and parcel of children with disabilities". Contrary to this, normal school teachers exhibited moderate level of awareness on all these aspects.

With regard to the awareness aspects under causes and characteristics of children with disabilities, the study showed that teachers working in VI, HI, MR and special school teachers together possessed high awareness (2.52, 2.58, 2.44 and 2.47 respectively) on the aspect hereditary and environmental factors causing disabilities in children (s. no. 8). For the same aspect, the teacher working in OH schools and normal schools showed moderate awareness (2.34 and 2.04 respectively). Exposure of women to hazardous environment in pre- and peri-natal period leads to disabilities in children. The special school teachers were fully aware of this aspect, whereas the normal school teachers' awareness is moderate on this. Special school teachers were moderately aware that children's exposure to lead coated toys, infectious diseases, and physical abnormalities leads to disabilities in children (VI-2.29, HI-2.31, MR-2.38, OH-2.37, special school teachers together-2.33). Similarly, except teachers working in schools for OH, other special school teachers showed moderate level of awareness on the aspect "mental retardation is the result of brain injuries and accidents in early years". Teachers working in schools for OH children possessed high awareness on this aspect. Contrary to this, normal school teacher awareness was low on s. no. 10 an 11 aspects (1.84 and 1.83 respectively). Faulty child bearing and rearing practices and faulty teaching learning practices lead to language learning disabilities in children. The teachers working in special schools (VI-2.47, HI-2.55, MR-2.42, OH-2.44 and special schools teachers together -2.47) possessed high awareness than their counterparts working in normal schools (1.87). Normal school teachers' awareness was moderate in these aspect. The teachers working in schools for HI, MR, OH and special school teachers put together had high awareness and teachers working in VI with moderate awareness on the aspect s. no. 13. On the otherhand, the normal school teachers' awareness was low (1.90) on the same aspect. Except teachers working in OH schools, the other special school teachers possessed moderate awareness on the hypo - and hyperactivity of children with disabilities. The normal school teachers too possessed moderate awareness (2.00) on this aspect. The teachers working schools for VI (1.65), schools for OH (1.78) and special schools together (1.81) showed low awareness on stereotypic behaviours of visually impaired children (s. no. 15). Moderate awareness was exhibited by the teachers working in the schools for HI (1.92), MR (1.90) and teachers working in normal schools 2.14 on the same aspect. Except teachers in OH schools, other teachers working in special schools for VI (2.35), HI (2.32), MR (2.31) and special school teachers together (2.35) and teachers working in normal schools (2.08) were moderately aware of the fact that the children with disabilities exhibit psychological problems such as inferiority complex, stress, strain, low span of attention and emotional instability etc. The special school teachers' awareness was low on the aspect s. no. 17 whereas, normal school teachers possessed moderate awareness.

A teacher with knowledge on 'identification and assessment of children with disabilities' is an asset to any educational institution. In the present study, the special school teachers, possessed high awareness (2.41) whereas normal school teachers' awareness was moderate (1.93). Teachers working in schools for VI (2.38) and schools for MR (2.40) too possessed moderate awareness on the aspect s. no. 18. On the aspect s. no. 19, the special school teachers showed low level of knowledge except teachers working in OH schools. On the otherhand, normal school teachers and teachers working in OH schools possessed moderate awareness (2.14 and 1.92 respectively). On s. no. 20, the teachers working in schools for VI, MR, OH and special school teachers together exhibited high awareness (2.52, 2.51, 2.46 and 2.46 respectively), whereas teachers working in schools for HI demonstrated moderate level of awareness (2.35) and normal school teachers with low level of awareness (1.83). On s.no. of the aspect 21, the special school teachers' awareness was high whereas, normal school teachers' awareness was moderate. On s. no. 22, the teachers exhibited moderate level of awareness, irrespective of the schools they were working. For s. no. of aspects 23 and 24, the special school teachers' awareness was low except the teachers working in schools for HI and normal schools who possessed moderate awareness.

A teacher having knowledge about teaching and training methods of educating children with disabilities will do better justice to them. The study shows that the teachers working in special schools except schools for OH possesses moderate awareness about the appropriate placement services for children with disabilities (s. no. 25). For the same aspect, normal school teachers' awareness was low. It is strange to note that teachers working in VI, OH and special school teachers together were not aware of the individualised educational programme based on the degree of disabilities. Whereas, the teachers working in the schools for HI, MR and normal schools demonstrated moderate level of awareness on this aspect (s. no. 26). The teachers working in VI, OH and special school teachers together demonstrated high level of awareness about the need for taking into account the performance ability of disabled children with providing teaching training programme to them. The teachers working HI, MR and normal schools showed moderate awareness on this aspect (s. no. 27). The moderate level of awareness was exhibited by HI, MR and normal school teachers on the need for short-term and long-term goal setting to educate children with disabilities. On the other hand, low level of awareness was exhibited by VI, OH and special school teachers together on this aspect (s. no. 28). Self-directed learning materials generally enhance gifted children's learning. This aspect was known to the teachers working in schools for VI, and OH whereas, the teachers working in HI, MR and special school teachers together were only moderately aware of this. The normal school teachers' awareness was very low on this aspect. All the special schools teachers except teachers working in schools for OH and normal school teachers were moderately aware of the fact that the MR and slow learners learn effectively when task or activity is broken into smaller sequential steps with short duration. High awareness was shown by the teachers working in OH schools. Speech and physical occupational therapy was needed for any educational programme for MR children. This fact was known to teachers working in VI, MR and OH schools whereas, the teachers in HI, special school teachers together and normal school teachers were moderately aware of the same (s. no. 31). The children with learning difficulties and slow learners can benefit from peer tutoring, group learning and multi-sensory approaches. Except teachers working in OH schools, other school teachers (VI, HI, MR, special school teachers together and normal school teachers) were having moderate awareness (s. no. 32). By using large print materials, magnifying devices and corrective lenses, the low vision children can enhance their learning. It is strange to note that the teachers working in VI and OH schools demonstrated low level of awareness on this aspect (s. no. 33). The teachers working in HI, MR, special school teachers together and in normal schools showed moderate awareness. Contrary to the s. no. 33 aspect, the teachers working in VI schools, MR schools, special school teachers together possessed higher level of awareness on the aspect that 'totally blind children are able to learn with the help of plus curriculum' (s. no. 34). For the same aspect, teachers working in HI and OH were having moderate awareness and teachers working in normal schools were with low awareness. The VI, HI, MR and special school teachers together were highly aware that talking books or audio tapes help the blind children in learning. The OH school teachers and normal school teachers' awareness was moderate and low respectively' (s. no. 35). Hearing impaired children can learn better through total communication approach. Similarly, through hearing aids the residual hearing can be used for learning in HI children. Further, group hearing aids will facilitate teaching learning process in the classroom set up for hearing impaired children. In all these aspects, the special school teachers except the teachers working in the schools for OH demonstrated high awareness (s. no. 36, 37 and 38). The normal school teachers possessed only moderate level of awareness on the aspect s. no. 36 and 37 and low awareness on the s. no. 38. Closed circuit television (CCTV) helps hearing impaired children in learning. This fact is well known to the teachers working in VI and HI schools, whereas moderate awareness was exhibited by the teachers in MR, OH special school teachers together and normal schools, on this aspect (s. no. 39). Orthotic devices help the orthopaedically handicapped children to function in a better way. The special school teachers' awareness was high on this aspect whereas the normal schools teachers demonstrated moderate awareness.

Guidance and counselling should be the integral part of any academic programme particularly for the children with disabilities. Such a programme not only involves children with disabilities but also their parents. A teacher with knowledge about the different aspects of guidance and counselling the children with disabilities and their parents will be an asset to the institution offering programmes for these children. In the present study, it is welcoming trend that out of 8 guidance and counselling activities the special school teachers possessed high awareness on 7 aspects (s. no. 41, 42, 43, 44, 45, 46 and 48). On all these aspects, the normal school teachers exhibited moderate level of awareness. For s. no. 47, except teachers working in VI schools, other special and normal school teachers demonstrated moderate level of awareness. The VI teachers' awareness was low in this aspect.

An overall analysis of Table 4.2 gives lead to draw the following conclusions:

(i) On the concept of disabilities in children, the special teachers were fully aware of different categories of disabilities in children (s. no. 1) and disabled children's difficulties in communication, language, perceptual and social development (s. no. 3). Their awareness was low on the aspects—children with disabilities do not differ significantly with other children (s. no. 2), children with disabilities do not have special abilities and they exhibit only disabilities (s. no. 4), disabled children's learning needs and learning styles are same as normal children and they need not require special attention in regular classroom (s. no. 5), children with physical disabilities may not possess equal IQ as par with average children (s. no. 6), slow learners and children with learning disabilities are not the part and parcel of children with disabilities (s. no. 7). From s. no. 1 to 7 the normal school teachers possessed moderate level of awareness. Awareness can be generated in special school teachers on the s. no. 2, 4, 5, 6 and 7 aspects, whereas for normal school teachers, eventhough their awareness is moderate, they need further sensitisation on all the aspects of concept of disabilities in children.

(ii) Under the dimension 'causes and characteristics of children with disabiiities', the special school teachers were fully aware that disabilities are the result of hereditary and environmental factors (s. no. 8), exposure of women to hazardous environment in pre- and peri-natal period leads to disabilities in children (s. no. 9), faulty child bearing and rearing practices,

teaching learning practices leads to language learning disabilities in children (s. no. 12) and children with disabilities exhibit perceptual motor co-ordination, cognitive, metacognitive and social skill deficits (s. no. 13). On the otherhand, their awareness was moderate with respect to the aspects—children's exposure to lead coated toys, infectious diseases, physical abnormalities leading to disabilities in children (s. no. 10), mental retardation is the result of brain injuries and accidents in early years (s. no. 11), children with disabilities exhibit hypo- and hyper-activity, psychological problems such as inferiority complex, stress, strain, low span of attention and emotional instability etc., (s. no. 14 and 16). Similarly, they exhibited low level of awareness about the stereotyped behaviours of visually impaired children and disabled children's abstract thinking (s. no. 15 and 17). On all the above aspects, the normal school teachers demonstrated moderate level of awareness (s. no. 8, 9, 12, 14, 15, 16 and 17) and low level of awareness on s. no. 10, 11 and 13. So any awareness programme must concentrate on the moderate and low awareness aspects for special and normal school teachers.

(iii) Under the dimension 'identification and assessment of children with disabilities' the special school teachers were fully aware of the primary tools for identification of children with disabilities (s. no. 18), intelligence test as the basis for identification of MR and gifted children (s. no. 20) and different tests to identify children with visual impairments (s. no. 21). On the otherhand, they were moderately aware that observation and hearing tests are essential to identify children with hearing impairment (s. no. 22). Their awareness was low on the informal tests to identify children with learning difficulties (s. no. 19), different language assessment tests (s. no. 23) and tests for assessment of social skill deficits in disabled children (s. no. 24). The normal school teachers possessed moderate level of awareness

on all these aspects (s. no. 18, 19, 21, 22, 23 and 24) except low awareness on s. no. 20. Awareness should be therefore generated in the special and normal school teachers on the moderate and low level awareness level aspects.

(iv) Under the dimension 'teaching and training methods', the special school teachers' awareness was high on the aspect in providing teaching and training programme the current performance ability of the disabled children should be taken into account (s. no. 27), use of plus curriculum for blind children (s. no. 34), need for talking books and audio tapes for blind children (s. no. 35), need for total communication approach, use of hearing aids for use of residual hearing, group hearing aids to facilitate teaching learning in the classroom, (s. no. 36, 37 and 38), and use of orthotic devices for orthopaedically handicapped children (s. no. 40). On the otherhand, their awareness was moderate on the aspects—appropriate placement services for children with disabilities (s. no. 25), use of self directed learning materials for gifted children's learning (s. no. 29), need for breaking the task into small sequential steps to make MR and slow learners learn effectively (s. no. 30), need for use of integrated therapy in the education of mentally retarded children (s. no. 31), use of peer tutoring, group learning and multisensory approaches for children with learning difficulties and slow learners (s. no. 32), need for large print materials, magnifying devices and corrective lenses for low vision children in learning (s. no. 33) and need for closed circuit television (CCTV) in the learning of hearing impaired children (s. no. 39). Similarly, special school teachers' awareness was low on the aspects—need for development of individualised education programme based on the degree of disability and the need for setting of long-term and short-term goals to educate children with disabilities (s. no. 26 and 28). As the normal school teachers possessed only moderate and low level of awareness on all the aspects under the dimension 'teaching and training methods' they should be given sensitisation of awareness generation programmes on teaching and training of disabled children.

(v). Under the dimension 'guidance and counselling', the special school teachers were fully aware that these activities promote self confidence in disabled children (s. no. 41), peer group guidance and counselling develop positive attitude towards children with disabilities (s. no. 43), need for guidance about pre-, peri- and pos-tnatal problems to the parents and community (s. no. 42), parents counselling to understand different aspects of difficulties faced by children with disabilities (s. no. 44), need for involving parents in planning, development and organisation of education programmes for children with disabilities (s. no. 45), need for community counselling (s. no. 46) and need for directing parents to the specialists such as audiologist, speech therapists, opthalmologist, physiologist, psychologist, and occupational therapist to understand their children with disabilities (s. no. 48). Their awareness was moderate with regard to the need for the PTA meetings, discussions and group work that give chance to know the progress of the children with disabilities (s. no. 47). On all the aspects under the dimension 'guidance and counselling', the normal school teachers demonstrated moderate awareness stating the need for sensitisation programmes.

In organising awareness/sensitisation programmes one can exploit the possible channels existing within the reach of formal and non-formal education. As a first step, sensitisation can be created by using the existing print and electronic media. Through pamphlets, wall posters and allotting the part of the page or page in a local newspaper that too in regional language definitely facilitate not only the teachers but also the parents and local community to develop sensitivity to the issues that promote the education of disabled. Similarly, subject experts and field practitioners can be invited for frequent radio talks which address the problems and prospects in disabled children's education. The Doordarshan Kendra should relay live programmes on the successful stories of the disabled people and the ways and means to help such people with real field experiences. In fact, no school or community is in dearth of resource and expertise. The only thing required is tapping the resources and the ways of utilising the same at optimum level and it will solve 50 perc ent of the problems in the field. One should develop such mindset in the personnel working in the organisation or school. In this respect, it is highly suggestive that the existing parent teacher associations can be exploited and the resource teacher can enlighten the other teachers and parents about the education of children with disabilities

The existing DIETs, College of Education and Departments of Education should organise short term orientation classes for the teachers already working and incorporate disability concepts in teacher training and B.Ed. curriculum, thereby the would be teachers will be sensitised.

Attitude of Special and Normal School Teachers towards Different Aspects of Children with Disabilities

Human behaviour is generally rational and such behaviour is moulded based on one's own awareness and attitudes towards a particular phenomena. Awareness refers to the feelings and believes one possess towards a particular aspect. Such feelings make the person behave in certain direction. In other words, attitude is the key factor for development and implementation of any educational programme. This is more true with regard to the programmes for the disabled children. The success of the programmes for these children in segregated settings like schools specially for VI, HI, MR and OH or integrated schools for the disabled or inclusive education for these children in normal schools depends to a large extent on the attitude of the teachers working in those schools. A teacher with right type of attitude will exhibit positive behaviours towards children with disabilities which in turn promotes the education of these children. In this study, an attempt is made to assess the attitude of the special and normal school teachers on various aspects of disabilities in children. The mean attitude score and level of awareness for different categories of special and normal school teachers under different dimensions of children with disabilities are presented in Table 4.3.

Table 4.3: Mean scores and level of attitude of special and normal school teachers towards each aspects of children with disabilities

Sl. No.	Attitude Statements	*Special School Teachers*								*Special School Teachers together (N = 660)*		*Normal School Teachers (N = 527)*	
		VI (N = 95)		*HI (N = 213)*		*MR (N = 293)*		*OH (N = 59)*					
		Mean Scores	*Level of Attitude*	*Mean Scores*	*Level of Attitude*	*Mean Scores*	*Level of Attitude*	*Mean Scores*	*Level of Attitude*	*Mean Scores*	*Level of Attitude*	*Mean Scores*	*Level of Attitude*
(1)	(2)	(3)	(4)	(5)	(6)	(7)	(8)	(9)	(10)	(11)	(12)	(13)	(14)
I.	**Concept of Disabilities**												
1.	Problems in visual, hearing motor and mental aspects leading to disabilities in children.	4.19	H	4.18	H	4.37	H	4.25	H	4.24	H	3.60	M
2.	The significant difference among children in learning represent disabilities in children.	3.36	M	3.33	M	3.68	M	3.07	M	3.36	M	3.24	M
3.	Difficulty in communication, language, perceptual and social development leads to disabilities in children.	3.44	M	3.35	M	3.64	M	3.07	M	3.38	M	3.20	M
4.	Disabilities in children do not lead to any special abilities.	2.86	L	2.92	L	2.69	L	3.69	M	3.04	L	2.81	L

(Contd...)

(1)	(2)	(3)	(4)	(5)	(6)	(7)	(8)	(9)	(10)	(11)	(12)	(13)	(14)
5.	The disabled children learning needs and learning style are same as normal children and they need not require special attention in regular classrooms.	2.77	L	3.08	M	2.72	L	2.73	L	2.82	L	2.70	L
6.	Physical disabilities in children leads to low intelligence quotient (IQ).	2.76	L	2.73	L	2.74	L	2.75	L	2.74	L	2.80	L
II.	**Causes and Characteristics of Children with Disabilities**												
8.	Hereditary and environmental factors contribute disabilities in children.	3.92	M	4.11	H	3.81	M	3.85	M	3.92	M	3.27	M
9.	Exposure of pregnant women to hazardous environment in pre- and peri-natal period leads to disabilities in children.	3.84	M	4.44	H	3.89	M	3.95	H	4.03	H	3.33	M
10.	Children's exposure to lead coated toys, infectious diseases and physical abnormalities leads to disabilities in children.	3.69	M	3.91	M	3.72	M	3.80	M	3.78	M	3.31	M
11.	Brain injuries and accidents leads to mental retardation in children.	3.85	M	4.20	H	3.92	M	4.05	H	4.00	H	3.26	M

(Contd...)

(1)	(2)	(3)	(4)	(5)	(6)	(7)	(8)	(9)	(10)	(11)	(12)	(13)	(14)
12.	Poor child bearing and rearing practices and faulty teaching learning practices leads to language learning disabilities in children.	3.83	M	4.11	H	3.81	M	3.61	M	3.84	M	3.77	M
13.	Perceptual and motor co-ordination, cognitive and metacognitive as well as social skill deficits are common in children with disabilities.	3.69	M	3.81	M	3.73	M	3.47	M	3.67	M	3.35	M
14.	Hydro and hyperactivity behaviours are usually exhibited by children with disabilities.	3.56	M	3.38	M	3.63	M	3.63	M	3.55	M	3.30	M
15.	Visual impairment in children may not lead to stereotyped behaviours.	2.62	L	2.73	L	2.50	L	2.63	L	2.62	L	2.76	L
16.	Disabilities in children leads to inferiority complex, stress, strain, low span of attention and emotional instability.	3.58	M	3.84	M	3.73	M	3.75	M	3.73	M	3.37	M
17.	The disabilities in children leads to better abstract thinking than the normal children.	2.99	M	3.59	M	3.34	M	2.92	L	3.21	M	3.06	M

(Contd...)

(1)	(2)	(3)	(4)	(5)	(6)	(7)	(8)	(9)	(10)	(11)	(12)	(13)	(14)
III.	**Identification and Assessment of Disabilities in Children**												
18.	The disabilities in children can be identified through direct observation and academic records.	3.84	M	4.12	H	3.69	M	3.81	M	3.87	M	3.35	M
19.	Language difficulties in children can be identified through informal tests (classroom tests such as oral, reading, writing, dictation etc.)	3.92	M	4.05	H	3.77	M	3.83	M	3.89	M	3.31	M
20.	Mental retardation and giftedness in children can be identified with intelligence tests.	3.80	M	4.08	H	3.95	H	3.78	M	3.90	M	3.29	M
21.	Visual impairment in children can be identified through classroom observation, visual screening and ophthalmological test.	3.96	H	4.13	H	3.96	H	3.98	H	4.01	H	3.17	M
22.	Hearing impairment in children can be identified through observation and hearing tests.	3.84	M	4.15	H	3.96	H	3.90	M	3.96	H	2.95	L
23.	Language learning difficulties in children need not be identified through language assessment tests.	2.45	L	2.97	L	2.69	L	3.05	M	2.79	L	2.66	L

(Contd...)

(1)	(2)	(3)	(4)	(5)	(6)	(7)	(8)	(9)	(10)	(11)	(12)	(13)	(14)
24.	Assessment of adaptive behaviour leads to the identification of social deficits.	3.63	M	3.67	M	3.56	M	3.58	M	3.61	M	3.38	M
IV.	**Teaching and Training Methods**												
25.	Children with disabilities may benefit from appropriate placement services.	4.07	H	4.15	H	3.89	M	4.02	H	4.03	H	3.34	M
26.	The degree of disability need not be the basis for organising the individualised Educational Programme (IEP).	2.60	L	2.92	L	2.77	L	2.90	L	2.80	L	2.68	L
27.	Teaching and training programmes for disabled children should be based on their current performance ability.	3.95	H	3.92	M	3.76	M	3.56	M	3.80	M	3.46	M
28.	Setting of long-term and short-term goals facilitate the education of children with disabilities.	3.78	M	4.05	H	3.69	M	3.81	M	3.83	M	3.31	M
29.	Self-directed learning materials facilitate learning in gifted children.	3.54	M	3.83	M	3.53	M	3.47	M	3.59	M	3.18	M

(Contd...)

(1)	(2)	(3)	(4)	(5)	(6)	(7)	(8)	(9)	(10)	(11)	(12)	(13)	(14)
30.	Breaking down a task or activity (task analysis) in a smaller sequential steps with short duration may not facilitate learning in mentally retarded and slow learners.	2.69	L	2.57	L	2.70	L	2.85	L	2.70	L	2.81	L
31.	Integrated therapy (speech, physical and occupational therapy) leads to better development in mentally retarded children.	4.03	H	3.71	M	3.83	M	3.68	M	3.81	M	3.35	M
32.	Children with learning difficulties and slow learning may benefit from peer tutoring, group learning and multi-sensory approaches.	3.84	M	3.91	M	3.92	M	3.90	H	3.89	M	3.38	M
33.	The learning of low vision children can be enhanced through large print materials, magnifying devices and corrective lenses.	4.11	H	4.09	H	3.98	H	3.71	M	3.97	H	3.32	M
34.	Plus curriculum (Braille reading, writing, orientation and mobility and sensory training) help totally blind children to learn 3 R's as well as orientation and mobility skills.	3.96	H	4.13	H	3.95	H	3.66	M	3.93	H	3.31	M

(Contd...)

(1)	(2)	(3)	(4)	(5)	(6)	(7)	(8)	(9)	(10)	(11)	(12)	(13)	(14)
35.	Use of audiotapes/talking books facilities learning in blind children.	4.05	H	4.18	H	3.87	M	3.64	M	3.94	H	3.33	M
36.	Total communication approach facilitate learning in hearing impaired children.	4.07	H	4.18	H	3.86	M	3.58	M	3.92	M-	3.25	M
37.	Residual hearing can be geared up with the help of hearing aids.	3.95	H	4.15	H	3.89	M	3.51	M	3.88	M	3.25	M
38.	In the classroom set up, use of group hearing aids facilitate teaching—learning process.	3.74	M	4.10	H	3.76	M	3.47	M	3.77	M	3.21	M
39.	Hearing impaired children's learning can be facilitated by CCTV.	3.47	M	3.89	M	3.58	M	3.19	M	3.53	M	3.17	M
40.	The daily living skills can be enhanced in the orthopedically handicapped children through the use of orthotic devices.	4 02	H	3.97	H	3.86	M	3.93	H	3.94	H	3.17	M
V.	**Guidance and Counselling Activities**												
41.	Guidance and counselling by a teacher leads self-confidence among children with disabilities.	4.06	H	4.27	H	3.93	H	4.12	H	4.09	H	3.30	M

(Contd...)

(1)	(2)	(3)	(4)	(5)	(6)	(7)	(8)	(9)	(10)	(11)	(12)	(13)	(14)
42.	The disabilities in children can be prevented by giving guidance about prenatal, perinatal and postnatal problems to the parents and community.	3.98	H	4.27	H	3.95	H	3.97	H	4.04	H	3.30	M
43.	The negative attitude of peer group towards the children with disabilities can be bypassed through peer group guidance and counselling.	4.02	H	4.11	H	3.88	M	3.82	M	3.98	H	3.29	M
44.	Parents counselling facilitates to overcome difficulties in disabled children.	4.06	H	4.23	H	3.93	H	3.83	M	4.04	H	3.28	M
45.	Involving parents in planning development and organisation of educational programmes for the children with disabilities leads to better understanding of their children's ability.	4.16	H	4.08	H	3.94	H	3.98	H	4.04	H	3.31	M
46.	Community counselling leads for development of positive attitude towards children with disabilities.	3.94	H	4.00	H	3.85	M	4.08	H	3.97	H	3.21	M

(Contd...)

(1)	(2)	(3)	(4)	(5)	(6)	(7)	(8)	(9)	(10)	(11)	(12)	(13)	(14)
47.	PTA meetings, discussion and group work may not facilitate the progress of children with disabilities.	2 54	L	2.72	L	2.72	L	3.20	M	2.79	L	3.20	M
48.	Directing parents to the specialists (Audiologist, Psychologist and Occupational therapist) leads better development of children with disabilities.	3.56	H	4.15	H	3.94	H	3.76	M	3.95	H	2.88	L

Note:

Level of Attitude

Low : Values from 2.97 and below.

Moderate : Values between 2.98 to 3.92.

High : Values from 3.93 and above.

From Table 4.3, it is inferred that the teachers working in special schools possessed positive attitudes on serial number of the aspect-1, under the dimension 'concept of disabilities in children', whereas normal school teachers' attitude was moderate level. Irrespective of the school they were working, the special and normal school teachers' attitude was moderate for serial number of the aspects 2 and 3. On the other hand, on serial number 4 and 5 attitude aspects, the special and normal school teachers demonstrated low level or negative attitude. Likewise, their attitude was also low for serial number of attitude aspects 6 and 7. In Table 4.3, also it is revealed that on majority of the aspects, the special school teachers possessed low awareness and normal school teachers possessed moderate level of awareness. Here, in attitude also on most of the aspects under the dimension the 'concept of disabilities in children' the teachers of normal and special schools demonstrated moderate and negative attitude. It is natural that awareness leads to better attitudes and better attitude leads to better performance. Here, the results reveal lower or moderate the level of awareness on the concept of disabilities in children, negative or moderate will be the attitude of the teachers.

Under the dimension 'causes and characteristics of children with disabilities', special school teachers together demonstrated positive attitude on serial number of aspects 9 and 11. In the same aspects the teachers working in VI and MR schools showed moderate or neutral attitude. For serial number of the aspects 8, 10, 12, 13, 14, 16 and 17, the special school teachers together demonstrated moderate attitude. For serial number 11, the teachers in HI schools and OH showed positive attitude. For serial number of aspects 15, the special school teachers together were having negative attitude. The teachers working in OH schools too possessed negative attitude for the serial number of aspects 17. Further, the table also reveals that the normal school teachers' attitude was at moderate level on all the aspects under the dimension 'causes and characteristics of children with disabilities', except on the aspect s. no. 15 with negative attitude or low attitude.

Under the dimension 'identification and assessment of children with disabilities 'the special school teachers demonstrated high or positive attitude on serial number of aspects 21and 22. Similarly, the VI and OH school teachers had moderate attitude on the serial number of aspect 22. On the serial number of the aspect 19 and 24, special school teachers together demonstrated moderate attitude only. For serial number 19, the teachers working in HI schools had positive attitude than their counterparts working in other schools. Contrary to this, for serial number 23, the special and normal school teachers' attitude was low or negative except teachers working in OH schools with neutral attitude. Normal school teachers had neutral attitude for the serial number of the aspects 18, 19, 20, 21 and 24, whereas for serial number 22 and 23 their attitude was negative.

Under the dimension 'teaching and training methods', the special school teachers together showed positive attitude for serial number of aspects 25, 33, 34, 35 and 40. But the teachers working in MR schools possessed neutral attitude on serial number of aspects 25, 35 and 40. Likewise, the teachers working in OH schools exhibited neutral attitude on the serial number of the aspect 35. On the other hand, the special school teachers together showed moderate level of attitude for serial number of aspects 27, 28, 29, 31, 32, 36, 37, 38 and 39. But, on serial number 28, 36, 37 and 38 the HI school teachers demonstrated positive attitude. For s. no. 27, 31, 36 and 37, the VI school teachers showed positive attitude. On the otherhand, for serial number 26 and 30, the special school teachers and normal school teachers had negative or low attitude. The attitudes of normal school teachers in the remaining serial number of aspects under the dimension 'teaching and training methods', were neutral. Under the dimension, 'guidance and counselling' the special school teachers', attitude together, was positive all together (s. nos. 41 to 46 and 48). Their attitude was low on the s. no. of aspect 47. Except for s. no. 48 (low attitude or negative attitude) the normal school teachers demonstrated neutral attitude.

An overall analysis of the trend of the results gives the following implications:

(i) The special school teachers were having positive attitude on the aspects—problems in visual, hearing, motor and mental aspects lead to disabilities in children (s. no. 1), whereas their attitude was neutral (moderate) on the aspects—significant difference among learning represent disabilities in children (s. no. 2) and difficulty

in communication, language, perceptual and social development leads to disabilities in children (s. no. 3), negative attitude on the aspects of disabilities in children do not lead any special abilities (s. no. 4), disabled children's learning needs and styles are same as normal children and they need not require special attention in regular classrooms (s. no. 5), physical disability will leads to low I.Q. (s. no. 6) and disabilities in children leads to slow learning and learning disabilities (s. no. 7), under the dimension 'concept of disabilities in children'. On all these aspects the normal school teachers' attitude was neutral (s. nos. 1 to 3) and negative (s. nos. 4 to 7).

(ii) Under the dimension, 'causes and characteristics' the special school teachers' attitude was high on the aspects—exposure of pregnant women into hazardous environment pre- peri-natal period leads to disabilities in children (s. no. 9) and brain injuries and accidents lead to mental retardation in children (s. no. 11); moderate attitude on the aspects hereditary and environmental factors contribute disabilities in children (s. no. 8), children's exposure to lead coated toys, infectious disease, and physical abnormalities leads to disabilities in children (s. no. 10), poor child bearing and rearing practices and faulty teaching learning practices leads to language learning disabilities in children (s. no. 12), perceptual and motor coordination, cognitive and metacognitive as well as social deficits are common in children with disabilities (s. no. 13). Hypo- and hyper-activity behaviours usually exhibited by children with disabilities (s. no. 14), disabilities in children lead to inferiority complex, stress, strain, low span of attention and emotional instability (s. no. 16), and disabilities in children lead to better abstract thinking than the normal children (s. no. 17), and low attitude or negative attitude about the aspect that visual impairment in children may not lead to stereotyped behaviours (s. no. 15). On all these aspects, the normal school teachers' attitude was neutral (s. nos. 8 to 16 and 18) and negative for the serial number of the aspect 15.

(iii) On the dimension 'identification and assessment of children with disabilities', the special school teachers' attitude was positive for the aspects—visual impairment in children can be identified through classroom observation, visual screening and ophthalmological tests (s. no. 21) and hearing impairment in children can be identified through classroom observation and hearing tests (s. no. 22). Contrary to this, their attitude is neutral on the aspects such as disabilities in children can be identified through observation and academic records (s. no. 18), informal tests for identification of hearing difficulties in children (s. no. 19), mental retardation and giftedness can be identified in children with intelligence tests (s. no. 20) and assessment of adaptive behaviour leads to identification of social deficits (s. no. 24). Similarly, they showed negative attitude on the aspect of identification of language learning difficulties in children through language assessment tests (s. no. 23). The normal school teachers' attitude was neutral (s. nos. 18 to 21 and 24) and negative (s. nos. 22 and 23).

(iv) With regard to the dimension 'teaching and training methods', the special school teachers together had positive attitude on the aspects—children with disabilities may benefit from appropriate placement services (s. no. 25), the learning of low vision children can be enhanced through large print materials, magnifying devices, and corrective lenses (s. no. 33). Use of plus curriculum for blind children to learn 3R's as well as orientation and mobility skills (s. no. 34), use of audio tapes and talking books for blind children (s. no. 35) and use of orthotic devices to facilitate the daily living skills of OH children (s. no. 40); neutral or moderate attitude on the aspects such as—teaching and training programmes for disabled children should be based on their current performance ability (s. no. 27), setting long-term and short-terms goals for the education of children with disabilities (s. no. 28), use of self directed learning materials for gifted children

(s. no. 29), need for integrated therapy to the mentally retarded children (s. no. 31), need for peer tutoring, group learning and multi-sensory approaches for children with learning difficulties and slow learning (s. no. 32), need for the use of total communication approach to the hearing impaired children, use of hearing aids to enhance the residual hearing use of group hearing aids to facilitate teaching learning process in the classroom and use of CCTV to facilitate the learning of HI children (s. nos. 36, 37, 38 and 39); negative attitude on the aspects-the need for taking into account the degree of disability in organising individualised education programme and breaking down the task or activity into smaller sequential steps with short duration to facilitate MR and slow learners learning (s. nos. 26 and 30). On all the teaching and training aspects the normal school teachers' attitudes was neutral (s. nos. 25, 27, 28, 29, 31 to 40) and negative (s. nos. 26 and 30).

(v) Positive attitude was shown by the special education teachers on the aspects—guidance and counselling by the teacher leads self confidence among children with disabilities, disabilities in children can be prevented by giving guidance about pre-, peri- and post-natal problems to the parents and community (s. nos. 41 and 42); need for peer group guidance and counselling, parent counselling (s. nos. 43 and 44) community counselling (s. no. 46), need to involve parents in planning, development and organisation of education programmes for children with disabilities (s. no. 45) and need for directing the parents of children with disabilities to the specialist—audiologist, psychologist and so on (s. no. 48); and they possessed negative attitude about the need for PTA meetings, discussion and group work to facilitate the progress of disabilities, under the dimension 'guidance and counselling activities'. The normal school teachers' attitude was neutral in most of the guidance and counselling activities except negative attitude in s. no. of the aspect 48.

Attitude building activities must be done in the following ways:

(i) For better attitudinal change there is a need to organise systematic sensitisation programmes by using popular media like print and electronic. A visit to the innovative and thought provoking activities or programmes organised by the specialised institutions in this area definitely facilitates positive attitudes in teachers. Video programming of such specialised school or institutional activities must be done and the same can be supplied to school libraries. Similarly, the Department of Education and DIETs can organise short duration orientation programmes to the existing teachers on different dimensions of disabilities with practical inputs.

Competencies Possessed by Special and Normal Teachers in Dealing Children with Disabilities

As already mentioned in 4.2.1. and 4.2.2., awareness and attitude of teachers play a vital role for the success of any educational programme to the children with disabilities. This awareness and positive attitudes lead to better competencies or performances. A competent teacher working in special schools or normal schools should be able to understand the different aspects of the concept of disabilities in children, be able to exhibit knowledge about the causes and characteristics of children with disabilities, have ability or skill in identification and assessment of children with disabilities, demonstrate skill in teaching and training methods and proficiency in providing guidance and counselling to the children with disabilities and their parents. Only such teachers facilitate the development of these children whether it is in segregated education or integrated education or inclusive education at school level. An attempt is made in this study to assess the extent of competencies possessed by the special and normal school teachers on different aspects of disabilities in children.

In Table 4.4, the mean competency scores and the level of competency of special and normal school teachers on different aspects of disabilities in children are presented.

Table 4.4: Mean scores and level of competency of special and normal school teachers towards each aspect of children with disabilities

Sl. No.	Competency Statements	Special School Teachers								Special School Teachers together (N = 660)		Normal School Teachers (N = 527)	
		VI (N = 95)		HI (N = 213)		MR (N = 293)		OH (N = 59)					
		Mean Scores	Level of Competency	Mean Scores	Level of Competency	Mean Scores	Level of Competency	Mean Scores	Level of Competency	Mean Scores	Level of Competency	Mean Scores	Level of Competency
(1)	(2)	(3)	(4)	(5)	(6)	(7)	(8)	(9)	(10)	(11)	(12)	(13)	(14)
I.	**Concept of Disabilities in Children**												
1.	Exhibit knowledge about visual, hearing, motor and mental deficiency problems in children.	2.68	H	2.62	H	2.65	H	2.80	H	2.68	H	2.07	M
2.	Able to understand the learning differences of disabled and normal children.	2.21	M	2.35	M	2.32	M	2.46	H	2.33	M	1.86	L
3.	Exhibit knowledge about the communication, language perceptual and social development difficulties in children with disabilities.	2.51	H	2.39	H	2.46	H	2.47	H	2.44	H	1.84	L

(Contd...)

(1)	(2)	(3)	(4)	(5)	(6)	(7)	(8)	(9)	(10)	(11)	(12)	(13)	(14)
4.	Able to know the special abilities of the disabled children.	2.38	M	2.34	M	2.36	M	2.56	H	2.41	H	1.85	L
5.	Knowledge about the learning needs and learning style of disabled children and need for special attention in regular classrooms.	2.57	H	2.43	H	2.47	H	2.51	H	2.49	H	1.91	L
6.	Knowledge about the intelligent quotient (IQ) of disabled and normal children.	2.33	M	2.31	M	2.23	M	2.27	M	2.28	M	1.83	L
7.	Knowledge about the slow learners and children with learning difficulties.	2.54	H	2.38	M	2.40	M	2.41	H	2.43	H	1.84	L
II.	**Causes and Characteristics of Children with Disabilities**												
8.	Exhibit knowledge about hereditary and environmental causes of disabilities in children.	2.33	M	2.46	H	2.25	M	2.47	H	2.37	M	1.97	L
9.	Demonstrate knowledge on disabilities in children due to exposure of women to hazardous environment in pre and perinatal periods.	2.59	H	2.36	M	2.47	H	2.53	H	2.48	H	1.92	L

(Contd...)

(1)	(2)	(3)	(4)	(5)	(6)	(7)	(8)	(9)	(10)	(11)	(12)	(13)	(14)
10.	Knowledge about lead coated toys, infectious diseases and physical, abnormalities causing disabilities in children.	2.28	M	2.36	M	2.30	M	2.17	M	2.27	M	1.86	L
11.	Knowledge about the causes of mental retardation in children.	2.42	H	2.36	M	2.39	H	2.41	H	2.39	H	1.91	L
12.	Knowledge about the relationship between child bearing and rearing practices, teaching-learning practices and language learning difficulties in children.	2.31	M	2.37	M	2.27	M	2.32	M	2.31	M	1.91	L
13.	Knowledge about the perceptual, motor co-ordination, cognitive, metacognitive as well as social skill deficits in disabled children.	2.54	H	2.37	M	2.31	M	2.39	H	2.40	H	1.95	L
14.	Demonstrate knowledge on hypo- and hyper-activity behaviour of children with disabilities.	2.43	H	2.46	H	2.51	H	2.54	H	2.48	H	1.87	L

(Contd...)

(1)	(2)	(3)	(4)	(5)	(6)	(7)	(8)	(9)	(10)	(11)	(12)	(13)	(14)
15.	Exhibit knowledge about the stereotype behaviours of visually impaired children.	2.24	H	2.24	M	2.29	M	2.29	H	2.26	M	1.97	L
16.	Knowledge about the psychological characteristics of children with disabilities.	2.43	H	2.32	M	2.34	M	2.44	H	2.38	M	1.66	L
17.	Knowledge about the different thinking abilities of disabled and non-disabled children.	2.32	M	2.37	M	2.27	M	2.44	H	2.35	M	1.80	L
III.	**Identification and Assessment of Children with Disabilities**												
18.	Ability to identify disabilities in children through direct observation and academic records.	2.53	H	2.57	H	2.43	H	2.58	H	2.52	H	2.05	M
19.	Skill in developing and using informal tests (classroom tests such as oral reading, writing and dictation etc.) to identify language difficulties.	2.40	H	2.45	H	231	M	2.46	H	2.40	H	1.90	L
20.	Skill in identifying mental retardation and giftedness in children.	2.42	H	2.45	H	2.33	M	2.36	M	2.39	H	1.78	L

(Contd...)

(1)	(2)	(3)	(4)	(5)	(6)	(7)	(8)	(9)	(10)	(11)	(12)	(13)	(14)
21.	Ability to use classroom observation and visual screening to identify visual impairment in children.	2.42	H	2.37	M	2.24	M	2.42	H	2.36	M	1.85	L
22.	Competency in identifying hearing impairment in children.	2.46	H	2.57	H	2.28	M	2.29	M	2.40	H	1.84	L
23.	Skill in identifying language learning difficulties in children.	2.43	H	2.46	H	2.27	M	2.34	M	2.55	M	1.76	L
24.	Proficiency in assessment of adaptive behaviour to identify social deficit skills in disabled children.	2.41	H	2.39	H	2.28	M	2.20	M	2.32	M	1.93	L
IV.	**Teaching and Training Methods**												
25.	Skill in providing appropriate placement services to the children with disabilities.	2.43	H	2.45	H	2.40	H	2.53	H	2.45	H	1.95	L
26.	Demonstrate skill in developing individualised educational plan to the disabled.	2.45	H	2.46	H	2.38	M	2.53	H	2.45	H	1.90	L
27.	Ability to plan teaching and training programmes for the disabled children based on their current performance.	2.37	M	2.54	H	2.42	H	2.51	H	2.46	H	1.88	L

(Contd...)

(1)	(2)	(3)	(4)	(5)	(6)	(7)	(8)	(9)	(10)	(11)	(12)	(13)	(14)
28.	Able to set long-term and short-term goals which facilities the education of children with disabilities.	2.48	H	2.37	M	2.35	M	2.41	H	2.40	H	1.93	L
29.	Skill in providing self-directed materials that facilitates learning in gifted children.	2.34	M	2.33	M	2.29	M	2.39	H	2.33	M	1.85	L
30.	Proficiency in teaching mentally retarded and slow learners.	2.35	M	2.27	M	2.42	H	2.46	H	2.37	M	1.86	L
31.	Knowledge about integrated therapy (speech, physical and occupational therapy) for better development of mentally retarded.	2.35	M	2.25	M	2.35	M	2.41	H	2.34	M	1.89	L
32.	Ability to organise peer tutoring, group learning and multi-sensory approaches for the children with learning difficulties and slow learning.	2.43	H	2.36	M	2.36	M	2.44	H	2.39	H	1.89	L
33.	Knowledge about large print materials, magnifying devices and corrective lenses for the low vision children in learning.	2.51	H	2.23	M	2.31	M	2.31	M	2.34	M	1.87	L

(Contd...)

(1)	(2)	(3)	(4)	(5)	(6)	(7)	(8)	(9)	(10)	(11)	(12)	(13)	(14)
34.	Knowledge and skill in using plus curriculum (Braille reading and writing, orientation and mobility and sensory training) for blind children.	2.45	H	2.24	M	2.30	M	2.27	M	2.31	M	1.79	L
35.	Skill in use of audiotapes/ talking books which facilities learning in blind children.	2.52	H	2.38	M	2.37	M	2.44	H	2.42	H	2.00	M
36.	Proficiency in total communication approach in teaching hearing impaired children.	2.32	M	2.55	H	2.34	M	2.32	M	2.38	M	1.91	L
37.	Knowledge about hearing aids to gear up residual hearing.	2.35	M	2.43	H	2.26	M	2.34	M	2.34	M	1.79	L
38.	Able to use group hearing aids in the classroom set-up to facilitate teaching learning process.	2.57	H	2.54	H	2.42	H	2.36	M	2.47	H	2.06	L
39.	Knowledge and skill in using CCTV for hearing impaired children's learning.	2.13	M	2.33	M	2.27	M	2.14	M	2.21	M	1.82	L

(Contd...)

(1)	(2)	(3)	(4)	(5)	(6)	(7)	(8)	(9)	(10)	(11)	(12)	(13)	(14)
40.	Knowledge and skill in use of orthotic devices to the orthopaedically handicapped children to promote daily living skills.	2.52	H	2.25	M	2.31	M	2.44	H	2.38	M	1.82	L
V.	**Guidance and Counselling Activities**												
41.	Able to develop self-confidence among children with disabilities.	2.38	M	2.46	H	2.37	M	2.46	H	2.41	H	1.86	L
43.	Skill in providing guidance and counselling to parents and community about prenatal, perinatal and postnatal problems.	2.66	H	2.50	H	2.39	H	2.56	H	2.52	H	1.87	L
43.	Ability to alleviate negative attitude of peer group towards children with disabilities.	2.33	M	2.45	H	2.32	M	2.47	H	2.39	H	1.81	L
44.	Proficiency in counselling the parents to overcome the difficulties of disabled children.	2.61	H	2.55	H	2.39	H	2.59	H	2.53	H	1.87	L
45.	Ability to involve parents in planning, development and organisation of educational programmes for the children with disabilities.	2.25	M	2.49	H	2.38	M	2.42	H	2.38	M	1.86	L

(Contd...)

(1)	(2)	(3)	(4)	(5)	(6)	(7)	(8)	(9)	(10)	(11)	(12)	(13)	(14)
46.	Able to give community counselling that leads to development of positive attitudes towards children with disabilities.	2.47	H	2.50	H	2.35	M	2.39	H	2.42	H	1.87	L
47.	Ability to conduct PTA meetings, discussion and group work to facilitate the development of children with disabilities.	2.27	M	2.49	H	2.30	M	2.34	M	2.35	M	1.84	L
48.	Ability to direct parents to the specialists (Audiologist, Psychologist and Occupational therapist) for better development of children with disabilities.	2.52	H	2.50	H	2.34	M	2.32	M	2.42	H	1.83	L

Note:

Level of Competency

Low : Value from 1.99 and below

Moderate : Values between 2.00 to 2.38

High : Values from 2.39 and above

In the present study, under the dimension 'concept of disabilities in children' the special school teachers together demonstrated high competency in serial numbers of the aspects 1, 3, 4, 5 and 7. For s. nos. 4 and 7, the VI, HI and MR school teachers and for s. no. 7, the HI and MR school teachers exhibited moderate competency. The competency level of the special school teachers together was moderate for serial number of the aspects 2 and 6. For s. no. 2, the OH school teachers' competency was high compared to their counterparts working in VI, HI and MR schools. On the other hand, the normal school teachers' competency level was moderate for s. no. 1 and low for s. no. of aspects 2 to 7.

Under the dimension 'causes and characteristics of children with disabilities', the special school teachers together demonstrated higher competency on serial number of aspects 9, 11, 13 and 14. But the teachers working in HI schools possessed moderate competency on s. no. 9 and 11 and HI and MR for s. no. 13. Contrary to this, their competency was at moderate level for s. nos. of the aspects 8, 10, 12, 15, 16 and 17. At the same time, the HI school teachers' competency was high for s. no. 8, VI and OH for s. no. 16, and OH for s. no. 17. On the otherhand, the normal school teachers' competency level was low on all the aspects under the dimension 'causes and characteristics of children with disabilities'. Under the dimension 'identification and assessment of children with disabilities', the special school teachers together exhibited high competency on s. nos. 18, 19, 20 and 22. The MR school teachers possessed moderate competency for s. no. 19, MR and OH for s. nos. 20 and 22. Contrary to this, the special school teachers together demonstrated moderate level of competency on s. nos. 21, 23 and 24. It is also noted that for s. nos. 21 the VI and OH school teachers competency is high, and for s. nos. 23 and 24 the VI and HI teachers' knowledge was also high. On the other hand, except for s. no. 18, the competency level of normal school teachers is low.

Under 'teaching and training methods', the special school teachers together demonstrated high level of competency on the s. nos. of aspects 25 to 28 , 32, 35 and 38. It is also observed that the MR teachers exhibited moderate competency for s. no. 26, VI school teachers for s. no. 27, MR and OH for s. nos. 28, 32 and 35 and OH school teachers for s. no. 38. Contrary to this, their competency level was moderate for the s. nos. of aspects 29, 30, 31, 33, 34, 36, 37, 39 and 40. It is also noted that, high competency was shown by OH teachers for s. no. 29, 31 and 40, MR and OH teachers for s. no. 30, VI teachers for s. no. 33, 34 and 40, HI teachers for s. no. 36 and 37. On other hand, in all the aspects under this dimensions, except s. no. 35 (moderate level) the normal school teachers showed low level of competency.

Under the dimension 'guidance and counselling' the special school teachers together demonstrated higher competency in the s. nos. 41 to 44, 46 and 48. Their competency was moderate on the aspects on s. nos. 45 and 47. Further, it is also observed that VI and MR school teachers exhibited moderate competency on s. nos. 41 and 43, MR for s. nos. 46, and 48 and OH for s. no. 48, for s. nos. 45 and 47 the HI school teachers and for s. no. 45 OH school teachers. On the otherhand, for all these aspects the normal school teachers' competency was very low.

An overall analysis reveals that, the aspects in which the special school and normal school teachers competencies are moderate and low should be given priority in organisations of training programmes for these teachers. Accordingly

(i) Under the dimension 'concept of disabilities in children', the aspects such as-able to understand the learning difference of disabled and non-disabled children and knowledge about intelligent quotient of disabled and non-disabled children and knowledge about intelligence quotient of disabled and non-disabled children should be given priority for special school teachers apart from the above two aspects, the normal school teachers should be given orientation about the different categories of disabilities in children, knowledge about communication, language, perceptual and social development difficulties ion children, the learning needs and learning styles of disabled children and knowledge about learners and children with learning difficulties.

(ii) Under 'causes and characteristics', the priority of special school teachers were hereditary and environmental factors related to disabilities in children, diseases and

physical abnormalities causing disabilities in children, relationship between child bearing and rearing practices, teaching learning practices and language learning difficulties in children, stereotyped behaviours in visually impaired children, psychological characteristics of children with disabilities and different thinking abilities of disabled and non-disabled children. Adding to this, the normal school teachers also require training in knowledge on disabilities in children due to hazardous environments in pre- and peri-natal periods, causes of mental retardation, perceptual, motor co-ordination, cognitive and metacognitive deficits as well as social skill deficits in disabled children, and hypo- and hyper-activity behaviours of children with disabilities.

(iii) Under the dimension 'identification and assessment, the special school teachers require training in use of classroom observation and visual screening to identify visual impairments in children, identifying language learning difficulties and assessment of adaptive behaviour to identify social deficit skills in disabled children. The normal school teachers too require orientation on this (as their competency level is low) apart from the aspects such as ability to identify disabilities in children through direct observation and academic records, use of informal tests to identify language difficulties, skill in identifying mental retardation and giftedness in children and identification of hearing impairment in children.

(iv) Under teaching and training, they need competency on the aspects of providing self directed materials to gifted children, teaching mentally retarded and slow learners, knowledge about speech, physical and occupational therapy, knowledge about large print materials, magnifying devices and corrective lenses, skill in using plus curriculum, knowledge about hearing aids to gear up residual hearing, proficiency in total communication approach, knowledge and skill in use of CCTV in HI

children's learning and use of orthotic devices to the orthopaedically handicapped children to promote daily living skills. Apart from the these aspects the normal school teachers require competencies on—skill in providing appropriate placement services to the disabled children, development of individualised education programme to the disabled, ability to plan teaching and training programmes to the disabled based on their current performance, able to set long- and short-term goals for the education of disabled, ability to organise peer tutoring, group learning and multi-sensory approach for children with learning difficulties and slow learning, skill in use of audio tapes/talking books to facilitate blind children's learning and able to use group hearing aids in the classroom set-up to facilitate teaching learning process.

(v) Under the dimension, guidance and counselling, the special school teachers require competencies on—involving parents in planning, development and organisation of educational programmes for the children with disabilities and ability to conduct PTA meetings, discussions and group work to facilitate the development of children with disabilities. Adding to these, normal school teachers require competencies in development of self-confidence in disabled children, providing guidance and counselling to the parents and community about pre-, peri- and post-natal problems, ability to alleviate negative attitude of peer group towards disabled children, proficiency in parent's counselling, able to provide community counselling to promote positive attitude towards disabled children and able to direct parents to the specialist such as audiologist, psychologist and occupational therapist for the betterment of children with disabilities.

To develop and promote the above said competencies in special and normal school teachers, the DIETs and the College of Education/Department of Education located in the particular locality should develop teaching and training materials, organise competency-based short duration training programmes. Likewise, the well structured teaching training programme in dealing each disability area should be documented and video taped, so that the same can be supplied to the DIETs and libraries located at district level so as to lend the same to different schools for viewing and practising the same. A visit by the teachers to the reputed institutions working in each disability area will add credit to their competencies.

Competencies Required by the Special and Normal School Teachers to deal Children with Disabilities

The performance of teacher to a great extent depends on knowledge, attitude and the competencies they possess in doing a particular activity. It is natural that higher the awareness, more will be the positive attitude and the competencies. A person who is sensitised with right type of awareness, attitude and competencies will always try to enrich his/her performance. This leads that individual to develop further zeal and quest for more perfection in his/her activities. The other way is that lower the awareness and attitude, lower will be the competency in doing the activity. The low awareness and attitude make the person to be more ignorant of what he/she needs to improve his/her activities effectively. If the third party specifies what they require to do their job more effectively, definitely this category of individuals will come out with their needs or requirements. Even after the third party intervention of explicitly spelling out the requirements, if they are not coming forward with their needs and requirements, there will be definitely urgency to sensitise them the need for awareness. That is what exactly the study tries to attempt. In the present study, an attempt is made to identify number and percentage of special and normal school teachers requiring and not requiring competency on each aspect of disabilities in children.

Table 4.5 clearly reveals that, more than 70 per cent of the special and normal school teachers expressed that they need competency on each aspect of children with disabilities specified under different dimensions. It means irrespective of their awareness, attitude and existing competencies on each aspect of disabilities in children (refer Tables 4.2, 4.3 and 4.4), the special and normal school teachers had opted for further training on all the aspects. This once again substantiated the thoughts that higher the awareness, more will be the attitude and competency. These three together add better sensitisation in the teachers paving way for seeking more competency. Similarly, when there is low awareness, attitude and lower will be the competency. Such a person may not go for enriching his competency by virtue of his ignorance. But in the present study, as the subjects are elites, in the sense that they are educated with rational thinking, they have gone for improving their competencies in the form of required competency.

This is the reason why the more percentage of teachers irrespective of their awareness and attitude had gone for further enhancement of their skills and abilities in dealing children with disabilities.

From the above, it can be concluded that, more than 70 per cent of the special and normal school teachers require competency on each aspect under different dimensions of disabilities in children. Any awareness generation programme , attitudinal building activities and competency based training programmes or activities for special and normal school teacher must incorporate appropriately the stated disability aspects studied in this investigation.

PART-II: DIFFERENTIAL ANALYSIS

Differential Analysis on the Awareness, Attitude and Existing Competencies of Special and Normal School Teachers in Dealing Children with Disabilities

In order to study the significant difference between two or more than two groups of samples, differential studies are made. In this part, as a first step to know the significant difference between special and normal school teachers' awareness, attitude and existing competencies to deal children with disabilities, mean and SD were calculated for awareness, attitude and existing competencies separately. Based on these means and SDs, t-values were worked out to know the significant difference, if any, between normal and special school teachers. The respective results are presented in Tables 4.6 to 4.8 and discussed.

Table 4.5: Number of percentage of special and normal schools teachers.requiring and competency in each aspect of dealing children with disabilities.

Sl. No.	Competency Statement	*Number and Percentage of Special and Normal School Teachers Requiring Competency*					
		Special School Teachers				*Special School Teachers together (N = 660)*	*Normal School Teachers (N = 527)*
		VI (N = 95)	*HI (N = 213)*	*MR (N = 293)*	*OH (N = 660)*		
(1)	(2)	(3)	(4)	(5)	(6)	(7)	(8)
I.	**Concept of Disabilities**						
1.	Exhibit knowledge about visual, hearing, motor and mental deficiency problems in children.	88 93%	188 88%	243 83%	44 75%	563 85%	379 72%
2.	Able to understand the learning differences of disabled and normal children.	80 84%	184 86%	235 80%	46 78%	545 85%	418 80%
3.	Exhibit knowledge about the communication, language perceptual and social development difficulties in children with disabilities.	82 86%	174 82%	232 79%	43 73%	531 80%	409 78%
4.	Able to know the special abilities of the disabled children.	82 86%	164 77%	226 77%	47 80%	519 79%	408 77%

(Contd...)

(1)	(2)	(3)	(4)	(5)	(6)	(7)	(8)
5.	Knowledge about the learning needs and learning style of disabled children and need for special attention in regular classrooms.	84 88%	168 79%	243 83%	3[illegible] 66%	534 81%	406 77%
6.	Knowledge about the intelligent quotient (IQ) of disabled and normal children.	83 87%	173 81%	233 80%	44 75%	533 81%	421 80%
7.	Knowledge about the slow learners and children with learning difficulties.	84 88%	171 80%	242 83%	47 80%	544 82%	425 81%
II.	**Causes and Characteristics of Children with Disabilities.**						
8.	Exhibit knowledge about hereditary and environmental causes of disabilities in children.	87 92%	169 79%	236 81%	46 78%	538 82%	399 76%
9.	Demonstrate knowledge on disabilities in children due to exposure of women to hazardous environment in pre and perinatal periods.	85 89%	171 80%	236 81%	49 83%	541 82%	429 81%
10.	Knowledge about lead coated toys, infectious diseases and physical abnormalities causing disabilities in children.	85 89%	165 77%	231 79%	47 80%	528 80%	400 76%

(Contd...)

(1)	(2)	(3)	(4)	(5)	(6)	(7)	(8)
11.	Knowledge about the causes of mental retardation in children.	88 93%	164 77%	227 77%	48 81%	527 80%	426 81%
12.	Knowledge about the relationship between child bearing and rearing practices, teaching-learning practices and language learning difficulties in children.	83 87%	171 80%	234 80%	47 80%	535 81%	427 81%
13.	Knowledge about the perceptual, motor co-ordination, cognitive, metacognitive as well as social skills deficits in disabled children.	86 91%	169 79%	237 81%	40 68%	532 81%	419 80%
14.	Demonstrate knowledge on hypo- and hyper-activity behaviour of children with disabilities.	83 87%	171 80%	255 87%	47 80%	556 84%	447 85%
15.	Exhibit knowledge about the stereotype behaviours of visually impaired children.	82 86%	167 78%	251 86%	38 64%	538 82%	448 85%
16.	Knowledge about the psychological characteristics of children with disabilities.	86 91%	175 82%	247 84%	47 80%	555 84%	449 85%

(Contd...)

(1)	(2)	(3)	(4)	(5)	(6)	(7)	(8)
17.	Knowledge about the different thinking abilities of disabled and non-disabled children.	86 91%	167 78%	247 84%	49 83%	549 83%	412 78%
III.	**Identification and Assessment of Children with Disabilities.**						
18.	Ability to identify disabilities in children through direct observation and academic records.	86 91%	169 79%	235 80%	46 78%	536 81%	360 68%
19.	Skill in developing and using informal tests (classroom tests such as oral reading, writing and dictation etc.) to identify language difficulties.	88 93%	165 77%	241 82%	44 75%	538 82%	417 79%
20.	Skill in identifying mental retardation and giftedness in children.	90 95%	169 79%	239 82%	43 73%	541 82%	440 83%
21.	Ability to use classroom observation and visual screening to identify visual impairment in children.	87 92%	168 79%	245 84%	50 85%	550 83%	411 78%
22.	Competency in identifying hearing impairment in children.	91 96%	169 79%	246 84%	48 81%	554 84%	415 79%
23.	Skill in identifying language learning difficulties in children.	89 94%	173 81%	245 84%	46 78%	553 84%	426 81%

(Contd...)

(1)	(2)	(3)	(4)	(5)	(6)	(7)	(8)
24.	Proficiency in assessment of adaptive behaviour to identify social deficit skills in disabled children.	87 92%	173 81%	227 7%	47 80%	534 81%	394 75%
IV.	**Teaching and Training Methods**						
25.	Skill in providing appropriate placement services to the children with disabilities.	85 89%	174 82%	245 84%	48 81%	552 84%	413 78%
26.	Demonstrate skill in developing individualised Educational Plan to the disabled.	84 88%	172 81%	247 84%	49 83%	552 84%	432 82%
27.	Ability to plan teaching and training programmes for the disabled children based on their current performance.	91 96%	167 78%	243 83%	49 83%	550 83%	422 80%
28.	Able to set long-term and short-term goals which facilitate the education of children with disabilities.	87 92%	176 83%	233 80%	50 85%	546 83%	403 76%
29.	Skill in providing self-directed materials that facilitates learning in gifted children.	89 94%	168 79%	230 79%	47 80%	534 81%	434 82%

(Contd...)

(1)	(2)	(3)	(4)	(5)	(6)	(7)	(8)
30.	Proficiency in teaching mentally retarded and slow learners.	82 86%	178 84%	238 81%	47 80%	545 83%	427 81%
31.	Knowledge about integrated therapy (speech, physical and occupational therapy) for better development of mentally retarded.	87 92%	183 86%	243 83%	47 80%	560 85%	428 81%
32.	Ability to organise peer tutoring, group learning and multi-sensory approaches for the children with learning difficulties and slow learning.	83 87%	174 82%	244 83%	46 78%	547 83%	416 79%
33.	Knowledge about large print materials, magnifying devices and corrective lenses for the low vision children in learning.	87 92%	180 85%	242 83%	47 80%	556 84%	427 81%
34.	Knowledge and skill in using plus curriculum (Braille reading and writing, orientation and mobility and sensory training) for blind children.	87 92%	184 86%	242 83%	47 80%	560 85%	445 84%
35.	Skill in use of audiotapes/ talking books which facilitates learning in blind children.	88 93%	177 83%	252 86%	50 85%	567 86%	417 79%

(Contd...)

(1)	(2)	(3)	(4)	(5)	(6)	(7)	(8)
36.	Knowledge about hearing aids to gear up residual hearing.	87 92%	171 80%	242 83%	47 80%	547 83%	431 82%
37.	Proficiency in total communication approach in teaching hearing impaired children.	85 89%	172 81%	246 84%	49 83%	552 84%	406 77%
38.	Able to use group hearing aids in the classroom set up to facilitate teaching learning process.	85 89%	167 78%	239 82%	44 75%	535 81%	390 74%
39.	Knowledge and skill in using CCTV for hearing impaired children's learning.	85 89%	172 81%	243 83%	47 80%	547 83%	438 83%
40.	Knowledge and skill in use of orthotic devices to the orthopedically handicapped children to promote daily living skills.	84 88%	173 81%	238 81%	48 81%	543 82%	395 75%
V.	**Guidance and Counselling Activities**						
41.	Able to develop self-confidence among children with disabilities.	87 92%	164 77%	231 79%	51 86%	533 81%	410 78%
42.	Skill in providing guidance and counselling to parents and community about prenatal, perinatal and postnatal problems.	86 91%	170 80%	232 79%	52 88%	540 82%	417 79%

(Contd...)

(1)	(2)	(3)	(4)	(5)	(6)	(7)	(8)
43.	Ability to alleviate negative attitude of peer group towards children with disabilities.	76 80%	169 79%	233 80%	45 76%	523 79%	423 80%
44.	Proficiency in parents counselling to overcome the difficulties of disabled children.	85 89%	167 78%	243 83%	43 73%	538 82%	418 79%
45.	Ability to involve parents in planning, development and organisation of educational programmes for the children with disabilities.	81 85%	166 78%	240 82%	46 78%	533 81%	420 80%
46.	Able to give community counselling that leads to development positive attitudes towards children with disabilities.	82 86%	168 79%	233 80%	49 83%	532 81%	415 79%
47.	Ability to conduct PTA meeting, discussion and group work to facilitate the development of children with disabilities.	78 82%	169 79%	211 72%	47 80%	505 77%	419 80%
48.	Ability to direct parents to the specialists (Audiologist, Psychologist and Occupational therapist) for better development of children with disabilities.	84 88%	163 77%	231 79%	49 83%	527 80%	429 81%

The t-values based on mean and SD of the awareness scores of each category of special school teachers and normal school teachers on various dimensions of children with disabilities are presented in Table 4.6.

Table 4.6: Mean and SD of the awareness scores of different categories of special and normal school teachers towards various dimensions of children with disabilities and the calculated t-values

Dimensions	*Special School Teachers*								*Special School Teachers together (N = 660)*		*Normal School Teachers (N = 527)*		*Calculated t-value*
	VI (N = 95)		*HI (N = 213)*		*MR (N = 293)*		*OH (N = 59)*						
	Mean	*SD*	*Mean*	*SD*	*Mean*	*SD*	*Mean*	*SD*	*Mean*	*SD*	*Mean*	*SD*	
(1)	*(2)*	*(3)*	*(4)*	*(5)*	*(6)*	*(7)*	*(8)*	*(9)*	*(10)*	*(11)*	*(12)*	*(13)*	*(14)*
Concept of disabilities	14.08	2.38	14.21	1.97	13.88	2.92	13.95	1.77	14.02	2.48	15.00	1.94	VI vs Nri 4.10** HI vs Nri 5.01** MR vs Nri 6.57** OH vs Nri 3.99** SST vs Nri 7.44**
Causes and characteristics	22.32	2.84	22.58	2.87	23.28	2.63	22.05	1.56	22.80	2.70	19.78	2.83	VI vs Nri 8.05** HI vs Nri 12.17** MR vs Nri 17.42** OH vs Nri 6.07** SST vs Nri 18.81**

(Contd...)

(1)	(2)	(3)	(4)	(5)	(6)	(7)	(8)	(9)	(10)	(11)	(12)	(13)	(14)
Identification and assessment	15.57	1.87	14.72	1.97	15.05	2.01	14.58	1.66	14.98	1.97	14.03	2.15	VI vs Nri 6.54** HI vs Nri 4.06** MR vs Nri 6.69** OH vs Nri 1.88@ SST vs Nri 7.91**
Teaching and training methods	37.48	5.48	35.69	4.66	37.58	3.46	36.75	2.80	36.88	4.24	31.30	4.21	VI vs Nri 12.55** HI vs Nri 12.47** MR vs Nri 21.77** OH vs Nri 9.70** SSI vs Nri 22.62**
Guidance and counselling	20.09	3.12	19.22	3.39	19.80	2.57	19.03	2.00	19.58	2.92	15.57	2.89	VI vs Nri 13.82** HI vs Nri 14.80** MR vs Nri 20.88** OH vs Nri 8.98** SST vs Nri 23.63**
Dimensions as a whole	109.55	10.21	106.43	9.24	109.59	8.75	106.36	4.48	108.27	8.97	95.68	8.74	VI vs Nri 13.85** HI vs Nri 14.90** MR vs Nri 21.82** OH vs Nri 9.24** SSI vs Nri 24.31**

Note: @ Not significant at 0.05 level. ** Significant at 0.01 level. SST Special Schools Teachers Together.

It means, the awareness of special and normal school teachers varied with respect to the concept of disabilities in children. It is strange to note that the teachers working in normal school possessed better awareness (mean value: 15.00) than the teachers working in special schools (VI-14.08, HI-14.21, MR-13.82, OH-13.95, special school teachers together-14.02). Similarly, the t-values with respect to the awareness of teachers on causes and characteristics of children with disabilities are significant at 0.01 level indicating variations in the awareness of different categories of special school teachers and normal school teachers (VI vs NS-8.05, HI vs Ns-12.17, MR vs Ns-17.42, OH vs Ns-6.07, special school teachers together vs Ns-18.81). Further, the awareness of teachers working in special schools was better than their counterparts working in normal schools on the causes and characteristics of children with disabilities. The mean values between the teachers working in VI vs NS (15.57 and 14.03), HI vs NS (14.72 and 14.03), MR vs NS (15.04 and 14.03), special school teachers together vs NS (14.98 and 14.03) schools were significantly varying with respect to their awareness on 'identification and assessment of children with disabilities'. As a result the t-values were significant at 0.01 level. The mean values of OH and normal schools were not bringing any significant differences in their awareness (t-value-1.88).

From Table 4.6, it is evident that the normal school teachers' awareness was significantly less on 'teaching and training methods (31.30), 'guidance and counselling (15.57) and dimensions as a whole (95.68) compared to the teachers working in the schools for VI (37.48, 20.09 and 109.55), HI (35.69, 19.22 and 106.43), MR (37.58, 19.80 and 109.59), OH (36.75, 19.03 and 106.36). As a result, the t-values were significant at 0.01 level. It means, the special school teachers demonstrated better awareness than their counterparts working in normal schools on teaching and training methods, guidance and counselling activities, and dimensions as a whole in dealing children with disabilities. Hence the formulated hypothesis 'there exists significant difference between the special and normal schools teachers' awareness on different dimensions of children with disabilities is accepted. The hypothesis is not accepted with reference to 'identification and assessment' dimensions as the teachers working in special schools for orthopaedically handicapped and normal schools as their t-value was not significant as 0.05 level in the awareness dimension identification and assessment of children with disabilities.

From Table 4.6 it can be concluded that, the significant differences existed between normal and special school teachers awareness on accept of disabilities in children, causes and characteristics, identification and assessment, teaching and training methods, guidance and counselling, and dimensions as a whole. No significant differences existed between the teachers working in schools for OH and normal schools on awareness of identification and assessment. Further, normal school teachers' awareness on concept of disabilities in children was higher than their counterparts working in special schools. Whereas, the awareness of teachers working in different categories of special schools, were higher in causes and characteristics, identification and assessment, teaching and training methods, guidance and counselling and dimensions as a whole than their counterparts working in normal schools.

Mean, SD and the calculated t-values of the attitude scores of each category of special and normal school teachers on various dimensions of children with disabilities are presented in Table 4.7.

The result of the t-test on the attitude of special and normal school teachers with regard to the concept of disabilities in children revealed the significant differences between the teachers working in VI vs NS (t-value : 4.84), HI vs NS (t-value: 6.68) and special schools put together vs NS (t-value: 4.50). It means, the teachers working in VI, HI schools and special schools teachers together significantly differed with normal school teachers in their attitude on the concept of disabilities in children.

Table 4.7: Mean and SD of the attitude scores of different categories of special and normal school teachers towards various dimensions of children with disabilities and the calculated t-values

Dimensions	*Special School Teachers*								*Special School Teachers together (N = 660)*		*Normal School Teachers (N = 527)*		*Calculated t-values*
	VI (N = 95)		*HI (N = 213)*		*MR (N = 293)*		*OH (N = 59)*						
	Mean	*SD*	*Mean*	*SD*	*Mean*	*SD*	*Mean*	*SD*	*Mean*	*SD*	*Mean*	*SD*	
(1)	*(2)*	*(3)*	*(4)*	*(5)*	*(6)*	*(7)*	*(8)*	*(9)*	*(10)*	*(11)*	*(12)*	*(13)*	*(14)*
Concept of disabilities	23.21	3.80	23.25	3.93	20.42	3.53	20.90	3.54	22.22	3.82	21.24	3.62	VI vs Nri 4.84** HI vs Nri 6.68' MR vs Nri 0.69@ OH vs Nri 0.72@ SST vs Nri 4.50**
Causes and characterisics	35.14	5.50	36.69	7.07	37.74	4.93	34.95	4.20	36.78	5.82	32.37	4.76	VI vs Nri 5.08** HI vs Nri 9.62** MR vs Nri 15.29** OH vs Nri 3.99** SSI vs Nri 14.03**
Identification and assessment	25.26	4.30	25.50	4.81	27.13	3.60	25.85	3.10	26.22	4.17	22.12	3.93	VI vs Nri 7.08** HI vs Nri 9.92** MR vs Nri 18.04** OH vs Nri 7.05** SST vs Nri 17.30**

(Contd...)

(1)	(2)	(3)	(4)	(5)	(6)	(7)	(8)	(9)	(10)	(11)	(12)	(13)	(14)
Teaching and training methods	58.98	10.00	58.90	11.04	61.22	6.60	59.02	5.54	59.95	8.76	51.49	7.76	VI vs Nri 8.25** HI vs Nri 10.33** MR vs Nri 18.12** OH vs Nri 7.24** SST vs Nri 17.38**
Guidance and counselling	30.60	6.10	29.66	6.30	31.93	4.40	30.00	3.51	30.83	5.35	25.58	4.71	VI vs Nri 9.10** HI vs Nri 9.62** MR vs Nri 18.97** OH vs Nri 6.99** SST vs Nri 17.70**
Dimensions as a whole	173.19	23.75	174.00	26.80	179.45	17.19	170.70	12.92	176.00	21.61	152.80	17.14	VI vs Nri 9.88** HI vs Nri 12.70** MR vs Nri 21.10** OH vs Nri 7.66** SST vs Nri 20.00**

Note: @ Not significant at 0.05 level.

** Significant at 0.01 level.

SST– Special School Teachers Together.

The t-values evinced significant differences in the attitude of special and normal school teachers with regard to the causes and characteristics of children with disabilities (t-value: VI vs NS-5.08, HI vs NS-9.62, MR vs NS-15.29, OH vs NS-3.99, and special school teachers together vs NS-14.03). It shows that the attitude of special and normal school teachers was not similar with regard to the causes and characteristics of children with disabilities. The mean values further revealed that the special school teachers (VI-35.14, HI-36.69, MR-37.74, OH-34.95 and special school teachers together-37.78) possessed better attitude than the normal school teachers (32.37). Similar trend was found with regard to identification and assessment, teaching and training methods, guidance and counselling and dimensions as a whole. The t-values were significant at 0.01 level in all the three dimensions evincing variations in the attitude of special and normal schools teachers. Hence the formulated hypothesis, 'there exist significant difference between special and normal school teachers' attitude towards different dimensions of children with disabilities' is accepted.

From Table 4.7, it is also observed that special school teachers irrespective of the type of school they are working possessed better attitude than the normal school teachers. This result gives rise the need for better awareness generation which lead for development of better attitude in normal school teachers on different dimensions of children with disabilities.

To sum up, the attitude of special and normal school teachers significantly varried with respect to the causes and characteristics of children with disabilities, identification and assessment, teaching and training, guidance and counselling and dimensions as a whole. The special school teachers possessed more positive attitude irrespective of the type of school they are working than the normal school teachers. Contrary to this, the teachers working in the schools for MR, and schools for OH did not significantly differ in their attitude with normal school teachers. But the teachers working in VI, HI and special school teachers together towards the concept of disabilities in children differed in their attitude than their counterparts working in normal schools. Here too, the teachers working in VI, HI and special school teacher together demonstrated better attitude than the normal school teachers.

The t-values based on mean and SD of the competency scores of each category special and normal school teachers on various dimensions of children with disabilities are presented in Table 4.8.

From Table 4.8, it is found that the obtained t-values with regard to the competency dimensions—concept of disabilities in children, (VI vs NS-11.31, HI vs NS-13.71, MR vs NS-24.49, OH vs NS-10.63, special school teachers together vs NS-25.26), causes and characteristics of children with disabilities (VI vs NS-9.20, HI vs NS-11.24, MR vs NS-23.00, OH vs NS-12.46 and special school teachers together vs NS-22.04), identification and assessment (VI vs NS-10.16, HI vs NS-11.23, MR vs NS-24.15, OH vs NS-12.36 and special school teachers together vs NS-23.04), teaching and training methods (VI vs NS-10.82, HI vs NS-11.58, MR vs NS-24.50, OH vs NS-12.49, and special school teachers together vs NS-23.47), guidance and counselling (VI vs NS-11.35, HI vs NS-13.40, MR vs NS-26.20, OH vs NS-12.02, and special school teachers together vs NS-23.68), and dimensions as a whole (VI vs NS-12.83, HI vs NS-14.83, MR vs NS-29.86, OH vs NS-14.63, and special school teachers together vs NS-28.95) were significant at 0.01 level. It indicates, that in existing competencies of special school teachers and normal school teachers were significantly varying in their competencies in dealing children with disabilities. The mean values also reveal that the normal school teachers exhibited low level of competency (13.20, 18.80, 13.12, 30.22, 14.81 and 90.14) compared to different categories of special school teachers (VI-16.61, 22.90, 16.19, 37.01, 19.23 and 111.93; HI-16.27, 22.30, 15.67, 35.77, 18.36 and 108.36; MR-17.65, 24.63, 17.41, 39.55, 20.16 and 119.40; OH-17.03, 25.02, 17.47, 39.34, 19.64 and 118.51 and special school teachers together-17.00, 23.66, 16.68, 37.94, 19.40 and 114.68). Hence the formulated hypotheses, 'there exists significant difference between the special and normal school teachers' existing competencies on different dimensions, to deal children with disabilities' is accepted.

Table 4.8: Mean and SD of the possessed competency scores of different categories of special and normal school teachers on various dimensions of children with disabilities and the calculated t-values

Dimensions	*Special School Teachers (Required)*								*Special School Teachers put together*		*Normal School Teachers*		*Calculated t-values*
	VI		*HI*		*MR*		*OH*						
	Mean	*SD*	*Mean*	*SD*	*Mean*	*SD*	*Mean*	*SD*	*Mean*	*SD*	*Mean*	*SD*	
(1)	*(2)*	*(3)*	*(4)*	*(5)*	*(6)*	*(7)*	*(8)*	*(9)*	*(10)*	*(11)*	*(12)*	*(13)*	*(14)*
Concept of disabilities	16.61	2.63	16.27	2.86	17.65	2.02	17.03	1.54	17.00	2.45	13.20	2.72	VI vs Nri 11.31** HI vs Nri 13.71** MR vs Nri 24.49** OH vs Nri 10.63** SST vs Nri 25.26**
Causes and characteristics	22.90	5.10	22.30	4.02	24.63	2.91	25.02	2.27	23.66	3.79	18.80	3.76	VI vs Nri 9.20** HI vs Nri 11.24** MR vs Nri 23.00** OH vs Nri 12.46** SSI vs Nri 22.04**
Identification and assessment	16.19	3.00	15.67	3.10	17.41	1.97	17.47	1.44	16.68	2.63	13.12	2.66	VI vs Nri 10.16** HI vs Nri 11.23** MR vs Nri 24.15** OH vs Nri 12.36** SST vs Nri 23.04**

(Contd...)

(1)	(2)	(3)	(4)	(5)	(6)	(7)	(8)	(9)	(10)	(11)	(12)	(13)	(14)	
													VI vs Nri	10.82**
													HI vs Nri	11.58**
Teaching and training methods	37.01	6.10	35.77	6.70	39.55	4.58	39.34	2.42	37.94	5.70	30.22	5.54	MR vs Nri	24.50**
													OH vs Nri	12.49**
													SST vs Nri	23.47**
													VI vs Nri	11.35**
													HI vs Nri	13.40**
Guidance and counselling	19.23	5.50	18.36	3.84	20.16	2.40	19.64	2.16	19.40	3.55	14.81	3.00	MR vs Nri	26.20**
													OH vs Nri	12.02**
													SST vs Nri	23.68**
													VI vs Nri	12.83**
													HI vs Nri	14.83**
Dimensions as a whole	111.93	17.60	108.36	15.98	119.40	10.65	118.51	5.33	114.68	14.30	90.14	14.77	MR vs Nri	29.86**
													OH vs Nri	14.63**
													SST vs Nri	28.95**

Note: @ Not significant at 0.05 level.

** Significant at 0.01 level.

SST– Special Schools Teachers Together.

From the above, it can be concluded that the special and normal school teachers significantly differed in their existing competencies on the concept of disabilities in children, causes and characteristics of children with disabilities, identification and assessment, teaching and training methods, guidance and counselling and dimensions as a whole. The special school teachers possessed better competencies than the normal school teachers in all the competency dimensions.

Effect of Gender, Age, Educational Qualification, Training in Special Education, Years of Experience, Location of School, Nature of School and Type of School on the Special and Normal School Teachers' Awareness, Attitude and Existing Competencies

One of the major objectives of the study was to find out the significant differences in the awareness, attitude and the existing competencies of special and normal school teachers in dealing children with disabilities due to variations in their independent variables. To know the significant differences, if any, in the awareness of special school teachers' and normal school teachers due to variation in their gender, age, educational qualification, training in special education, years of experience, location of school, nature of school, and type of school they are working, mean and SD were calculated for each group in a variable. Based on these means and SD, t-value/F-value was worked out to know the significant differences in the awareness, of special school teachers and normal school teachers. The same procedure was adopted for attitude and existing competencies of special school teachers and normal school teachers to know the significant differences due to variations in their independent variables under study. The obtained results are presented in Tables 4.9 to 4.11 and discussed.

The mean and SD and calculated t-values of special and normal school teachers awareness due to variations in their independent variables are presented in Table 4.9.

Table 4.9: Mean and SD of the awareness scores of special and normal school teachers towards children with disabilities and the calculated t/F-values

Independent Variable	N	*Special Schools*		*Calculated t/F-values*	N	*Normal Schools*		*Calculated t/F-values*
		Mean	*SD*			*Mean*	*SD*	
(1)	(2)	(3)	(4)	(5)	(6)	(7)	(8)	(9)
Gender								
Men	206	106.54	7.58		265	94.18	6.86	
				3.38**				4.01**
Women	454	109.06	9.44		262	97.19	10.09	
Age								
20-30 years	241	107.51	8.41		221	97.29	9.04	
31-40 years	306	108.07	8.51		219	94.89	8.62	
41-50 years	80	109.70	10.60	3.57*	68	92.28	5.67	7.35**
51 years & above	33	112.30	1.52		19	98.32	11.26	
Educational Qualification								
Teacher Training	217	107.43	8.37		255	94.50	8.61	
Graduate with B.Ed.	325	107.90	9.03		168	97.91	8.41	

(Contd...)

(1)	(2)	(3)	(4)	(5)	(6)	(7)	(8)	(9)
Graduate with B.Ed. & M.Ed.	66	110.33	8.13		66	94.36	8.13	
				3.30*				4.66**
Postgraduate with B.Ed.	35	111.77	1153		22	94.77	9:34	
Postgraduate with B.Ed. & M.Ed.	17	111.12	10.02		16	97.69	11.68	
Training in Special Education								
One month training by RCI	109	107.91	6.16		95	96.71	7.49	
Diploma in Special Education	441	108.97	9.28		45	101.49	8.34	
				5.78**				6.98**
B.Ed. in Special Education	49	108.27	8.76		33	93.64	5.76	
M.Ed. in Special Education	6	112.00	14.07		76	95.54	7.24	
Others Specify	55	103.05	9.14		278	94.67	9.47	
Years of Experience								
1-5 years	291	108.43	8.48		187	98.71	9.71	
6-10 years	222	107.65	8.25		166	94.46	8.36	

(Contd...)

(1)	(2)	(3)	(4)	(5)	(6)	(7)	(8)	(9)
11-15 years	78	109.22	10.21	0.52@	49	92.86	6.02	9.65**
15-20 years	36	108.69	10.93		58	93.98	5.62	
21 years and above	33	108.42	12.17		67	93.76	8.59	
Location of School								
Rural	44	107.59	8.28		11	99.00	10.35	
				0.52@				1.27@
Urban	616	108.32	9.02		516	95.61	8.70	
Nature of School								
Government School	39	106.15	7.65		438	93.16	6.21	
				1.52@				19.14**
Private/Voluntary Organisation School	621	108.41	9.03		89	108.10	8.82	
Type of School								
VI	95	107.49	6.55					
HI	213	109.56	8.76					
				2.76*				
MR	293	107.98	10.01					
OH	59	106.32	6.93					

Note: @ Not Significant at 0.05 level
* Significant at 0.05 level
** Significant at 0.01 level

In Table 4.9, the t-values obtained with respect to gender for special schools (3.38) and normal schools (4.01) were significant at 0.01 level, indicating variations in the awareness of men and women teachers. Further, the mean values indicate that women teachers were having better awareness than their counterparts in special as well as normal schools. The mean awareness scores of teachers working in rural and urban schools did not significantly differ both in special and normal schools. The t-values obtained for special schools (0.52) and normal schools (1.27) were not significant at 0.05 level. Similarly, the awareness of teachers working in government and voluntary organizations with reference to special schools, was not significant (1.52) at 0.05 level. In case of normal schools, there was a wide gap in the awareness of teacher's working in government schools (93.16) and teachers working in voluntary organisation or private schools (108.10). Consequently, the t-value (19.14) was significant at 0.01 level. The teachers working in voluntary sector possessed better awareness (108.10) than the teachers working in government schools (93.16). Hence, the formulated hypothesis, 'there exists significant difference in the special school teachers' awareness on different dimensions of children with disabilities due to variation in their gender, age, educational qualification, training in special education, years of experience, locations of school, nature of school, category of school and type of school they are working' is accepted with respect to the variable gender in both the schools and the variable nature of school in case of normal school teachers only. The stated hypothesis is rejected with respect to the variable 'location of the special and normal schools' and 'the nature of special school' the teachers working.

The Table 4.9 also reveals that the F-values obtained with respect to age and educational qualifications are significant at 0.01 level in case of age (7.35) and educational qualification (4.66) for normal school are significant at 0.01 level and in case of special schools (3.57 and 3.30) are significant at 0.05 level. It means, variations in age of the teachers were bringing significant difference in their awareness. The trend of the mean values also revealed that more the qualifications higher will be the awareness, higher the age the more will be the awareness in special school teachers.

In normal schools the trend was mixed in nature. The teachers with 51 years and above age group possessed higher awareness (98.32) followed by 21 years to 30 years (97.29), 31 years to 40 years (94.89) and 41 years to 50 years (92.28) age group. Similarly, teachers having graduation with B.Ed. demonstrated higher awareness (97.91) followed by teachers with P.G., B.Ed. and M.Ed. (97.69), P.G. with B.Ed. (94.77), teacher training (94.50) and graduation with B.Ed. and M.Ed. (94.36). With respect to the variable 'training in special education', the obtained F-value (6.98) was significant at 0.01 level indicating the variation in the awareness of special school teachers on various aspects of disabilities in children, due to the different types of training they received in special education. The mean values also reveal that the teachers with diploma in special education (101.49) were higher in their awareness followed by the teachers with one month training (96.71), teachers with M.Ed. in special education (95.54), teachers with other training (94.67) and teachers with B.Ed. in special education (93.64). The F-values obtained in case of special school with reference to years of experience was not significant at 0.05 level (0.52), indicating that the years of experience of the teacher was not having any bearing on their awareness. Whereas, the F-value was significant (9.65) with respect to the same variables in case of normal schools. It shows that the awareness of teachers differed based on their years of experience in normal schools. It shows that the awareness of teachers differed based on their years of experience in normal schools. Teachers with 1-5 years of experience possessed higher awareness (98.71) followed by 6 to 10 years (94.46), 16 to 20 years (93.98), 21 years and above (93.76) and 11 to 15 years (92.86) of experience.

The obtained F-value 2.76 with respect to the variable 'type of schools is significant at 0.05 level. It means, the awareness of teachers working in different special schools varried. The teachers working in the schools for hearing impaired were better informed about the different aspects of disabilities in children (109.56) followed by the teachers working in MR schools (107.98), schools for VI (107.49) and schools for OH (106.32). Hence the formulated hypothesis, there exists significant difference in the special teachers' awareness on different dimensions of children with disabilities due to variation in their gender, age, educational qualification, training in special education, years of experience, location of school, nature of school, category of school and type of school they are working' is accepted with respect to age, educational qualification, training in special education and the type of special school the teacher working only. The stated hypothesis is also accepted with respect to 'years of experience of teachers working in normal schools, but rejected in case of special schools.

From the above, it can be concluded that the variables gender, age, educational qualification, training in special education, type of school the teachers working had significantly influenced the special and normal school teachers' awareness on different aspects of disabilities in children. The variables 'years of experience' and 'nature of school' the teachers working had not significantly influenced the special school teachers awareness on different dimensions of disabilities in children.

Table 4.10 presents mean, SD and calculated t-values of special and normal schools teachers' attitude due to variation in their independent variables.

The stated hypothesis Table 4.10, 'there exist significant differences in the special school teachers' attitude towards different dimensions of children with disabilities due to variation in their gender, age, educational qualification, training in special education, years of experience, location of school, nature of school, category of school and type of school' is accepted with respect to gender, training in special education and type of special schools the teachers working, only. In Table 4.10, the respective t-value 2.44 with reference to gender and, F-values with respect to training in special education and type of special school the teachers working (11.69 and 7.75) are significant at 0.05 and 0.01 level. It means, variations in gender, training in special education and type of special school the teachers working were significantly influencing the special school teachers' attitude on different aspects of disabilities in children. The mean values indicate that women teachers possessed more favourable attitude (117.38) than men teachers (172.97). The teachers who received one month training by RCI demonstrated more favourable attitude (183.87) followed by the teachers with M.Ed. in special education (181.00), B.Ed. in special education (176.29), diploma in special education (175.92)

Table 4.10: Mean and SD of the attitude scores of special and normal school teachers towards children with disabilities and the calculated t/F-values based on the variation in independent variables

Independent Variable	*N*	*Special Schools*		*Cal. t/F-values*	*N*	*Normal Schools*		*Cal. t/F-values*
		Mean	*SD*			*Mean*	*SD*	
(1)	*(2)*	*(3)*	*(4)*	*(5)*	*(6)*	*(7)*	*(8)*	*(9)*
Gender								
Men	206	172.97	20.61		265	150.65	14.17	
				2.44*				2.87**
Women	454	177.38	21.94		262	154.97	19.97	
Age								
20-30 years	241	175.31	20.27		221	154.49	16.98	
31-40 years	306	177.22	21.56		219	151.75	17.98	
				0.78@				3.92**
41-50 years	80	173.46	26.01		68	148.38	13.10	
51 years and above	33	175.94	20.04		19	161.11	24.28	
Educational Qualification								
Teacher Training	217	174.01	23.52		255	152.64	17.93	
Graduate with B.Ed.	325	176.19	19.99		168	154.72	15.66	
Graduate with B.Ed. & M.Ed.	66	180.20	22.80		66	148.68	16.61	
				1.21@				3.67**

(Contd...)

(1)	(2)	(3)	(4)	(5)	(6)	(7)	(8)	(9)
Postgraduate with B.Ed.	35	177.20	23.31		22	145.45	19.74	
Postgraduate with B.Ed. & M.Ed.	17	179.18	16.46		16	162.25	20.67	
Training in Special Education								
One month training by RCI	109	183.87	16.18		95	154.61	13.51	
Diploma in Special Education	441	175.92	20.52		45	158.84	18.16	
				11.69**				9.30**
B.Ed. in Special Education	49	176.29	21.91		33	146.52	11.69	
M.Ed. in Special Education	6	181.00	21.48		76	143.51	19.61	
Others Specify	55	160.27	29.93		278	154.49	17.42	
Years of Experience								
1-5 years	291	176.38	18.67		187	158.14	19.31	
6-10 years	222	177.68	21.69		166	150.52	16.63	
11-15 years	78	174.78	25.35		49	148.22	14.23	
				1.57@				8.61**
15-20 years	36	170.81	29.25		58	146.03	13.40	
21 years & above	33	170.03	25.20		67	152.75	14.94	
Location of School								
Rural	44	178.09	20.15		11	163.73	21.19	
				0.66@				2.11*
Urban	616	175.86	21.72		516	152.57	17.28	

(Contd...)

(1)	(2)	(3)	(4)	(5)	(6)	(7)	(8)	(9)
Nature of School								
Government School	39	178.54	20.71		438	148.38	12.51	
				0.76@				15.63**
Private/Voluntary Organisation School	621	175.85	21.67		89	174.55	21.45	
Type of School								
VI	95	173.87	17.34					
HI	213	181.73	17.76					
				7.75*				
MR	293	173.43	23.81					
OH	59	171.56	25.10					

Note: @ Not Significant at 0.05 level.
* Significant at 0.05 level.
** Significant at 0.01 level.

and teachers with other training (160.27). Likewise, the teachers working in schools for the hearing impaired showed more favourable attitude (181.73) followed by the teachers working in schools for VI (173.87), MR (173.43) and OH (171.56).

On the other hand, the variables age (0.78), educational qualification (1.21), years of experience (1.57), location of school (0.66) and nature of school (0.76) the teachers working had not significantly influenced the special school teachers attitude towards children with disabilities, as the obtained F-values are not significant at 0.05 level. Hence the stated hypotheses, 'there exists significant difference in the special school teachers' attitude towards different dimensions of children with disabilities' due to variations in gender, age, educational qualification, training in special education, years of experience, location of school, nature of school, category of school and type of school' is rejected with reference to age, educational qualification, years of experience, location of school and nature of school.

The Table 4.10 also reveals that the t-values obtained with respect to gender (2.87), location of the school (2.11), nature of school (15.63) and F-value with respect to age (3.92), educational qualification (3.67), training in special education (9.30) and years of experience (8.61) are significant at 0.01 level. It means, the attitude of normal school teachers differed due to variations in these variables. Hence the formulated hypothesis there exists significant difference in the normal school teachers 'attitude towards different dimensions of children with disabilities due to variation gender, age, educational qualification, training in special education, years of experience, location of school, nature of school, category of school and type of school' is accepted with reference to gender, age, educational qualification, training in special education, years of experience, location of school and nature of school.

Further women teachers possessed better attitude (154.97) than men teachers (150.65). Teachers with 51 years and above age group exhibited more favourable attitude (161.11) followed by teachers in the age group of 21 to 30 years (154.49), 31 to 40 years (151.75) and 41 to 50 years (148.38). Teachers with P.G., B.Ed. & M.Ed. qualification demonstrated better attitude (162.25) followed by the teachers having graduate with B.Ed. (154.72), teacher training (152.64), graduate with B.Ed. (154.72), teacher training (152.64), graduate with B.Ed. & M.Ed. (148.68) and postgraduate with B.Ed. (145.45). Further, the teachers with diploma in special education demonstrated better attitude (158.84) followed by the teachers with one month training in special education (154.61), teachers with other training (154.49), teachers with B.Ed. in special education (146.52) and teachers with M.Ed. in special education (143.51). The normal school teachers with 1-5 years of experience showed more favourable attitude (158.14) followed by 21 years and above (152.75), 6-10 years (150.52), 16 to 20 years (148.22) and 11-15 years (146.03) experienced teachers. Teachers working in rural schools possessed more favourable attitude than their counterparts. Similarly, teachers working in voluntary or private sector demonstrated more favourable attitude (174.55) than teachers working in government schools (148.38).

From the above, it can be concluded that the variables gender, training in special education, type of special school the teachers working are significantly influenced their attitude towards children with disabilities. On the other hand, the variables age, educational qualification, years of experience, location of school and nature of school had not significantly influenced the special school teachers' attitude towards children with disabilities.

In normal schools, variations in teachers' gender, age, educational qualification, training in special education, years of experience, location of school and nature of school had brought significant differences in their attitude towards children with disabilities.

Mean, SD and the obtained t-values of special and normal school teachers' existing competencies due to variation in their independent variables are presented in Table 4.11.

In Table 4.11, the F-values obtained with respect to age (5.00) and training in special education (5.17) are significant at 0.01 level; educational qualification (2.60), years of experience (2.86) and type of school (2.85) are significant at 0.05 level indicating the differences in the existing competencies of special school teachers. Further, an analysis of mean values reveals that when the age increases the competency level of the teachers also increase. The teachers having graduation with B.Ed. and M.Ed. demonstrated better

Table 4.11: Mean and SD of the existing competency scores of special and normal school teachers towards children with disabilities and the calculated t/F-values based on the variation in independent variables

Independent Variables	N	*Special Schools*		*Cal. t/F-values*	N	*Normal Schools*		*Cal. t/F-values*
		Mean	*SD*			*Mean*	*SD*	
(1)	(2)	(3)	(4)	(5)	(6)	(7)	(8)	(9)
Gender								
Men	206	114.73	11.75		265	87.90	11.25	
				0.064@				3.54**
Women	454	114.66	15.32		262	92.41	17.37	
Age								
20-30 years	241	115.08	13.22		221	91.85	14.96	
31-40 years	306	115.30	13.56		219	89.95	15.73	
				5.00**				4.78**
41-50 years	80	109.36	17.06		68	84.40	16.65	
51 years and above	33	118.91	18.15		19	93.11	17.58	
Educational Qualification								
Teacher Training	217	114.64	14.91		255	85.56	14.93	
Graduate with B.Ed.	325	115.01	12.86		168	94.10	15.14	
Graduate with B.Ed. & M.Ed.	66	116.65	16.08		66	87.82	11.88	
				2.60*				4.64**

(Contd...)

(1)	(2)	(3)	(4)	(5)	(6)	(7)	(8)	(9)
Postgraduate with B.Ed.	35	107.54	16.96		22	86.95	10.46	
Postgraduate with B.Ed. and M.Ed.	17	116.06	16.41		16	87.75	17.25	
Training in Special Education								
One month training by RCI	109	116.56	12.70		95	91.84	13.69	
Diploma in Special Education	441	115.91	13.06		45	98.11	13.33	
				8.29**				4.99**
B.Ed. in Special Education	49	109.20	15.88		33	87.33	9.35	
M.Ed. in Special Education	6	101.67	22.07		76	90.75	10.30	
Others Specify	55	107.36	19.77		278	88.44	16.39	
Years of Experience								
1-5 years	291	115.65	11.54		187	96.34	17.77	
6-10 years	222	115.12	15.21		166	87.45	87.45	
11-15 years	78	113.38	16.09	2.86*	49	85.27	85.27	14.36**
15-20 years	36	107.50	16.30		58	86.88	86.88	
21 years and above	33	114.12	20.40		67	85.91	85.91	
Location of School								
Rural	44	113.50	13.79		11	98.00	18.56	
				0.57@				1.79@
Urban	616	114.76	14.33		516	89.97	14.66	

(Contd...)

(1)	(2)	(3)	(4)	(5)	(6)	(7)	(8)	(9)
Nature of School								
Government School	39	116.23	11.42		438	85.48	9.73	
				0.70@				22.47**
Private/Voluntary Organisation School	621	114.58	14.45		89	113.07	13.97	
Type of School								
VI	95	116.22	10.58					
HI	213	116.13	14.86					
				2.85*				
MR	293	112.87	14.39					
OH	59	115.95	16.12					

Note: @ Not Significant at 0.05 level.

* Significant at 0.05 level.

** Significant at 0.01 level.

competencies (116.65) followed by postgraduate with B.Ed. and M.Ed. (116.06), graduation with B.Ed. (115.01), teacher training (114.64) and post graduate with B.Ed. (107.54). Teachers with one month training received from RCI exhibited better competencies (116.56) followed by the teachers with diploma in special education (115.91), B.Ed. in special education (109.20), other specify (107.36) and M.Ed. in Special Education (101.67). Teachers with less years of experience possessed better competencies (115.65) followed by 6-10 years (115.12), 21 years and above (114.12), 11-15 years (113.38) and 16-20 years (107.50). Likewise, the teachers working in the schools for visually impaired showed better competencies (116.22) followed by the teachers working in schools for HI (116.13), OH (115.95) and MR (112.87).

On the otherhand, the t-values obtained were not significant with reference to gender (0.064), location of school (0.57) and nature of school (0.70). It means, the variations in these variables had not brought any significant differences in the teacher competencies to deal children with disabilities. Hence the stated hypothesis, 'there exists significant difference in the existing competencies of special school teachers' on different dimensions to deal children with disabilities due to variations in their gender, age, educational qualification, training in special education, years of experience, location of school, nature of school and type of school' is rejected in case of gender, location and nature of school.

Table 4.11 also indicates that the t-values of gender (3.54) and nature of school (1.79), F-values of age (4.78), educational qualification (4.64), training in special education (4.99) and years of experience (14.36) are significant at 0.01 level and the t-value for the variable 'location of school' (1.79) is not significant at 0.05 level. It implies that, normal school teachers differed in their existing competencies due to variations in their gender, nature of school working, age, educational qualification, training in special education and years of experience. Hence, the formulated hypothesis 'there exists significant difference in the existing competencies of normal schools teachers on different dimensions to deal children with disabilities due to variation in their 'location of school' is rejected whereas it is accepted for the other variables.

Further, mean values show that women teachers possessed better competencies (92.41) than men teachers (87.90). The teachers working in voluntary or private organisations demonstrated better competencies (113.07) than the teachers working in government schools (85.48). The teachers with 51 years and above age exhibited better competencies (93.11) followed by 21-30 years (19.85), 31-40 years (89.95) and 41-50 years (84.40) of experience.

Graduate teachers with B.Ed. demonstrated better competencies (94.10) followed by graduation with B.Ed. and M.Ed. (87.82), postgraduate with B.Ed. and M.Ed. (87.75), postgraduate with B.Ed. (86.95) and teacher training (88.56). Similarly, teachers with diploma in special education had better competencies (98.11), followed by the teachers who received one month training from RCI (91.84), M.Ed. in special education (90.75), other training (88.44) and B.Ed. in special education (87.33). Likewise, less experienced teachers demonstrated better competencies (96.34) followed by the teachers with 6-10 years (87.45), 16-20 years (86.88), 21 years and above (85.91) and 11-15 years (85.27) of experience.

From the above, it can be concluded that the variables age, educational qualification, training in special education, years of experience and type of school the teachers working had significantly influenced the special school teachers existing competencies. Contrary to this, the variables gender, location of school and nature of the school the teachers working had not significantly influenced their existing competencies in dealing children with disabilities. In normal schools, except the variable 'locations of the school', all the other variables had significantly influenced the competencies of teachers.

Correlational Studies

One of the objectives of the study was to find out the relationship between awareness and attitude, awareness and extent of competencies possessed and attitude and extent of competencies possessed by the special school teachers and normal school teachers in dealing children with disabilities. To realise this objective, r-values were calculated and presented in Tables 4.12 and 4.13.

Table 4.12: Relationship between awareness and attitude, awareness and existing competencies and attitude and existing competencies of special school teachers on each dimension of children with disabilities

Variables	*Concept of Disabilities*	*Causes and Characteristics*	*Identification and Assessment*	*Teaching and Training*	*Guidance and Counselling*	*Dimensions as a Whole*
Awareness and Attitude	0.164**	0.312**	0.151**	0.351**	0.407**	0.457**
Awareness and Existing Competencies	0.052@	0.140**	0.145**	0.132**	0.253**	0.221**
Attitude and Existing Competencies	0.069@	0.211**	0.325**	0.184**	0.308**	0.298**

Note: @ Not Significant at 0.05 level

** Significant at 0.01 level

Correlations were computed based on special school teachers' awareness and attitude, awareness and existing competencies and attitude and existing competencies of special school teachers on each dimension of children with disabilities.

From Table 4.12, it is evident that r-values of awareness and attitude of special school teachers with regard to the concept of disabilities (0.164), causes and characteristics (0.312), identification and assessment (0.151), teaching and training methods (0.351), guidance and counselling (0.407) and dimensions as a whole (0.457) are significant at 0.01 level. It indicates that there is a significant positive relationship between the special school teachers' awareness and attitude towards children with disabilities. It means, higher the awareness, higher the attitude of special school teachers. Hence, the stated hypotheses, 'there exists significant relationship between awareness and attitude of special school teachers towards children with disabilities' is accepted.

The Table 4.12 also reveals the significant relationship between awareness and existing competencies of special school teachers in the area 'causes and characteristics of children with disabilities (0.140), identification and assessment (0.145), teaching and training methods (0.132), guidance and counselling (0.253), dimensions as a whole (0.221) at 0.01 level. Here too, the trend is higher the awareness higher the existing competencies in special school teachers. Contrary to this, there was no significant relationship between awareness and existing competencies of special school teachers on the dimension, 'concept of disabilities in children' (0.052). Hence the stated hypothesis 'there exists significant relationship between awareness and extent of competencies possessed by the special school teachers in dealing children with disabilities' is accepted in case of causes and characteristics, identification and assessment, teaching and training methods and guidance and counselling but it is rejected with regard to the concept of disabilities in children.

Similarly, the r-values show the existence of positive relationship between attitude and existing competencies of special school teachers (causes and characteristics of children with disabilities (0.211), identification and assessment (0.325), teaching and training methods (0.184), guidance and counselling (0.308) and dimensions as a whole (0.298). Here too, no significant relationship was observed between attitude and existing competencies of special school teachers towards children with disabilities with regard to the dimension-concept of disabilities in children. Hence, the formulated hypothesis 'there exists significant positive relationship between attitude and extent of competencies possessed by special school teachers in dealing children with disabilities' is rejected only in case of concept of disabilities in children.

To conclude, there is a significant positive relationship between the awareness and attitude; awareness and extent of competencies possessed, and attitude and extent of competencies possessed by the special school teachers on each dimension of disabilities in children except for the concept of disabilities in children with reference to awareness and extent of competencies possessed and attitude and extent of competencies possessed. Further, higher the awareness, attitude and extent of competencies possessed, then higher the attitude, higher the extent of competencies possessed.

In Table 4.13, the r-values on each dimension of children with disabilities based on normal school teachers' awareness and attitude, awareness and extent of competencies possessed and attitude and extent of competencies possessed are presented.

The obtained r-values for normal school teachers' awareness and attitude on concept of disabilities in children (0.043) is not significant at 0.05 level. Contrary to this, there existed significant relationship between normal school teachers awareness and attitude on causes and characteristics (0.237), identification and assessment (0.124), teaching and training methods (0.421), guidance and counselling (0.412), dimensions as a whole (0.522). It means, awareness of normal school teachers towards children with disabilities had significant bearing on their attitude. Hence, the stated hypothesis, 'there exists significant relationship between awareness and attitude of normal school teachers towards children with disabilities' is accepted, except the dimension 'concept of disabilities' in children.

Table 4.13: Relationship between awareness and attitude, awareness and existing competencies and attitude and existing competencies of normal school teachers on each dimensions of children with disabilities

Variables	*Concept of Disabilities*	*Causes and Characteristics*	*Identification and Assessment*	*Teaching and Training*	*Guidance and Counselling*	*Dimensions as a Whole*
Awareness and Attitude	0.043@	0.237**	0.124**	0.421**	0.412**	0.522**
Awareness and Existing Competencies	0.215**	0.482**	0.182**	0.640**	0.595**	0.754**
Attitude and Existing Competencies	0.036@	0.238**	0.306**	0.394**	0.416**	0.492**

Note: @ Not Significant at 0.05 level

** Significant at 0.01 level

The stated hypothesis 'there exists relationship between awareness and extent of competencies possessed by the normal school teachers in dealing children with disabilities' is accepted with respect to all dimensions. It means, the r-values on the concept of disabilities (0.215), causes and characteristics (0.482), identification and assessment (0.182), teaching and training methods (0.640), guidance & counselling (0.595), and dimensions as a whole (0.754) are significant at 0.01 level indicating the positive relationship between awareness and extent of competencies possessed by the normal school teachers.

The obtained r-value is not significant at 0.05 level for attitude and extent of competencies possessed by the normal school teachers only on the dimension 'concept of disabilities in children' (0.036). On the other hand, the r-values are significant at 0.01 level on causes and characteristics (0.238), identification and assessment (0.306), teaching and training methods (0.394), guidance and counselling (0.416), and dimensions as a whole (0.492). It indicates the positive relationship between the attitude and extent of competencies possessed by the normal school teachers in dealing children with disabilities. Hence, the formulated hypothesis 'there exist significant relationship between the attitude and extent of competencies possessed by normal school teachers' in dealing children with disabilities is rejected with respect to concept of disabilities in children only.

To sum up, the correlation studies reveal the significant positive relationship between awareness and attitude; awareness and extent of competencies possessed and; attitude and extent of competencies possessed by the normal school teachers in dealing children with disabilities on the dimensions causes and characteristics, identification and assessment, teaching and training methods, guidance and counselling and dimensions as a whole. But, on the concept of disabilities in children, there existed significant relationship between awareness and extent of competencies possessed by the normal school teachers, but not between awareness and attitude and, attitude and extent of competencies possessed.

Stepwise Multiple Regression

Stepwise multiple regression is used to identify how far and to what extent the independent variables are contributing to the dependent variables.

In this part of analysis, stepwise multiple regression analysis was applied to know how far and to what extent the independent variables contribute to the dependent variables. The independent variables such as gender, age, educational qualifications, training in special education, years of experience, location of school, nature of school, type of school and category of school the teachers working were included in the study. Awareness, attitude and existing competencies of special and normal school teachers were the dependent variables.

Influence of Independent Variables on the Dependent Variables

To know how far and to what extent the independent variables were contributing to each dependent variable, stepwise multiple regression was applied. The following multiple regression equation was used to explain the contribution of independent variables to the unit increase in the dependent variable.

$$R_1 = a + B_1 X_1 + B_2 X_2 + \ldots\ldots + B_z X_z$$

With the use of the above equation for stepwise multiple regression, β co-efficient, the individual contribution of the variable and the percentagewise individual contribution to the dependent variables are presented in Table 4.14.

Table 4.14 reveals that the contribution of independent variable 'category of school' accounted to 9 per cent followed by years of experience—8 per cent, age—7 per cent, gender—6 per cent, educational qualification—4 per cent, and training in special education—1 per cent to the awareness of special school teachers on various aspects of children with disabilities. In other words, the independent variables—category of school, years of experience, age, gender, and educational qualification are the major predictors to the awareness of special education teachers. The variable 'training in special education' is the least predictor.

Table 4.14: Summary of stepwise multiple regression analysis

Dependent variable: Awareness, Attitude and Existing Competencies of Special and Normal School Teachers.

Independent variables: Gender, Age, Educational Qualification, Training in Special Education, Years of Experience, Location of School, Nature of School, Category of School and Type of School.

Dependent Variable	*Independent Variable*	*β Coefficient*	*Individual contribution of the Variable (R^2)*	*Percentagewise Individual contribution of the Variable*
1	2	3	4	5
Special Schools				
Awareness	Training in Special Education	-0.168	0.017	1%
	Educational Qualification	0.176	0.041	4%
	Gender	0.142	0.064	6%
	Age	0.228	0.075	7 %
	Years of Experience	-0.161	0.087	8%
	Category of School	0.082	0.094	9%
Attitude	Training in Special Education	-0.262	0.056	5%
	Educational Qualification	0.135	0.070	7%
	Gender	0.110	0.082	8%
Existing Competencies	Training in Special Education	-0.178	0.036	3%
	Category of School	0.106	0.047	4%

(Contd...)

1	2	3	4	5
Normal Schools				
Awareness	Nature of School	0.566	0.411	41%
	Training in Special Education	-0.185	0.439	43%
	Gender	0.085	0.446	44%
Attitude	Nature of School	0.564	0.318	31%
Existing Competencies	Nature of School	0.640	0.490	49%
	Training in Special Education	-0.190	0.523	52%

The variable gender contributed 8 per cent, educational qualification-7 per cent and training in special education 5 per cent to the attitude of special school teachers towards children with disabilities. It reveals that, gender is the foremost predictor followed by training in special education and educational qualification to the attitude of special school teachers towards children with disabilities.

Similarly, the variables—category of school and training in special education accounted to 4 per cent and 3 per cent respectively to the existing competencies of special school teachers. It indicates that, category of school is the significant predictor followed by training in special education to the existing competencies of special school teachers to deal children with disabilities.

In normal schools, the contribution of independent variable 'gender' was 44 per cent training in special education accounted 43 per cent and the nature of school 41 per cent to the awareness of normal school teachers. It means, gender, training in special education and nature of school the teachers working are the major predictors of awareness of normal school teachers on the different dimensions of disabilities in children.

Similarly, nature of school had contributed 31 per cent and 49 per cent to the dependent variables attitude and existing competencies of normal school teachers respectively. The variable 'training in special education' accounted for 52 per cent of variance to the existing competencies of normal school teachers. In other words, nature of school is the significant predictor to the attitude of normal school teachers only. The variable 'training in special education' (52%) is the foremost predictor followed by nature of school to the existing competencies of normal school teachers.

To sum up, the variable 'category of school' is the major predicator followed by years of experience, age, gender educational qualification and training in special education to the awareness of special school teachers towards children with disabilities. Gender followed by educational qualification and training in special education are the predictors of special school teachers attitude towards children with disabilities. Likewise, category of school and training in special education are the major predictor to the existing competencies of the special school teachers in dealing children with disabilities. In normal schools, teachers gender, training in special education and nature of school are the foremost predictors to the awareness; nature of school as a major predictor for attitude and; training in special education and nature of school are the predictors for the existing competencies in dealing children with disabilities. While organizing the need based teacher training programmers the above significant and foremost predicting variables that are contributing to the awareness, attitude and existing competencies of special and normal school teachers in dealing children with disabilities are to be considered and given due importance.

Infrastructure Facilities Available in Special and Normal Schools for Education of Children with Disabilities

One of the major objectives of the study was to identify the infrastructure facilities available in special schools and normal schools and to find out the dropout rate in those schools, keeping in mind the infrastructure facilities available. For this at the first stage, the number and percentage of special and normal schools having each infrastructure facility were worked out and presented in Table 4.15 and discussed.

In the second stage, mean and SD had been calculated for infrastructure facilities in each school. Based on mean ±1 SD, the number of good infrastructure facility schools, moderate infrastructure facility schools and poor infrastructure facility schools were identified with reference to special schools and normal schools. The corresponding dropout rate in percentage had been worked out. The obtained results are presented in Table 4.16.

Slate and stylus help the totally blind children to write Braille letter effectively. This facility was available in 67 per cent of special schools for VI followed by 20 per cent of special schools for OH, 13 per cent of special schools for MR, 8 per cent of special schools for HI. Overall, only 18 per cent of special schools together were with slate and stylus. On the other hand, only 3 per cent of normal schools were having this facility. As these were useful to the totally blind, it should be available in special schools for VI. But these

Table 4.15: Number and percentage of special and normal schools with and without infrastructure facilities

Nature of Infrastructure Facilities	Number and Percentage of Schools with and without Infrastructure Facilities (ISF)											
	Schools for VI (N = 9)		Schools for HI (N = 26)		Schools for MR (N = 40)		Schools for OH (N =10)		Special School together (N = 84)		Normal Schools (N = 76)	
	With ISF	Without ISF	With ISF	Without ISF	With ISF	Without ISF	With ISF	Without ISF	With ISF	Without ISF	With ISF	Without ISF
(1)	(2)	(3)	(4)	(5)	(6)	(7)	(8)	(9)	(10)	(11)	(12)	(13)
1. Slate and stylus to the totally blind children	6 (67)	3 (33)	2 (8)	24 (92)	5 (13)	35 (87)	2 (20)	8 (80)	15 (18)	69 (82)	2 (3)	74 (97)
2. Magnifying devices, lenses and large print and coloured materials for low vision children	6 (67)	3 (33)	4 (15)	22 (85)	5 (13)	35 (87)	2 (20)	8 (80)	17 (20)	67 (80)	1 (1)	75 (99)
3. Mathematical aids like abacus, Taylor frame etc.	8 (89)	1 (11)	13 (50)	13 (50)	7 (18)	33 (82)	4 (40)	6 (60)	32 (38)	52 (62)	22 (29)	54 (71)
4. Embossed teaching learning materials	8 (89)	1 (11)	14 (54)	12 (46)	20 (50)	20 (50)	7 (70)	3 (30)	49 (58)	35 (42)	8 (11)	68 (89)
5. Audiotapes/talking books	7 (78)	2 (22)	18 (69)	8 (31)	23 (58)	17 (42)	8 (80)	2 (20)	56 (67)	28 (33)	8 (11)	68 (89)
6. Orientation and mobility materials for blind children	7 (78)	2 (22)	20 (77)	6 (23)	22 (55)	18 (45)	6 (60)	4 (40)	55 (65)	29 (35)	7 (9)	69 (91)
7. Hearing aids for hearing-impaired children	3 (33)	6 (67)	23 (88)	3 (12)	22 (55)	18 (45)	1 (10)	9 (90)	48 (57)	36 (43)	7 (9)	69 (91)

(Contd...)

(1)	(2)	(3)	(4)	(5)	(6)	(7)	(8)	(9)	(10)	(11)	(12)	(13)
8. Facilities to use group hearing aids in the classroom	4 (44)	5 (56)	22 (85)	4 (15)	24 (60)	16 (40)	1 (10)	9 (90)	50 (60)	34 (40)	3 (4)	73 (96)
9. Facilities to curtail extra noises thereby facilitating the hearing of children with moderate hearing loss	3 (33)	6 (67)	23 (88)	3 (12)	26 (65)	14 (35)	3 (30)	7 (70)	54 (64)	30 (36)	23 (30)	53 (70)
10. Overhead projector	3 (33)	6 (67)	22 (85)	4 (15)	30 (75)	10 (25)	4 (40)	6 (60)	58 (69)	26 (31)	25 (33)	1 (67)
11. Audiovideo instructional materials for slow learners and children with learning difficulties	4 (44)	5 (56)	16 (62)	10 (38)	29 (73)	11 (27)	4 (40)	6 (60)	52 (62)	32 (38)	31 (41)	45 (59)
12. Computer assisted instruction	4 (44)	5 (56)	18 (69)	8 (31)	29 (73)	11 (27)	7 (70)	3 (30)	58 (69)	26 (31)	38 (50)	38 (50)
13. Orthotic and prosthetic devices for orthopaedically handicapped children	5 (56)	4 (44)	20 (77)	6 (23)	31 (78)	9 (22)	7 (70)	3 (30)	63 (75)	21 (25)	9 (12)	67 (88)
14. Physiotherapy and occupational therapy materials for orthopaedically handicapped and mentally retarded	4 (44)	5 (56)	15 (58)	11 (42)	32 (80)	8 (20)	9 (90)	1 (10)	60 (71)	24 (29)	17 (22)	59 (78)
15. Lighting arrangements in the classroom for low vision children	5 (56)	4 (44)	16 (62)	10 (38)	26 (65)	14 (35)	8 (80)	2 (20)	55 (65)	29 (35)	32 (42)	44 (58)

(Contd...)

(1)	(2)	(3)	(4)	(5)	(6)	(7)	(8)	(9)	(10)	(11)	(12)	(13)
16. Low cost multimedia materials for slow learners	6 (67)	3 (33)	21 (81)	5 (19)	31 (78)	9 (22)	10 (100)	0 (0)	68 (81)	16 (19)	14 (18)	62 (82)
17. School transport facilities for disabled children	9 (100)	0 (0)	19 (73)	7 (27)	32 (80)	8 (20)	8 (80)	2 (20)	68 (81)	16 (19)	6 (8)	70 (92)
18. Adopted play materials for the disabled children	8 (89)	1 (11)	21 (81)	5 (19)	35 (88)	5 (12)	6 (60)	4 (40)	69 (82)	15 (18)	7 (9)	69 (91)
19. Speech therapy and effective use of residual hearing	8 (89)	1 (11)	23 (88)	3 (12)	33 (83)	7 (17)	8 (80)	2 (20)	71 (85)	13 (15)	4 (5)	72 (95)
20. Equipment and materials to identify children with different disabilities	7 (78)	2 (22)	23 (88)	3 (12)	32 (80)	8 (20)	7 (70)	2 (20)	68 (81)	15 (18)	3 (4)	73 (96)
21. Speech synthesizers for children with disabilities	6 (67)	3 (33)	15 (58)	11 (42)	17 (43)	23 (57)	4 (40)	6 (60)	42 (50)	42 (50)	5 (7)	71 (93)
22. Talking calculators and Braille typewriters	7 (78)	2 (22)	6 (23)	20 (77)	11 (28)	29 (72)	2 (20)	8 (80)	26 (31)	58 (69)	38 (50)	38 (50)

Note:

(1) Figures in brackets are in percentage.

(2) The total number of special schools together are 84 only.

(3) One school is working for both HI and MR and hence this school is added to MR totalling 40 schools.

materials were also available in special schools for HI, MR and OH. It means, the children with other disabilities also have visual impairment. This may be the reason that these schools also possess slate and stylus to meet the needs of children multiple with disabilities. Magnifying devices, lenses and large print and coloured materials for low vision children help to read learning materials. This material makes the low vision children to cope up within the regular classroom teaching-learning process. 67 per cent of special schools for VI possess this materials followed by 20 per cent of schools for OH, 15 per cent of schools for HI and 13 per cent of schools for MR. But only 20 per cent of special together possessed this facility. Contrary to this, only one normal school was having magnifying devices, lenses and la.ge print and coloured materials for low vision children.

Abacus and Taylor frame are rendering helping hands for visually impaired to solve mathematical problems. In the study area, nearly 89 per cent of special schools were having abacus and taylor frame for their VI children. On the other hand, to meet the needs of children with additional disabilities, 50 per cent of special schools for HI followed by 40 per cent of schools for OH and 18 per cent of schools for MR and 38 per cent of schools together were with abacus and taylor frame materials etc. Now a days, as the abacus is also used by normal school children, 29 per cent of normal schools were having mathematical aids like abacus and taylor frame. Embossed teaching learning materials make the totally blind to sensitise and understand the concept in right direction. 89 per cent of special schools for VI were having this facility followed by 70 per cent of schools for OH, 54 per cent schools for HI, 50 per cent of schools for MR, and 58 per cent of special schools together.

Audiotapes/talking books are useful for both the children with hearing impairment and visual impairment. Realizing the need for this facility 80 per cent of schools for OH, followed by 78 per cent of schools for VI, 69 per cent of schools for HI and 58 per cent of schools for MR were equipped with audiotapes and talking books. These facilities helped even children with MR and OH to develop their listening capacity and provide sensory training. Overall, 67 per cent of special schools together had audiotapes and talking books. 11 per cent of normal schools were also possessing audiotapes/talking books which help the hard of hearing to use his/her residual hearing and sensory training to VI children.

78 per cent of special schools were with orientation and mobility training materials for blind children. These materials helped the totally blind children to move around within and outside the school with more confidence. These materials were also available in other categories of special schools [HI—77 per cent, OH—60 per cent, MR—55 per cent and special schools together—65 per cent]. Contrary to this, only 9 per cent if normal schools were having orientation and mobility materials for blind children.

Hearing aid is the device used to enhance the residual hearing of hearing impaired children. Realizing the importance in educational activities, 88 per cent of special schools for HI were provided with hearing aids for their hearing impaired children followed by 55 per cent of schools for MR, 33 per cent of schools for VI and 10 per cent of schools for OH. Totally 57 per cent of special schools together were equipped with hearing aids. Only in 9 per cent of normal schools, this facility was available. Provision of group hearing aids in the classroom will enrich teaching-learning process. Apart from special schools for HI, 60 per cent of schools for VI and 10 per cent of special schools for OH possessed these facilities. Therefore, 60 per cent of special schools together were equipped with group hearing aids in the classroom to develop residual hearing. Here too, only 4 per cent of normal schools were provided with group hearing aid.

88 per cent of special schools for HI, 65 per cent of schools for MR, 33 per cent of schools for VI, and 30 per cent of schools for OH had curtailed extra noises to facilitate the moderate hearing-loss children's classroom learning. Overall, there were 64 per cent of special schools which were promoting better learning in children by taking appropriate steps for avoiding extra noises. Likewise, 30 per cent of normal schools had provision to avoid extra noises, which may not disturb both hearing impaired and normal children.

Overhead projector is a technological device which plays a vital role in teaching-learning process. It gives opportunity to the hearing impaired to visualize the letters, words and sentences. Similarly, it also helps the children with other disabilities in other special schools. 85 per cent of schools for HI followed by 75 per cent for MR, 40 per cent for OH and 33% for VI and 69 per cent special schools together had the OHP. As it is also very useful for the normal children, 33 per cent of normal schools possessed overhead projector in their schools.

Audiovideo instructional materials for slow learners and children with learning difficulties are also much useful to the children with visual impairment, hearing impairment and mental retardation. Audio instructional materials help in sensory training for VI and HI. They promote motivation in mentally retarded to learn step by step. 73 per cent of such for MR, followed by 62 per cent for HI, 44 per cent for VI and 40 per cent for OH and 62 per cent special schools together were having audio video instructional materials. As these materials were very useful for slow learners and children with learning difficulties, 41 per cent of normal schools were having this materials, as the bulk of students in any classroom of normal school consist of these students.

Availability of computer assisted instruction was present in 73 per cent of special schools for MR, 70 per cent of schools for OH, 69 per cent of schools for HI, and 44 per cent of schools for VI. Thus, totally 69 per cent of special schools possessed computer assisted instruction. Similarly, 50 per cent of normal schools were also having computer assisted instruction, as per the study.

Orthotic and Prosthetic devices for orthopaedically handicapped children help them to move more easily within and outside the classroom. These devices help them to overcome their physical disabilities. 70 per cent of schools for orthopaedically handicapped were equipped with orthotic and prosthetic devices. At the same, 73 per cent of schools for MR and 77 per cent of schools for HI were having orthotic and prosthetic devices than the schools for OH. Many of the mentally retarded children were having additional physical deformities which warrant orthotic and prosthetic devices. This may be reason for more number of MR and HI schools having this facility. 56 per cent of special schools for VI also had these orthotic and prosthetic devices to serve the visually impaired children with additional deformities. Overall, 75 per cent of special schools were having orthotic and prosthetic devices for OH children. Only 12 per cent of normal schools were having this facility.

Physiotherapy and occupational therapy is a must for orthopaedically handicapped and mentally retarded children. Knowing the importance of these therapies, 80 per cent of special schools for MR and 90 per cent of schools for OH were equipped with the materials required for this. Even in special schools for HI and VI (58% and 44%) these materials were available. Thus 71 per cent of special schools were having this facility but only 22 per cent of normal schools possessed the same.

Proper lighting arrangements in the classroom for low-vision children is required for effective reading and writing. But only 56 per cent of special schools for VI were having proper lighting arrangements. On the other hand, 80 per cent of schools for OH, 65 per cent of schools for MR, and 62 per cent of schools for HI were with the provision of proper lighting arrangements in the classroom. On the Other hand 42 per cent of normal schools at primary level possessed good lighting arrangements in the classrooms. 100 per cent of special schools for OH followed by 81 per cent of schools for HI, 78 per cent of schools for MR and 67 per cent of schools for VI had low cost multimedia materials for slow learners. It involved using of multisensory approach in teaching-learning process. Totally, 81 per cent of special schools together had low cost multimedia materials. On the otherhand, only 82 per cent of normal schoois were in dearth of these materials.

Transport facilities help children with disabilities to come to school without any hurdles. 100 per cent of special schools for VI followed by 80 per cent of schools for MR and OH and 73 per cent of schools for HI have school transport facilities. Over all, 81 per cent of special schools together had transport facilities to the children with disabilities, whereas only 8 per cent of normal schools had provision for school transport facilities.

Adopted play materials help the disabled children learning by doing. These materials are of much use in the education of mentally retarded and visually impaired children. Realising the need the schools for VI and MR in the study area had 89 per cent and 88 per cent of adopted play materials for the disabled children. Likewise, 81 per cent of schools for HI, 60 per cent of schools for OH and 82 per cent special schools together had adopted play materials for the disabled children. Only 9 per cent of normal schools possessed the same. Speech therapy will enhance effective communication for the children with disabilities particularly for MR and OH. 89 per cent and 88 per cent of special school for VI and HI had provision for speech therapy and effective use of residual hearing followed by 83 per cent of special schools for MR and 80 per cent of schools for OH. But only 5 per cent of normal schools had provision of speech therapy.

Equipment and materials for identification of children with disabilities are important facilities that every school should possess. 88 per cent of schools for HI, 80 per cent of schools for MR, 78 per cent of schools for VI, 70 per cent of schools for OH and 81 per cent of special schools together had this basic facility, which helps to identify the degree of disability and provide appropriate placement services. This provision was available in only 4 per cent of normal schools. 67 per cent and 58 per cent of special school for VI and HI were equipped with speed synthesiser. Voice input with speech synthesiser supportive system facilitates the education of children with disabilities. It is evident that it is useful in the education of MR and OH. 43 per cent and 40 per cent of special schools for MR and OH possessed speech synthesiser. Contrary to this, the availability of speech synthesiser was very low in normal schools (7%). The availability of this facilitating was urban primary schools.

Talking calculators and Braille typewriters are useful for visually impaired children. 78 per cent of special schools for VI were having the provision for talking calculators of Braille typewriters. But 28 per cent of special schools for MR, 23 per cent of schools for HI, and 20 per cent of schools for OH and 31 per cent of special schools together had talking calculators and Braille typewriter to meet the needs of children with multiple disabilities. Likewise, 50 per cent of normal schools were also equipped with this facility to serve better to the children with disabilities.

To sum up, out of 22 infrastructure facilities needed for education of children with disabilities, 9 facilities such as slate and stylus, magnifying devices, lenses and large print and coloured materials for low vision children, mathematical aids like abacus, taylor frame etc, embossed teaching learning materials, audiotapes/talking books, orientation and mobility materials, lighting arrangements in the classroom for low vision children, equipment and materials to identify children with different disabilities and talking calculators and Braille typewriters are important in educating visually impaired children. These facilities help the visually impaired children to learn better and cope up with normal children. 56 to 89 per cent of special schools for VI were having the different infrastructure facilities mentioned above. As some of the children studying in some of the special schools were with multiple disabilities, such schools possessed the above said infrastructure facilities, which are needed for children with visual impairment. Here, it is imperative to say that irrespective of the type of school these facilities are essential to all the schools. This is the reason why a common infrastructure checklist is developed for all the schools to identify the infrastructure.

Facilities such as hearing aids for hearing-impaired children, group hearing aids in the classroom, providing conducive environment to the students with moderate hearing loss, with overhead projector, speech therapy equipment and speech synthesisers and materials to identify children with disabilities are very important for meeting the education of hearing impaired children. Special schools for HI possessed 58 to 88 per cent of these facilities to use their residual hearing of HI children and enhance their learning. On the otherhand, schools for VI, MR and OH were equipped to certain extent with these facilities to overcome the hearing loss in the children with multiple disabilities.

Special schools for MR should possessed facilities such as physiotherapy and occupational therapy materials, low cost multimedia materials, school transport facilities, adopted play materials, speech therapy equipment and materials. Such facilities promote provision for better intervention to the children with mental retardation. These facilities were available in 78 per cent to 88 per cent of special schools for MR. 44 per cent to 100 per cent of special schools for VI, 58 per cent to 88 per cent of schools for HI, and 70 per cent to 100 per cent of special schools for OH possessed these facilities. Here too, children with multiple disabilities were served better with the availability of these facilities. Similarly, 70 per cent to 90 per cent of special schools for OH were with orthotic and prosthetic devices, physiotherapy and occupational therapy, school transport facilities, adopted play materials, equipment and materials to identify children with different disabilities. 56 per cent to 100 per cent of special schools for VI, 58 per cent to 88 per cent of schools for HI and 78 per cent to 88 per cent of schools for MR were served better with the above infrastructure facilities. Contrary to this, normal schools possessed only a limited number of all the above stated infrastructure facilities. It reveals the dearth of infrastructure facilities available in normal schools for the education of children with disabilities. For better integrated or inclusive educational practices, the above mentioned basic infrastructure facilities in the normal schools are the need of the hour. Similarly, for special schools depending upon the need that is specific disability and multiple disabilities, the stated infrastructure facilities should be provided to give better quality education to the disabled children.

Table 4.16 presents the number of schools with good, moderate and poor infrastructure facilities and the corresponding dropout rate in special and normal schools.

Table 4.16: Number and percentage with poor, moderate and good infrastructure facilities and their corresponding dropout percentage

Type of School	*No. of Schools*	*Percentage of Dropout Rate*
Special Schools (N = 84)		
Good Facility Schools	35	2.25
Moderate Facility Schools	48	6.83
Poor Facility Schools	1	10.00
Normal Schools (N = 76)		
Good Facility Schools	1	2.00
Moderate Facility Schools	49	6.69
Poor Facility Schools	26	10.54

Table 4.16 clearly shows that out of 84 special schools, 35 were with good infrastructure facilities and their corresponding dropout rate is 2.25 per cent. Similarly, there were 48 moderate facility schools with 6.83 drop out rate. Only one school was coming under poor facility school and 10 per cent was the drop out rate. It reveals that better the infrastructure facilities lower will be the dropout rate.

In normal schools, only one school was with good infrastructure facilities and the dropout rate was 2 per cent. There were 49 schools with moderate infrastructure facilities and the corresponding dropout rate was 6.69 per cent. 26 schools were falling under poor facility schools with 10.54 as dropout rate. The results indicate that poor the infrastructure facilities, higher is the dropout rate. It means, there is an inverse relationship between infrastructure facilities and the dropout rate in special and normal schools. The result clearly says that to arrest the dropout rate, the schools should be equipped with proper infrastructure facilities.

The table also reveals that there were 35 special schools with good infrastructure facilities and only one normal school with good facilities. With moderate facilities, there were 48 special schools and 49 normal schools. Likewise, 26 normal schools were with poor infrastructure whereas only one special school was under the category of poor infrastructure. A close look at Table 4.16 also reveals that the trend of the dropout rate is almost same irrespective of the category of the school (special and normal). Further, the table explicitly reveals that whether it is normal or special school more the facilities l[illegible] is the dropout rate and poorer the facilities more will be the dropout rate. It once again reinstates the need for provision of better infrastructure facilities to arrest dropout and wastage at primary level irrespective of special or normal school. Moreover, it clearly reveals the need for provision of more facilities in normal schools for better integration of children with different disabilities.

Attitude of Non-Disabled Peers towards their Disabled Peers

To know the attitude of non-disabled peers towards their disabled peers, the number and percentage of normal school pupils who exhibited positive attitude or negative attitude on each attitude statement were calculated. The results are presented in Table 4.17 and discussed.

Table 4.17: Number and percentage of non-disabled peers (in normal schools) having positive and negative attitude towards their disabled peers

Sl. No.	*Attitude Statements*	*Number and Percentage of Non-disabled Peers having*			
		Positive Attitude		*Negative Attitude*	
		No.	*%*	*No.*	*%*
1	2	3	4	5	6
1.	Disabled children can be adjusted in normal classrooms	273	72	107	28
2.	Studying along with disabled children hampers learning of normal children	290	76	90	24
3.	Helping disabled children's learning promotes self-satisfaction in normal children	320	84	60	16
4.	Allowing disabled children in normal schools do not lead poor learning in other students	296	78	84	22
5.	Integration helps the normal children to understand the difficulties of disabled children	187	49	193	51
6.	Interaction with disabled children leads to the development of positive attitude in the normal children	185	49	195	51
7.	Studying with disabled children in regular classroom hampers adjustment in normal children	227	60	153	40
8.	Integrated education helps for better emotional stability in children	333	88	47	12

(Contd...)

1	2	3	4	5	6
9.	Disabled children can not compete with normal children in an integrated setup	232	61	148	39
10.	Integrated education promote better motivation in disabled children	305	80	75	20
11.	Studying with disabled children in normal classroom facilitate better social relationships	315	83	65	17
12.	Disabled children are different from others and cannot perform regular school activities	228	60	152	40
13.	Getting education is the right of every child irrespective of disability	312	82	68	18
14.	Disabled children can not learn better in segregated environment	285	75	95	25
15.	Disabled children are differently abled	336	88	44	12
16.	Disability is not a factor to be considered for better peer group relationships	345	91	35	9

Man is a social animal. His or her existence depends on how well he or she adjusts or accommodates in different environments. Such healthy adjustment tendencies must be developed through education and training. It is easy to develop such things through education particularly at the early years. Primary education is the right stage to inculcate such values. When the world is changing rapidly, human values for better existence are also changing from time to time. The present concept throughout the world is helping others to help ourself. If it is so, such universal values can be inculcated in students at primary level. This can be done by following certain inclusive education practices at school level. Inclusive education is nothing but integration of children with certain physical, mental and learning disabilities into the mainstreaming classrooms. For effective integration one should take into consideration the different aspects of school setting such as teachers' awareness, attitude, competencies, infrastructure facilities available and so on. Apart from the above, the attitude of non-disabled towards their disabled peers is one of the aspects that should be kept in mind while going for integration. In fact, the philosophy behind integration is development of self-confidence, better self concept and self esteem to alleviate inferiority complex and to promote independence in the disabled children. Whether it is general education or special education, peer tutoring or peer learning promotes better achievement not only in academics but also in personal and social life. Integration of disabled children at primary stage itself promotes better learning in the disabled by adopting peer tutoring and peer learning. Once again, it is needless to say that the attitude of non-disabled peers towards the disabled peers play a vital role in the success of the concept of integration. In this study an attempt is made to study the normal school children's attitude towards their disabled peers.

Table 4.17 reveals the non-disabled peers' attitude towards the disabled peers. The idea of integration and inclusive education is gaining ground all over the world. The successful integration of children with disabilities warrants non-disabled peers' co-operation, more favourable attitude and helping tendencies towards the disabled peers. 72 per cent of non-disabled peers had positive attitude that the disabled children could be adjusted in normal classroom and the remaining 28 percent not. 76 per cent of non-disabled peers felt that, studying along with disabled children would not hamper learning of normal children but 24 per cent of non-disabled peers exhibited negative attitude. Self-satisfaction was achieved by helping disabled children's learning. 84 per cent of non-disabled peers felt that self-satisfaction is achieved by helping their disabled peers while learning and 16 per cent demonstrated negatively. 22 per cent of non-disabled peers felt that allowing disabled children in normal schools leads to poor learning in other students. At the same time, 78 per cent showed favourable attitude towards this attitude statement. Integration helps the disabled children to mingle within the society effectively. Integration is successful only if normal children accept and understand the difficulties of disabled children.

88 per cent of non-disabled peers accepted that, integrated education helps for better emotional stability in children and 12 per cent had not accepted (s. no. 8). With supportive devices and materials, disabled children can compete and cope up with normal children in an integrated set up. Normal peers (61%) had accepted this but the remaining felt that disabled children can not compete (s. no. 9).

The study reveals that 49 per cent of non-disabled peers felt that integration helps the normal children to understand the difficulties of disabled children (s. no. 5) and interaction with disabled children leads to the development of positive attitude (s. no. 6) and the rest felt otherwise. On s. no. 7, 60 per cent of the children felt that the adjustment in normal children will hamper by studying with the disabled children in regular classroom and only 40 per cent felt that their adjustment may not hamper.

Eventhough emotional stability is a psychological concept, it can be moulded in children in proper social settings. In integrated education, normal children will have the opportunity to know and understand the problems of disabled peers thereby developing emphatic attitude towards them. In the process of education they share their feelings, interest and with disabled and vice versa that promotes emotional stability in both the groups.

80 per cent non-disabled peers expressed that integrated education promote better motivation in disabled children and the remaining 20 per cent felt negatively. (s. no. 10). 83 per cent of the non-disabled peers showed positive feelings the remaining 17 per cent showed unfavourable attitude on s. no. of item 11. Only 40 per cent of peers felt that disabled children are different from others and cannot perform regular school activities and the remaining were against it (s. no. 12). 82 per cent of non-disabled peer felt that getting education is the right of every child irrespective of disability and the remaining were otherwise (s. no. 13) and 75 per cent of non disabled peers expressed that disabled children can not learn better in segregated environment 88 per cent of non-disabled peers accepted that disabled childıen are differently abled but the remaining 12 per cent were not. For s. no. 16, 91 per cent of non-disabled peers felt that disability is not a factor to be considered for better peer group relationship and only 9 per cent felt otherwise.

To sum up, more than 75 per cent of non-disabled peers possessed positive attitude on the attitude statements such as studying along with disabled children hampers learning in normal children (s. no. 2), helping disabled children's learning promotes self-satisfaction (s. no. 3), allowing disabled children in normal school do not lead poor learning in other students (s. no. 4), integrated education helps for better emotional stability (s. no. 8), and promote better motivation in disabled children (s. no. 10), studying with disabled children in normal classroom facilitates better social relationship (s. no. 11), education is the right of every child irrespective of disability (s. no. 13), disabled children can not learn better in segregated environments (s. no. 14), disabled children are differently abled (s. no. 15) and disability is not a factor to be considered for better peer group relationships (s. no. 16). Only 50-74 per cent of non-disabled peers demonstrated positive attitude on the attitude statement aspects—disabled children can be adjusted on normal classrooms (s. no. 1). studying with disabled children in regular classroom hampers adjustment in normal children (s. no. 7), disabled children cannot compete with normal children in integrated setup (s. no. 9) and disabled children are different from others and cannot perform regular school activities (s. no. 12). On the otherhand on attitude statements—integrating helps the normal school children to understand the difficulties of disabled children (s. no. 5) and integration with the disabled children leads to the positive attitude (s. no. 6), only 49 per cent of the normal school students showed positive attitude and the rest in the opposite direction. This gives rise to the need for the development of better attitudes in normal students by informing them the right things and better human values. At this point, it is needless to say that teachers and parents play a vital role. Hence once again, it is stressed that parent sensitisation and teacher awareness programmes on different aspects of disabilities in children are the need of the hour.

Summary and Suggestions

Introduction

Every individual is unique and hence 'special'. Education is bound to cater to the needs of all the individuals in compliance with the constitutional provision of equal opportunity. There are some individuals who by virtue of their physical and mental abilities require a more relevant or appropriate instruction than is usually available within formal and informal educational structures. A domain of education has been constructed to satisfy their learning requirements (Laura and Ashman, 1985). This domain is called 'Special Education'. Reddy et al. (2000) define special education as 'specifically designed instruction that meets the unusual needs of special children'. It requires special materials, teaching techniques or equipment and/or facilities. The prime aim of special education is drawing out and strengthening the special children abilities. Related services like special transportation, psychological assessment, physical and occupational therapy, medical treatment and counseling also go hand in hand with special education.

The National Policy on Education (1986) has made a significant contribution towards developing educational opportunity for the disabled children. The centrally sponsored scheme of integrated education for the disabled children (IED) is geared to realise this objective.

Education of disabled children has basic concepts and goals in common with the education of all children. The children with visual impairment, hearing impairment, mentally retarded and orthopaedically handicapped have feelings, drives, emotions and motives common to normal children in general. Along with those common characteristics there are some specific characteristics that warrant special services in their educational programmes. It can be provided either in regular classroom or special classes within the regular school and in special schools to strengthen their abilities and grow according to their potentialities. Such special services or special education may vary depending upon the type of disabilities.

There are children with mild and moderate degrees of visual impairments, hearing impairments, mental retardation and orthopaedically handicapped, emotional or behaviour disorders apart from children with learning difficulties. A child with seriously defective vision requires different techniques of instruction than the child who has normal vision. Reddy and Sujathamalini (2000) pointed out that there are number of general factors that need to be considered when devising an appropriate teaching style for use to the child with a visual impairment. They are: (1) position, (2) presentation, (3) experiences, (4) expectations, (5) giving information and (6) speed of working. Similarly, Reddy and Kusuma (2001) highlighted that proper lighting arrangements, wearing glasses, magnifying devices, and proper seating arrangements may help the children with visual impairment.

Hearing impairment reduces or distorts our perception or knowledge of the world around us. A hearing impairment whether permanent or fluctuating, adversely affects the child's performance in learning. Hearing impairment as a generic term indicates a hearing disability, which ranges in severity from mild to profound; it includes the subsets of deaf and hard of hearing. Educational programmes for hearing impaired children include oral approach and total communication approach. Oral approach includes auditory training and speech training. Total communication approach makes use of both oral approach and manual approach. Use of hearing aids helps to gear up residual hearing. Providing conducive environment, instructional modifications, peer tutoring and bodily system are some important techniques to teach speech and hearing impaired children in general education classroom.

Children with mental retardation may be markedly different from the children in the next door in some ways, but also like them in others. Mental retardation refers to significantly sub-average general intellectual functioning resulting in or associated with impairments in adaptive behavior and manifested during the developmental period. Mental retardation is classified into three groups namely— educable, trainable and custodial. An educational programme for mentally retarded children varies according to their degree of disability. The emphasis on academic skills (Basic 3R's) will be more for educable mentally retarded, whereas training in self help skills, community living and vocational training are centered in the educational programmes for trainable mentally retarded and concentration is on self help skills for the custodial group.

Orthopaedically handicapped are having interference with the normal functioning of the bones, joints, muscles to such an extent that special arrangements are required to accommodate him/her in regular classes. These children are easily identified as this disability is more visible than others like partially sighted, hearing impaired etc. The OH children are assisted with suitable prosthetic and orthotic devices and function as normal as possible. These children do not have any learning problems whereas; they face problems in participation in regular classroom activities. Wheel chairs, hoists, canes, walkers and crutches help the OH children to move either vertically or horizontally in and outside the classroom.

Thus, different categories of disabled children require different type of educational modifications. A teacher with multi-talents will provide well-designed educational programme based on the nature, type and degree of disability to circumvent their disabilities and capitalise their abilities.

Need for the Study

Teacher's role is indispensable in any educational system. Teacher is an artist who moulds and shapes physical, mental and moral powers of the mind. To accomplish this task effectively, a teacher should be highly competent. In general, the teachers of children with disabilities should first obtain education and experience in teaching normal children and in addition, should become specialists in the area of special education. Special education, as it is a developing field of professional activity, it warrants more competent teachers. Children with disabilities are to be identified at an early stage for early intervention. This is possible only if the teacher at primary level possess knowledge on different aspects of children with disabilities, such as concept of disabilities, causes and characteristics of children with disabilities, identification and assessment of children with disabilities, teaching and training methods and guidance and counselling.

A competent teacher should possess right type of knowledge and positive attitude and exhibit multiple skills to handle children with disabilities. The multiple skills that are to be exhibited by them require specific competencies. A teacher with kindness, patience, and positive attitude will be an asset to the special education field. Intensive training and education help him/her to perform the diversified roles more effectively. As it is a growing field, the strong base should be laid down. As a first step, the present awareness, attitude and possessed competencies have to be assessed.

Number of studies has been quoted on teacher awareness (Dharmaraj, 2000; Sarojini, 2000; Selvakani, 2000; Kusuma Harinath, 2000 and Nagomi Ruth, 2000) and teacher competencies (Sujathamalini, 2002 and Jeevanantham, 2002). Reddy and Ramar studied the effectiveness of multimedia based modular approach in teaching science and mathematics to slow learners (1999 and 1998), low achievers (1995 and 1995a), teaching social science to low achievers (1994), slow learners (2000) and English to slow learners (1997). Santhakumari (2003), Jayaprabha (2003) and Shyamala (2004) conducted studies on instructional strategies like cognitive, metacognitive and cognitive behaviour modification to overcome learning disabilities, behaviour disorders and antisocial behaviours in children respectively. Sivakami (2000) studied the effectiveness of certain strategies to overcome learning disabilities in English. Kusuma Harinath (2000) studied the factors related to learning disabilities in English and their parents and teacher's awareness and attitude.

Reddy et al. (2001) studied the relative effectiveness of tangible materials (Braille) and talking books (audio cassettes) in learning social science concepts by the visually impaired children in secondary schools. Reddy and Kanchanamala (2002) found the effectiveness of multimedia based modular approach in learning botany by the slow learners.

In foreign context, Brent and Margery (2003), Swartz (1995), Hoffman, Barbara (1995), Drury (1994) conducted studies on awareness of teachers towards children with disabilities. Cook et al. (2000), Brownlee (2000) Treder David (2000), Praisner (2003), Westwood and Graham (2003) studied the attitude of teachers towards children with disabilities. Similarly, a good number of studies had been quoted on teacher competencies. Some of them are Blanchett (2001), McNicholas, Jim (2001), Knowlton (1999), Blackhurst et al. (1977) and Hudson et al. (1987) and Jairrels, Veda (1993).

From the above studies, it is evident that only limited number of studies has been conducted in India on teacher awareness, attitude and competencies to deal children with disabilities. In the western world the research in this area is far better than the Indian scenario. The success of integration programmes for children with special needs require careful planning, and organisation of physical as well as academic environment. As stated, the research done in special education particularly on teacher awareness, attitude and competencies to deal children with disabilities is very limited in India and such studies are more warranted. Studies that focus their attention to assess the awareness, attitude and competencies of special school and normal school teachers will give a clear cut picture about the existing scenario and will pave way for better policy planning for teachers working in special and normal schools. Further, it also gives an idea about the effect of independent variables on the teacher's awareness, attitude and competencies so as to plan for the development of specific need based and situation-oriented training programmes to the teachers working in special and normal schools.

The present study is an attempt to identify awareness, attitude and competencies of special and normal schools teachers to deal children with disabilities. Such a study facilitates to develop proper educational policies and programme planning for children with disabilities. The study also concentrates on studying the relationship between independent (gender, age, educational qualification, training in special education, years of experience, location of school, nature of school, category of school and type of school) and dependent variables (awareness, attitude and existing competencies) paving way for organisation of awareness and sensitization programmes apart from attitudinal building activity to the special and normal school teachers dealing children with disabilities. The study also directed to see how far and to what extent the independent variables influence the dependent variables, thereby paving the way for taking care of these aspects while organising training programmes. Finally, the thrust is on studying the infrastructure facilities available for the education of children with disabilities in special and normal schools and the dropout rate existing in these schools, which in turn leads to provision of better facilities. On the whole, the present study gives better insight for policy planning, development and implementation of educational programmes for the disabled.

Statement of the Problem

Keeping the above discussion in mind, the statement of the problem is given as follows.

"Awareness, attitude and competencies required for special and normal school teachers in dealing children with disabilities"

Operational Definition of the Terms Used in the Study

Awareness

In the Hutchinson Encyclopedic Dictionary (1994) aware is explained as ' having knowledge or realisation'.

The New Roget's Thesaurus (1985) defines aware as 'appreciative, conscious, cognizant (knowledge)'.

Oxford Advanced Learner's Dictionary (1996) defines aware, as 'having knowledge of realising, be fully aware of'.

Concise Oxford Dictionary (1990) also states that 'aware is conscious, not ignorant, having knowledge, well informed'. Awareness is noun of aware.

In the present study, awareness is defined as having knowledge or being fully aware of or well informed about the concept of disabilities in children, causes and characteristics of children with disabilities, identification and assessment of children with disabilities, teaching & training methods, and guidance and counselling to the children as well as to the parents and community.

Attitude

Chambers Concise Dictionary (1992) defines attitude as 'position expressing some thoughts or feelings'.

Larousse Science and Technology Dictionary (1996) defines attitude as an inferred disposition to feel, think and act in certain ways which is used to explain the variation between individuals in their response to similar situation. Attitudes are assumed to represent the effect of past experience on behaviour, through their effects on the cognition, emotional and structuring of perception.

According to Encyclopedic Dictionary of Psychology and Education (1996), attitude is a 'learned disposition to act in a consistent way towards particular persons, objects or conditions'. Likewise, Oxford Advanced Learner's Dictionary (1996) defines attitude 'as a way of thinking about or behaving towards'. Similarly, the Hutchinson Encyclopaedic Dictionary (1994) defines attitude 'as a way of regarding, a disposition or reaction'.

In the present study, attitude refers to the special and normal school teachers' beliefs, feelings and behaviours towards the different aspects of children with disabilities.

Competencies

In Oxford Advanced Learner's Dictionary (1996) competence is 'being able to do'. It also defines competent as 'having the necessary ability, authority, skill, knowledge etc'.

The Hutchinson Encyclopedic Dictionary (1994) defines competency 'as being competent'. Similarly, Concise Oxford Dictionary (1990) states 'competence as ability, the state of being competent, competent as adequately qualified or capable, effective'.

In this study, competencies refer to the knowledge, attitude, skill and performance of special and normal school teachers in dealing children with disabilities.

Children

Encyclopaedic Dictionary of Psychology and Education (1996) defines children ' as young persons of either sex before puberty'.

In this study, children refer to the young persons from I to IV standard or at primary level.

Disabilities

Oxford Advanced Learner's Dictionary (1996) defines disability 'as the state of being disabled'.

Encyclopedic Dictionary of Psychology and Education (1996) explains disability 'as something that disables or disqualifies a person, a physical incapacity caused by injury, disease etc'. Similarly, Concise Oxford Dictionary (1990) explains disability 'as physical incapacity either congenital or caused by injury, disease etc'.

In this study, disabilities refer to physical and sensory impairments like visual impairment, hearing impairment, mental retardation and orthopaedically handicapped.

Objectives of the Study

1. To assess the awareness and attitude of special school teachers (VI, HI, MR and OH) working at primary level on different dimensions of children with disabilities.
2. To assess the awareness and attitude of primary school teachers working in normal schools towards different dimensions of children with disabilities.
3. To assess the extent of competencies possessed by the special school teachers and normal school teachers on different dimensions to deal children with disabilities.
4. To identify the competencies required for the teachers of special and normal schools on different dimensions to deal children with disabilities.

5. To find out the significant difference, if any, between the special school and normal school teachers' awareness on different dimensions (concept of disabilities in children, causes and characteristics of children with disabilities, identification and assessment of children with disabilities, teaching and training methods, and guidance & counselling) of children with disabilities.

6. To find cut the significant difference, if any, between the special school and normal school teachers' attitude towards different dimensions of children with disabilities.

7. To find out the significant difference, if any, between the special school and normal school teachers' existing competencies on different dimensions to deal children with disabilities.

8. To find out the significant differences, if any, in the awareness of special school teachers on different dimensions of children with disabilities due to variation in their gender, age, educational qualification, training in special education, years of experience, location of school, nature of school, category of the school and type of school they are working.

9. To find out the significant differences, if any, in the awareness of normal school teachers on different dimensions of children with disabilities due to variation in their gender, age, educational qualification, training in special education, years of experience, location of school, nature of school, category of the school and type of school they are working.

10. To find out the significant differences, if any, in the attitude of special school teachers on different dimensions of children with disabilities due to variation in their gender, age, educational qualification, training in special education, years of experience, location of school, nature of school, category of the school and type of school they are working.

11. To find out the significant differences, if any, in the attitude of normal school teachers on different dimensions of children with disabilities due to variation in their gender, age, educational qualification, training in special education, years of experience, location of school, nature of school, category of the school and type of school they are working.

12. To find out the significant differences, if any, in the existing competency of special school teachers, on different dimensions to deal children with disabilities due to variation in their gender, age, educational qualification, training in special education, years of experience, location of school, nature of school, category of the school and type of school they are working.
13. To find out the significant differences, if any, in the existing competency of normal school teachers on different dimensions to deal children with disabilities due to variation in their gender, age, educational qualification, training in special education, years of experience, location of school, nature of school, category of the school and type of school they are working.
14. To find out the relationship between:
    (a) Awareness and attitude of special school teachers towards children with disabilities.
    (b) Awareness and attitude of normal school teachers towards children with disabilities.
    (c) Awareness and extent of competencies possessed by the special school teachers in dealing children with disabilities.
    (d) Awareness and extent of competencies possessed by the normal school teachers in dealing children with disabilities.
    (e) Attitude and extent of competencies possessed by the special school teachers in dealing children with disabilities.
    (f) Attitude and extent of competencies possessed by the normal school teachers in dealing children with disabilities.
15. To study how far and to what extent the independent variables (gender, age, educational qualification, training in special education, years of experience, location of school, nature of school, category of the school and type of school)

influence the dependent variables (awareness, attitude, and existing competencies) of special and normal school teachers in dealing children with disabilities.

16. To find out the infrastructure facilities available in special schools and normal schools for children with disabilities.
17. To find out the relationship between the infrastructure facilities and dropout rate in special and normal schools.
18. To study the attitude of non-disabled peers towards their disabled peers in special schools.

Hypotheses of the Study

1. There exists significant difference between the special and normal school teachers' awareness on different dimensions of children with disabilities.
2. There exists significant difference between the special and normal school teachers' attitude towards different dimensions of children with disabilities.
3. There exists significant difference between the special and normal school teachers existing competencies on different dimensions (concept of disabilities, causes and characteristics of children with disabilities, identification and assessment of children with disabilities, teaching and training methods, and guidance and counselling) to deal children with disabilities.
4. There exists significant difference in the special school teachers' awareness on different dimensions of children with disabilities due to variation in their gender, age, educational qualification, training in special education, years of experience, location of school, nature of school, category of school and type of school they are working.
5. There exists significant difference in the normal school teachers' awareness on different dimensions of children with disabilities due to variation in their gender, age, educational qualification, training in special education, years of experience, location of school, nature of school, category of school and type of school they are working.

6. There exists significant difference in the special school teachers' attitude towards different dimensions of children with disabilities due to variation in their gender, age, educational qualification training in special education, years of experience, location of school, nature of school, category of school and type of school they are working.

7. There exists significant difference in the normal school teachers' attitude towards different dimensions of children with disabilities due to variation in their gender, age, educational qualification training in special education, years of experience, location of school, nature of school, category of school and type of school they are working.

8. There exists significant difference in the existing competencies of special school teachers' on different dimensions to deal children with disabilities due to variation in their gender, age, educational qualification, training in special education, years of experience, location of school, nature of school, category of the school and type of school they are working.

9. There exists significant difference in the existing competencies of normal school teachers' on different dimensions dealing children with disabilities due to variation in their gender, age, educational qualification, training in special education, years of experience, location of school, nature of school, category of the school and type of school they are working.

10. There exists significant relationship between:
    (a) awareness and attitude of special school teachers towards children with disabilities.
    (b) awareness and attitude of normal school teachers towards children with disabilities.
    (c) awareness and extent of competencies possessed by the special school teachers' in dealing children with disabilities.
    (d) awareness and extent of competencies possessed by the normal school teachers' in dealing children with disabilities.

(e) attitude and extent of competencies possessed by the special teachers towards children with disabilities.

(f) attitude and extent of competencies possessed by the normal school teachers towards children with disabilities.

11. There exists positive relationship between infrastructure facilities and the dropout rate in special schools and normal schools.

Methodology

The methodology followed in this study comprising construction of research tools, reliability of the tools, sampling procedures, data collection and statistical techniques used is discussed here under.

Construction of Research Tools

The result of any scientific investigation depends upon the tools used in the study. Considering the nature and purpose of the study, the researcher selected rating scales to measure the awareness, attitude and competencies required for special and normal school teachers dealing children with disabilities.

Development of Research Tools

The objectives of the study were to assess the awareness attitude, existing and required competencies of special and normal school teachers to deal children with disabilities. To achieve these objectives, the researcher developed the following tools:

(i) Rating Scale to assess the Awareness of Special and Normal School Teachers towards various aspects of children with disabilities.

(ii) Attitude Scale to assess the Attitude of Special and Normal School Teachers towards various aspects of children with disabilities.

(iii) Competency Assessment Rating Scale to assess the Existing Competencies of Special and Normal School Teachers in dealing children with disabilities.

(iv) Checklist to identify the Required Competencies of Special and Normal School Teachers to deal children with disabilities.

(v) Peer Attitude Scale to identify the Attitude of Normal school children towards their disabled peers.

(vi) Checklist to identify the infrastructure facilities available for disabled children in special and normal school.

(i) *Rating Scale to assess the Awareness of Special and Normal school Teachers Towards Various Aspects of Children with Disabilities*

To develop rating scale to assess the awareness of special and normal school teachers on various aspects of children with disabilities, the investigator made a thorough and indepth study of relevant literature, consultation with educationists, discussion with special education experts, professionals working in disability area etc. A draft pool of awareness statements was thus prepared in a clear and concise form with better understanding. Care was taken to avoid ambiguity and repetition.

Thus the drafted statements were given to a panel of experts to review, restructure or reword the items, if necessary. They were also requested to arrange the items under different areas (dimensions) such as concept of disabilities in children, causes and characteristics of children with disabilities, identification and assessment of children with disabilities, teaching and training methods and guidance and counseling. Based on their comments the items were restructured, reworded and certain items were deleted and added. At this stage, there were 48 statements falling under the above dimensions. Against each statement 3 gradations were given namely 'aware to great extent', 'aware to certain extent' and 'not aware' having the scores 3, 2 and 1 respectively for positive statements and reverse scoring for negative statements.

To know the personal information about the teachers', particulars such as gender, age, educational qualification, training in special education, years of experience, location of school, nature of school, category of school and type of school were included in the part-1 of the rating scale.

(ii) *Attitude Scale to assess the Attitude of Special and Normal school Teachers Towards Various Aspects of Children with Disabilities*

To assess the attitude of the special and normal school teachers towards children with disability, an attitude scale was developed by the investigator. The procedure followed for the development of awareness scale was adopted and finally the attitude scale too consisted of 48 statements falling under the five attitudinal dimensions. Against each statement, 5 gradations were given namely, 'strongly agree', 'agree' 'agree to certain extent, 'disagree' and strongly disagree' with scores 5, 4, 3, 2 and 1 respectively for positive statements and 1, 2, 3, 4 and 5 for negative statements.

(iii) *Competency Assessment Rating Scale and Checklist to Assess the Existing and Required Competencies of Special and Normal school Teachers in Dealing Children with Disabilities*

The researcher had developed the competency assessment rating scale to assess the existing competencies of special and normal school teachers in dealing children with disabilities. In developing this scale, the investigator transformed the awareness statements into competency statements. The statements or aspects in the awareness, attitude and competency scale were the same but they structured in such a way to measure awareness, attitude and competency of the teachers'. There were 48 competency statements falling under 5 competency dimensions, as in case of awareness and attitude. Against each competency statement, three ratings were given, namely, 'competency to greater extent', 'competency to certain extent' and 'no competency' having scores 3, 2 and 1 respectively.

To identify the required competencies of special and normal school teachers in dealing children with disabilities, the same competency statements were used. But rating was given in the form of 'Yes' or 'No' type. The scoring was '1' for 'Yes' and '0' for 'No'.

(iv) *Peer Attitude Scale to Identify the Attitude of Normal School Children Towards their Disabled Peers*

Peer attitude statements were drafted in consultation with experts, educationists and professionals. The statements were prepared with utmost care to avoid ambiguity, repetitions and inaccuracies. At the end, 16 attitude statements were constructed in a clear and concise form. Against each peer attitude statement 'Yes' and 'No' was given. The normal school children were asked to say 'Yes' if they possess positive attitude on that particular statement and say 'No' if they have negative attitude. The scoring for 'Yes' was '1' and '0' for 'No'.

(v) Checklist to Identify the Infrastructure Facilities Available for the Education of Disabled Children in Special and Normal Schools

A checklist was developed to identify the infrastructure facilities available in special and normal schools for the education of disabled children. Against each infrastructure facility, 'Yes' or 'No' was given. The school heads were requested to put 'tick' mark on 'Yes' if the particular infrastructure facility is available or otherwise put 'tick' mark on 'No'. The infrastructure facilities checklist consisted of 22 statements.

Reliability of the Tools used in the Study

In the present study, split-half method was used to establish the reliability of the rating scales and checklists. In this method, the tool was divided into two equivalent halves and the correlation was found for these half-tests by using Karl Pearson's Correlation Co-efficient formula.

$$r = \frac{N\Sigma xy - \Sigma x \Sigma y}{\sqrt{\left(N\Sigma x^2 - (\Sigma x)^2\right)\left(N\Sigma y^2 - (\Sigma y)^2\right)}}$$

From the reliability of the half test, the self correlation of the whole test was then estimated by using spearman brown prophecy formula.

$$r_{11} = \frac{2r_{½}\,1/11}{1 + r_{½}\,1/11}$$

r_{11} = Reliability co-efficient of the whole test

$r_{½}$ = Reliability co-efficient of the half test found experimentally

The obtained reliability values for the tools used in the study presented here under.

(a) Awareness Rating Scale

$r_{½}$ = Half test reliability = 0.61

r_{11} = Whole test reliability = 0.76

(b) Attitude Scale

$r_{½}$ = Half test reliability = 0.76

r_{11} = Whole test reliability = 0.86

(c) Competency Assessment Rating Scale

$r_{½}$ = Half test reliability = 0.84

r_{11} = Whole test reliability = 0.91

(d) Checklist to identify the required competencies

$r_{½}$ = Half test reliability = 0.84

r_{11} = Whole test reliability = 0.92

(e) Peer Attitude Scale

$r_{½}$ = Half test reliability = 0.73

r_{11} = Whole test reliability = 0.84

(f) Checklist to identify the infrastructure facilities

$r_{½}$ = Half test reliability = 0.48

r_{11} = Whole test reliability = 0.65

The r-values of half test and the whole test with respect to each tool used in the study were high and hence the research tools used in the study were highly reliable.

Validity of the Tools Used in the Study

Based on the expert's consultations and opinion, it can be said that the tools used in the study possessed content validity and face validity. The obtained intrinsic validity of the awareness rating scale (0.87), attitude scale (0.93), competency assessment rating scale (0.95), checklist to identify the required competencies (0.96), peer attitude scale (0.81) and checklist to identify the infrastructure facilities in special and normal schools (0.92) were high and hence the tools used in the study possessed intrinsic validity.

Sample of the Study

The area of the study comprised both Andhra Pradesh and Tamil Nadu states in south India. For the purpose of the study, the investigator selected randomly two districts in each state where all categories of special schools (VI, HI, MR and OH) are existing. In Andhra Pradesh, Hyderabad and Chittoor districts were selected as the study area. In Tamil Nadu, Chennai and Madurai districts were selected. The selected districts have all the four categories of special schools.

In 1995, the National Information Centre on Disability and Rehabilitation, Ministry of Welfare, Govt. of India had prepared a Directory Compiling the list of institutions working for the disabled. According to this Directory, there are 31 institutions for VI, 46 institutions for HI, 63 institutions for MR and 37 institutions for OH functioning in the selected four districts.

Out of these 177 institutions, 84 institutions are running schools for different categories of disabled children. There are 660 teachers working in 84 special schools. All the 660 teachers working in these schools form the sample of the study.

The number of schools and teachers working in each category of disability in the selected four districts of AP and Tamilnadu states are presented in Table 5.1.

The normal schools located in the area where the special schools are functioning also formed the sample of the study. There were 76 primary schools existing for normal children in the special schools localities. All the 527 teachers working in those schools formed the sample of the study. Thus the study covered 84 special schools with 660 teachers and 76 Normal primary schools with 527 teachers in the four districts of the Andhra Pradesh and Tamil Nadu States in south India.

Table 5.1: Number of Schools and Teachers Working in Different Category of Special Schools

	Schools for VI	*No. of Teachers*	*Schools for HI*	*No. of Teachers*	*Schools for MR*	*No. of Teachers*	*Schools for OH*	*No. of Teachers*	*Total Number of Schools*	*Total Number of Teachers*
Madurai	2	16	–	–	3	23		1	5	40
Chennai	4	47	7	88	21	167	7	50	39	352
Chittoor	1	8	2	26	2	12	–	–	5	46
Hyderabad	2	24	17	99	14	91	3	8	35	222
Total	**9**	**95**	**26**	**213**	**40**	**293**	**10**	**59**	**84**	**660**

Note:

(1) The total number of special schools together are 84 only.

(2) One school is working for both HI and MR and hence this school is added to MR totaling 40 schools.

To know the attitude of non-disabled peers towards children with disabilities, 5 non-disabled children from each primary school were selected randomly by using simple random sampling technique. Thus the total number of non-disabled children covered in the study was 380.

All the school heads of special and normal schools (160) were also selected to rate the infrastructure checklist.

Overall, 1187 teachers, 380 peers and 160 school heads formed the sample for the study.

Data Collection

The research investigators of the project personally visited the schools and got permission from the school heads to collect data from their teachers. Good rapport was established with the heads and teachers of special and normal schools before administering the tools. The developed awareness rating scale, attitude scale, competency assessment rating scale, checklist to identify the required competencies, were administered to the special and normal schools teachers to know their awareness, attitude, possessed and required competencies.

Teachers were asked to go through each statement and rate their awareness, attitude, existing and required competencies on different aspects of children with disabilities. They were also asked to give their personal information in Part-I of the awareness rating scale.

For peer attitude scale, each attitude statement was explained by the research investigators to the sample pupils in normal schools. Their responses were then noted down.

Checklist to identify the infrastructure facilities was given to the schools heads of special and normal schools with a request to state the facilities available in the schools for the education of children with disabilities and also requested to mention the dropout rate. The filled in scales and checklists were collected and scored.

Findings of the Study

The results of descriptive analysis in Part-I and differential analysis in Part-II presented reveals the following findings.

PART-I

1. On the concept of disabilities in children, the special teachers were fully aware of different categories of disabilities in children (s. no. 1) and disabled children's difficulties in communication, language, perceptual, and social development (s. no. 3). Their awareness was low on the aspects—children with disabilities do not differ significantly with other children (s. no. 2), children with disabilities do not have special abilities and they exhibit only disabilities (s. no. 4), disabled children's learning needs and learning styles are same as normal children and they need not require special attention in regular classroom (s. no. 5), children with physical disabilities may not possess equal IQ as par with average children (s. no. 6) , slow learners and children with learning disabilities are not the part and parcel of children with disabilities (s. no. 7). From s. no. 1 to 7 the normal school teachers possessed moderate level of awareness. Awareness can be generated in special school teachers on the s. no. 2, 4, 5, 6 and 7 aspects, whereas for normal school teachers even though their awareness was moderate they need further sensitisation on all the aspects of concept of disabilities in children.

   Under the dimension 'causes and characteristics of children with disabilities', the special school teachers were fully aware that disabilities are the result of hereditary and environmental factors (s. no. 8), exposure of women to hazardous environment in pre- and peri- natal period leads to disabilities in children (s. no. 9), faulty child bearing and rearing practices, teaching learning practices leads to language learning disabilities in children (s. no. 12) and children with disabilities exhibit perceptual motor co-ordination, cognitive, metacognitive and social skill deficits (s. no. 13) . On the other hand, their awareness was moderate with respect to the aspects—children's exposure to lead coated toys, infectious diseases, physical abnormalities leading to disabilities in children (s. no. 10), mental retardation is the result of brain injuries and accidents in early years (s. no. 11), children with disabilities exhibit hypo- and hyper-activity, psychological problems such as inferiority complex, stress, strain, low span of attention and emotional instability etc., (s. nos. 14 and 16). Similarly, they had exhibited low level of awareness about the stereotyped behaviours of visually impaired children and disabled children's abstract thinking (s. nos. 15 and 17). On all the above aspects, the normal school teachers demonstrated moderate level of awareness (s. nos. 8, 9, 12, 14, 15, 16 and 17) and low level of awareness on s. no. 10, 11 and 13. So any awareness programme must concentrate on the moderate and low awareness aspects for special and normal school teachers.

Under the dimension 'identification and assessment of children with disabilities', the special school teachers were fully aware of the primary tools for identification of children with disabilities (s. no. 18), intelligence test as the basis for identification of MR and gifted children (s. no. 20) and different tests to identify children with visual impairments (s. no. 21). On the otherhand, they were moderately aware that observation and hearing tests are essential to identify children with hearing impairment (s. no. 22). Their awareness was low on the informal tests to identify children with learning difficulties (s. no. 19), different language assessment tests (s. no. 23) and tests for assessment of social skill deficits in disabled children (s. no. 24). The normal school teachers possessed moderate level of awareness on all these aspects (s. nos. 18, 19, 21, 22, 23 and 24) except low awareness on s. no. 20. Awareness should be generated in the special and normal school teachers on the moderate and low level awareness level aspects.

Under the dimensions 'teaching and training methods', the special school teachers awareness was high on the aspects in providing teaching and training programme the current performance ability of the disabled children should be taken into account (s. no. 27), use of plus curriculum for blind children (s. no. 34) , need for talking books and audio tapes for blind children (s. no. 35), need for total communication approach, use of hearing aids for use of residual hearing, group hearing aids to facilitate teaching learning in the classroom, (s. nos. 36, 37 and 38), and use of orthotic devices for orthopaedically handicapped children (s. no. 40). On the otherhand, their awareness was moderate on the aspects-appropriate placement services for children with disabilities (s. no. 25), use of self-directed learning materials for gifted children's learning (s. no. 29), need for breaking the task into small sequential steps to make MR and slow learners learn effectively (s. no. 30), need for use of integrated therapy in the education of mentally retarded children (s. no. 31), use of peer tutoring, group learning and multisensory approaches for children with learning difficulties and slow learners (s. no. 32), need for large print materials, magnifying devices and corrective lenses for low vision children in learning (s. no. 33) and need for closed circuit television (CCTV) in the learning of hearing impaired children (s. no. 39). Similarly, special school teachers' awareness was low on the aspects—need for development of individualised education programme based on the degree of disability and the need for setting of long-term and short-term goals to educate children with disabilities (s. no. 26 and 28). As the normal school teachers possessed only moderate and low level of awareness on all the aspects under the dimension 'teaching and training methods' they should be given sensitisation of awareness generation programmes on teaching and training of disabled children.

Under the dimension 'guidance and counselling', the special school teachers were fully aware that these activities promote self confidence in disabled children (s. no. 41), peer group guidance and counselling develop positive attitude towards children with disabilities (s. no. 43), need for guidance about pre-, peri- and post-natal problems to the parents and community (s. no. 42), parents counselling to understand different aspects of difficulties faced by children with disabilities (s. no. 44), need for involving parents in planning, development and organisation of education programmes for children with disabilities (s. no. 45), need for community counselling (s. no. 46) and need for directing parents to the specialists such as audiologist, speech therapists, ophthalmalogist, physiologist, psychologist, and occupational therapist to understand their children with disabilities (s. no. 48). Their awareness was moderate with regard to the need for the PTA meetings, discussions and group work that give chance to know the progress of the children with disabilities (s. no. 47). On all the aspects under the dimension 'guidance and counselling', the normal school teachers demonstrated moderate awareness stating the need for sensitisation programmes. (refer Table 4.2).

2. The special school teachers were having positive attitude on the aspects—problems in visual, hearing, motor and mental aspects lead to disabilities in children (s. no. 1), whereas their attitude was neutral (moderate) on the aspects—significant difference among learning represent disabilities in children (s. no. 2) and difficulty in communication, language, perceptual and social development leads to disabilities in children (s. no. 3), negative attitude on the aspects of disabilities in children do not lead any special abilities (s. no. 4), disabled children's learning needs and styles are same as normal children and they need not require special attention in regular classrooms (s. no. 5), physical disability will leads to low I.Q. (s. no. 6) and disabilities in children leads to slow learning and learning disabilities (s. no. 7), under the dimension 'concept of disabilities in children'. On all these aspects the normal school teachers' attitude was neutral (s. nos. 1 to 3) and negative (s. nos. 4 to 7).

   Under the dimension 'causes and characteristics', the special school teachers' attitude was high on the aspects—exposure of pregnant women into hazardous environment pre- peri-natal period reads to disabilities in children (s. no. 9) and brain injuries and accidents leads to mental retardation in children (s. no. 11); moderate attitude on the aspects hereditary and environmental factors contribute disabilities in children (s. no. 8), children's exposure to lead coated toys, infectious disease, and physical abnormalities leads to disabilities in children (s. no. 10), poor child bearing and rearing practices and faulty teaching learning practices leads to language learning disabilities in children (s. no. 12), perceptual and motor co-ordination, cognitive and metacognitive as well as social deficits are common in children with disabilities (s. no. 13). Hypo- and hyper-activity behaviours usually exhibited by children with disabilities (s. no. 14), disabilities in children leads to inferiority complex, stress, strain, low span of attention and emotional instability (s. no. 16), and disabilities in children leads to better abstract thinking than the normal children (s. no. 17), and low attitude or negative attitude about the aspect that—visual impairment in children may not lead to stereotyped behaviours (s. no. 15). On all these aspects, the normal school teachers' attitude was neutral (s. nos. 8 to 16 and 18) and negative for the serial number of the aspect 15.

On the dimension 'identification and assessment of children with disabilities', the special school teachers' attitude was positive for the aspects—visual impairment in children can be identified through classroom observation, visual screening and ophthalmological tests (s. no. 21) and hearing impairment in children can be identified through classroom observation and hearing tests (s. no. 22). Contrary to this, their attitude was neutral on the aspects such as—disabilities in children can be identified through observation and academic records (s. no. 18), informal tests for identification of hearing difficulties in children (s. no. 19), mental retardation and giftedness can be identified in children with intelligence tests (s. no. 20) and assessment of adaptive behaviour leads to identification of social deficits (s. no. 24). Similarly, they showed negative attitude on the aspect of identification of language learning difficulties in children through language assessment tests (s. no. 23). The normal school teachers' attitude was neutral (s. nos. 18 to 21 and 24) and negative (s. nos. 22 and 23).

With regard to the dimension 'teaching and training methods', the special school teachers together had positive attitude on the aspects—children with disabilities may benefit from appropriate placement services (s. no. 25), the learning of low vision children can be enhanced through large print materials, magnifying devices, and corrective lenses (s. no.

33). Use of plus curriculum for blind children to learn 3R's as well as orientation and mobility skills (s. no. 34), use of audio tapes and talking books for blind children (s. no. 35) and use of orthotic devices to facilitate the daily living skills of OH children (s. no. 40); neutral or moderate attitude on the aspects such as—teaching and training programmes for disabled children should be based on their current performance ability (s. no. 27), setting long-term and short-term goals for the education of children with disabilities (s. no. 28), use of self-directed learning materials for gifted children (s. no. 29), need for integrated therapy to the mentally retarded children (s. no. 31), need for peer tutoring, group learning and multi-sensory approaches for children with learning difficulties and slow learning (s. nos. 32), need for the use of total communication approach to the hearing impaired children, use of hearing aids to enhance the residual hearing use of group hearing aids to facilitate teaching learning process in the classroom and use of CCTV to facilitate the learning of HI children (s. no. 36, 37, 38 and 39); negative attitude on the aspects—the need for taking into account the degree of disability in organising individualised education programme and breaking down the task or activity into smaller sequential steps with short duration to facilitate MR and slow learners learning (s. nos. 26 and 30). On all the teaching and training aspects the normal school teachers' attitudes was neutral (s. nos. 25, 27, 28, 29, 31 to 40) and negative (s. nos. 26 and 30).

Positive attitude was shown by the special education teachers on the aspects—guidance and counselling by the teacher leads self confidence among children with disabilities, disabilities in children can be prevented by giving guidance about pre-, peri- and post-natal problems to the parents and community (s. nos. 41 and 42); need for peer group guidance and counselling, parent counselling (s. nos. 43 and 44) community counselling (s. no. 46), need to involve parents in planning, development and organisation of education programmes for children with disabilities (s. no. 45) and need for directing the parents of children with disabilities to the specialist—audiologist, psychologist and so on (s. no. 48) ; and possessed negative attitude about the need for PTA meetings, discussion and group work to facilitate the progress of disabilities, under the dimension 'guidance and counselling activities'. The normal school teachers' attitude was neutral in most of the guidance and counselling activities except negative attitude in s. no. of the aspect 48. (refer Table 3).

3. The aspects in which the special school and normal school teachers' competencies were moderate and low should be given priority in organisations of training programmes for these teachers. Accordingly, under the dimension 'concept of disabilities in children', the aspects such as—able to understand the learning difference of disabled and non-disabled children and, knowledge about intelligence quotient of disabled and non-disabled children should be given priority for special school teachers. Apart from the above two aspects, the normal school teachers should be given orientation about the different categories of disabilities in children, knowledge about communication, language, perceptual and social development difficulties non children, the learning needs and learning styles of disabled children and knowledge about learners and children with learning difficulties.

   Under 'causes and characteristics', the priorities of special school teachers were hereditary and environmental factors related to disabilities in children, diseases and physical abnormalities causing disabilities in children, relationship between child bearing and rearing practices, teaching learning practices and language learning difficulties in children, stereotyped behaviours in visually impaired children, psychological characteristics of children with disabilities and different thinking abilities of disabled and non-disabled children. Adding to this, the normal school teachers also required training in knowledge on disabilities in children due to hazardous environments in pre- and peri-natal periods, causes of mental retardation, perceptual, motor co-ordination, cognitive and metacognitive deficits as well as social skill deficits in disabled children, and hypo- and hyper-activity behaviours of children with disabilities.

Under the dimension 'identification and assessment, the special school teachers required training in use of classroom observation and visual screening to identify visual impairments in children, identifying language learning difficulties and assessment of adaptive behaviour to identify social deficit skills in disabled children. The normal school teachers too required orientation on this (as their competency level is low) apart from the aspects such as ability to identify disabilities in children through direct observation and academic records, use of informal tests to identify language difficulties, skill in identifying mental retardation and giftedness in children and identification of hearing impairment in children.

Under teaching and training, they needed competency on the aspects of providing self directed materials to gifted children, teaching mentally retarded and slow learners, knowledge about speech, physical and occupational therapy, knowledge about large print materials, magnifying devices and corrective lenses, skill in using plus curriculum, knowledge about hearing aids to gear up residual hearing, proficiency in total communication approach, knowledge and skill in use of CCTV in HI children's learning and use of orthotic devices to the orthopaedically handicapped children to promote daily living skills. Apart from these aspects, the normal school teachers required competencies on—skill in providing appropriate placement services to the disabled children, development of individualised education programme to the disabled, ability to plan teaching and training programmes to the disabled based on their current performance, able to set long- and short-term goals for the education of disabled, ability to organise peer tutoring, group learning and multi-sensory approach for children with learning difficulties and slow learning, skill in use of audio tapes/talking books to facilitate blind children's learning and able to use group hearing aids in the classroom set up to facilitate teaching learning process.

Under the dimension 'guidance and counselling, the special school teachers required competencies on—involving parents in planning, development and organisation of educational programmes for the children with disabilities and ability to conduct PTA meetings, discussions and group work to facilitate the development of children with disabilities. Adding to these, normal school teachers required competencies in development of self confidence in disabled children, providing guidance and counselling to the parents and community about pre-, peri- and post-natal problems, ability to alleviate negative attitude of peer group towards disabled children, proficiency in parent's counselling, able to provide community counselling to promote positive attitude towards disabled children and able to direct parents to the specialist such as audiologist, psychologist and occupational therapist for the betterment of children with disabilities (refer Table 4.4).

4. More than 70 per cent of the special and normal school teachers required competency on each aspect under different dimensions of disabilities in children (refer Table 4.5).

PART-II

1. Significant differences existed between normal and special school teachers awareness on aspect of disabilities in children, causes and characteristics, identification and assessment, teaching and training methods, guidance and counselling, and dimensions as a whole. No significant differences existed between the teachers working in schools for OH and normal schools on awareness of identification and assessment. Further, normal school teachers' awareness on concept of disabilities in children was higher than their counterparts working in special schools. Whereas, the awareness of teachers working in different categories of special schools, were higher in causes and characteristics, identification and assessment, teaching and training methods, guidance and counselling and dimensions as a whole than their counterparts working in normal schools (refer Table 4.6).

2. The attitude of special and normal school teachers significantly varied with respect to the causes and characteristics of children with disabilities, identification and

assessment, teaching and training, guidance and counselling and dimensions as a whole. The special school teachers possessed more positive attitude irrespective of the type of school they are working than the normal school teachers. Contrary to this, the teachers working in the schools for MR, and schools for OH did not significantly differed in their attitude with normal school teachers. But the teachers working in VI, HI and special school teachers together towards the concept of disabilities in children differ in their attitude than their counterparts working in normal schools. Here too, the teachers working in VI, HI and special school teacher together demonstrated better attitude than the normal school teachers. (refer Table 4.7).

3. The special and normal school teachers significantly differed in their existing competencies on the concept of disabilities in children, causes and characteristics of children with disabilities, identification and assessment, teaching and training methods, guidance and counselling and dimensions as a whole. The special school teachers possessed better competencies than the normal school teachers in all the competency dimensions (refer Table 4.8).
4. The variables gender, age, educational qualification, training in special education, type of school the teachers working' had significantly influenced the special and normal school teachers' awareness on different aspects of disabilities in children. The variable 'years of experience' and 'nature of school' the teachers working has not significantly influenced the special school teachers awareness on different dimensions of disabilities in children (refer Table 4.9).
5. The variables gender, training in special education, type of special school the teachers working had significantly influenced their attitude towards children with disabilities. On the other hand, the variables age, educational qualification, years of experience, location of school and nature of school had not significantly influenced the special school teachers' attitude towards children with disabilities. In normal schools, variations in teachers' gender, age,

educational qualification, training in special education, years of experience, location of school and nature of school had brought significant differences in their attitude towards children with disabilities (refer Table 4.10).

6. The variables age, educational qualification, training in special education, years of experience and type of school the teachers' working had significantly influenced the special school teachers existing competencies. Contrary to this, the variables gender, location of school and nature of the school the teachers working had not significantly influenced their existing competencies in dealing children with disabilities. In normal schools, except the variable 'locations of the school', all the other variables had significantly influenced the competencies of teachers (refer Table 4.11).

7. Correlational studies reveal that there was a significant positive relationship between the awareness and attitude; awareness and extent of competencies possessed, and attitude and extent of competencies possessed by the special school teachers on each dimension of disabilities in children except for the concept of disabilities in children with reference to awareness and extent of competencies possessed and attitude and extent of competencies possessed. Further, higher the awareness, attitude and extent of competencies possessed, then higher will be the attitude and higher the extent of competencies possessed (refer Table 4.12).

8. There was a significant positive relationship between awareness and attitude; awareness and extent of competencies possessed and; attitude and extent competencies possessed by the normal school teachers in dealing children with disabilities on the dimensions causes and characteristics, identification and assessment, teaching and training methods, guidance and counselling and dimensions as a whole. But, on the concept of disabilities in children, there existed significant relationship between awareness and extent of competencies possessed by the normal school teachers, but not between awareness and attitude and attitude and extent of competencies possessed (refer Table 4.13).

9. The variable 'category of school' is the major predicator followed by years of experience, age, gender educational qualification and training in special education to the awareness of special school teachers towards children with disabilities. Gender followed by educational qualification and training in special education are the predictors of special school teachers attitude towards children with disabilities. Likewise, category of school and training in special education are the major predictor to the existing competencies of the special school teachers in dealing children with disabilities. In normal schools, teachers gender, training in special education and nature of school are the foremost predictors to the awareness; nature of school as a major predictor for attitude and; training in special education and nature of school are the predictors for the existing competencies in dealing children with disabilities (refer Table 4.14).

10. Out of 22 infrastructure facilities needed for education of children with disabilities, 9 facilities such as slate and stylus, magnifying devices, lenses and large print and coloured materials for low vision children, mathematical aids like abacus, taylor frame etc, embossed teaching learning materials, audiotapes/talking books, orientation and mobility materials, lighting arrangements in the classroom for low vision children, equipment and materials to identify children with different disabilities and talking calculators and Braille typewriters are important in educating visually impaired children. These facilities help the visually impaired children to learn better and cope up with normal children. 56 to 89 per cent of special schools for VI were having the different infrastructure facilities mentioned above. As some of the children studying in some of the special schools were with multiple disabilities, such schools possessed the above said infrastructure facilities, which are needed for children with visual impairment. Here, it is imperative to say that irrespective of the type of school these facilities are essential to all the schools. This is the reason why a common infrastructure checklist is developed for all the schools to identify the infrastructure facilities.

Facilities such as hearing aids for hearing impaired children, group hearing aids in the classroom, providing conducive environment to the students with moderate hearing loss, with overhead projector, speech therapy equipment and speech synthesisers and materials to identify children with disabilities are very important for meeting the education of hearing impaired children. Special schools for HI possessed 58 to 88 per cent of these facilities to use the residual hearing of HI children and enhance their learning. On the other hand, schools for VI, MR and OH were also equipped to certain extend with these facilities to overcome the hearing loss in the children with multiple disabilities.

Special schools for MR should possess facilities such as physiotherapy and occupational therapy materials, low cost multimedia materials, school transport facilities, adopted play materials, speech therapy equipment and materials. Such facilities promote provision for better intervention to the children with mental retardation. These facilities were available in 78 per cent to 88 per cent of special schools for MR. 44 per cent to 100 per cent of special schools for VI, 58 per cent to 88 per cent of schools for HI, and 70 per cent to 100 per cent of special schools for OH possessed these facilities. Similarly, 70 per cent to 90 per cent of special schools for OH were with orthotic and prosthetic devices, physiotherapy and occupational therapy, school transport facilities, adopted play materials, equipment and materials to identify children with different disabilities. 56 per cent to 100 per cent of special schools for VI, 58 per cent to 88 per cent of schools for HI and 78 per cent to 88 per cent of schools for MR served better with the above infrastructure facilities.

Contrary to this, normal schools possessed only a limited number of all the above stated infrastructure facilities. It reveals the dearth of infrastructure facilities available in normal schools for the education of children with disabilities. For better integrated or inclusive educational practices, the above mentioned basic infrastructure facilities in the normal schools are the need of the hour. Similarly, for special schools depending upon the need that is specific disability and multiple disabilities, the stated infrastructure facilities should be provided to give better quality education to the disabled children (refer Table 4.15).

11. Whether it is normal or special school, more the facilities less is the dropout rate and poorer the facilities more will be the dropout rate. It once again reiterated the need for provision of better infrastructure facilities to arrest dropout and wastage at primary level irrespective of special or normal school. Moreover, it clearly reveals the need for provision of more facilities in normal schools for better integration of children with different disabilities. (refer Table 4.16).

12. More than 75 per cent of non-disabled peers possessed positive attitude on the attitude statements such as—studying along with disabled children hampers learning in normal children (s. no. 2), helping disabled children's learning promotes self-satisfaction (s. no. 3), allowing disabled children in normal school do not lead poor learning in other students (s. no. 4), integrated education helps for better emotional stability (s. no. 8), and promote better motivation in disabled children (s. no. 10), studying with disabled children in normal classroom facilitate better social relationship (s. no. 11), education is the right of every child irrespective of disability (s. no. 13), disabled children can not learn better in segregated environments (s. no. 14), disabled children are differently abled (s. no. 15) and disability is not a factor to be considered for better peer group relationships (s. no. 16). Only 50-74 per cent of non-disabled peers demonstrated positive attitude on the attitude statement aspects—disabled children can be adjusted on normal classrooms (s. no. 1), studying with disabled children in regular classroom hampers adjustment in normal children (s. no. 7), disabled children cannot compete with normal children in integrated setup (s. no. 9) and disabled children are different from others and cannot perform regular school activities (s. no. 12). On the other hand on attitude statements-integrating helps the normal school children to understand the difficulties of disabled children (s. no. 5) and integration with the disabled children leads to the positive attitude

(s. no. 6) only 49 per cent of the normal school students showed positive attitude and the rest in the opposite direction. This gives rise to the need for the development of better attitudes in normal students by informing them the right things and better human values. At this point, it is needless to say that teachers and parents play a vital role. Hence once again, it is stressed that parent sensitisation and teacher awareness programmes on different aspects of disabilities in children are the need of the hour (refer Table 4.17).

Implications of the Study

1. The study revealed that, out of 48 aspects, in more than the half of the aspects the special school teachers possessed moderate and low level of awareness, indicating the need for sensitisation programmes on the other hand, for all the aspects, the normal school teachers awareness is moderate and low. In organizing awareness/sensitisation programmes, one can exploit the possible channels existing within the reach of formal and non-formal education. As a first step, sensitisation in teachers can be done by using the existing print and electronic media. Through pamphlets, wall-posters and allotting the part of the page or page in a local newspaper that too in regional language definitely facilitate not only the teachers but also the parents and local community who develop sensitivity to the issues that promote the education of the disabled. Similarly, subject experts and field practitioners can be invited for frequent radio talks, which address the problems in disabled children's education. The Doordharshan kendras should broadcast live programmes on the success stories of the disabled people and ways and means to help such people with real field experience. In fact, no school or community is in dearth of resource and expertise. The only thing required is tapping the resources and the ways of utilising the same will solve 50 per cent of the problems. One should develop such mindset in the personnel working in the organisation or school. In this respect, it is highly suggestable that the existing parent-teacher associations can be exploited and the resource teacher can enlighten the other

teachers and parents about the education of children with disabilities. The existing DIETs and Colleges of Education, Departments of Education/Special Education should organise short-term orientation classes for the teachers already working and incorporate disability concepts in teacher training and B.Ed., curriculum, thereby, the would be teachers will be sensitized.

In nutshell, any awareness/sensitisation programme at the first stage must tune the policy makers to think where to intervene, how to intervene and when to intervene, to set right the things. At this point, they should first sensitize the media, both print and electronic, about the need for relaying and broadcasting of programmes for the education of the disabled by taping human and material resources available in their reach. In the next stage, as already mentioned, awareness can be generated through well structured campaigns by using formal and non-formal education channels. Education of children with disabilities should not be done in isolation. The concerned people like teachers parents and community should be given due weightage in planning, organisation and management of activities. Such is the case, it is inevitable to generate awareness in these groups. The existing community Radio Listening Centres and community TV viewing Centers can be profitably utilised for this purpose. The community educator/adult educator working in the local community should inform the community about the time of relay/broadcast of the programme on disability aspects and after hearing/viewing the same, he/she can generate lively discussion to sensitize them on various aspects of disabilities in children. With such an approach, the parents and community will act as supportive agents to the teachers working with disabled children. There are various developmental programmes such as ICDS, non-formal education for girls, adult-education programmes for 15-35 age group, non-formal education for women, workers education and so on are in implementation in different parts of the country. Disability issues should be the part and parcel of these programmes so that the sensitization can be done at every point. Such a wholistic approach is the need of the hour to promote the education of the disabled whether it is in integrated education or inclusive education or in special education.

2. In attitude also, the special school teachers demonstrated neutral and negative attitude on 37 aspects, out of 48 giving scope for attitudinal building activities. On all the attitudinal aspects, the normal school teacher attitude was neutral and negative. This once again raises the scope for organisation of systematic sensitization programme by using popular medias like print and electronic. A visit to the innovative and thought provoking activities or programmes organised by the specialized institutions in this area definitely facilitates to develop positive attitude in teachers. Video programming of such specialised school or institutional activities must be done and the same can be supplied to school libraries. Similarly, the Department of Education DIETs, RCI can organise short duration orientation programmes to the existing teachers on different dimensions of disabilities with practical inputs.

3. The study revealed that in more than 50 per cent of the aspects, the special school teachers' competency was low and moderate. Whereas in all the competency aspects the normal school teachers competency was low and moderate. To develop and promote the competencies identified and studied in this investigation in special and normal school teachers, the DIETs and the Colleges of Education/ Departments of Education and RCI should develop teaching and training materials, organise competency based short duration training programmes. The NCERT should take the responsibility of developing a handbook for teachers to deal children with disabilities. Likewise, well structured teaching training programme in dealing each disability area should be documented and video-taped, so that the same can be supplied to the DIETs and Libraries, located at district level, so as to lend the same to different schools for viewing and practicing the same. A visit by the teachers to the reputed institutions/schools working in each disability area will add credit to their competencies. Short term orientation course

(say for one or two months) should be made mandatory for all the teachers working in schools and this training should develop competency based activities to deal children with disabilities.

4. With regard to the required competencies the study once again ascertained that, more than 70 per cent of special and normal school teachers felt that the required competency on each aspect under different dimensions of disabilities in children. Any awareness generation programme, attitudinal building activities and competency based training programmes or activities for special and normal school teachers must incorporate appropriately the stated disability aspects studied in this investigation.

5. The study revealed that there was significant difference in the awareness of special and normal school teachers on different dimensions of disabilities in children. Similar trend was followed for attitude and the existing competencies. This gives raise to the question that normal school teachers need more intensive training on different aspects of disabilities in children than the special school teachers. It implies that while planning awareness, attitude and competency based programmes, the duration should be more with highly intensified practical components. Such activities provide for better competencies to normal school teachers to join with their counterparts.

6. The differential analysis with reference to the effect of independent variables on teachers' awareness, attitude and competencies revealed that variations in special education training and type of school the teachers working had brought significant difference in their awareness attitude and competencies.

   (a) The teachers who possessed M.Ed., in special education had better awareness than the diploma, B.Ed., and one month RCI training in special education. In attitude, the teachers with one month RCI training possessed better attitude than the teachers with M.Ed., B.Ed., and Diploma in special education. The teachers with one month RCI training exhibited better competencies than the teachers with diploma B.Ed., and M.Ed., with special education. It is strange to note that teachers with higher special education qualification had low awareness, positive attitude and low competency than the teachers with less qualification in special education. This trend is attributed to so many reasons. One such popular reason is that when the project staff visited the schools for data collection, in informal discussion with the teachers it is revealed that most of the teachers are working in special schools on consolidated basis, but not on regular scale. There is no job security. These special schools are mostly organised in private or voluntary sector. Such a situation might have contributed for negative interest in the teachers towards their profession and this in turn resulted in low attitude and competency than the teachers with less training. Hence, steps are to be taken needed to streamline the salary structure and to provide job security to the teachers working in special schools.

The teachers working in schools for HI possessed better awareness and attitude followed by MR, VI and OH. When it comes to the competencies, teachers in VI schools were better followed by HI, OH and MR. The reason, as it is observed, is that in most of the OH schools the teachers with general qualification are employed and moreover they need not require the knowledge of different aspects of VI, HI and MR. This may be the reason that their awareness and attitude are low compared to their counterparts. It is also observed that OH children too possess multiple disabilities and teachers require different training to deal such things in children. In organisation of educational training programmes for the teachers of OH and MR schools these things should be kept in mind.

(b) In normal schools, the results revealed the need for generation of awareness, development of positive attitude and better competencies in men teachers. Similarly, the programme planners and implementers must concentrate more on the teachers with 31 to 50 age groups, as their awareness, attitude and competencies are low. Likewise, the teachers with P.G. with B.E., and M.Ed., P.G. with B.Ed., teacher training, graduation with B.Ed., and M.Ed., require more orientations as their awareness, attitude and competencies are less. With regard to the years of experience the teachers with more than six years of experience and teachers working in govt. schools must be given priority in the participation of training programmes.

7. The study revealed that there is a positive correlation between awareness and attitude; awareness and competency ; and attitude and competencies in both special and normal school teachers. This result bears an implication to the policy-makers that while planning educational programmes for the disabled children, environmental building must be done in the form of awareness raising and attitudinal development particularly for teachers and the community. Only in such environment, the programmes can flourish.

8. The result of the stepwise multiple regression analysis clearly indicated that the variables, category of the school, educational qualification, training in special education and gender are the predictors to the awareness, attitude and existing competencies of special education teachers. Likewise, years of experience are also the contributors for teachers awareness. The variable 'nature of school, where the teacher is working' is the foremost predictor for normal school teachers' awareness attitude and existing competencies. The variable 'training in special education' also is the significant predictor for awareness and existing competencies of normal school teachers. Gender is the predictor only to the awareness of teachers. It implies that while selecting teaching personnel and giving training programme to them, these variables must be kept in mind.

9. The study revealed that around 20 per cent to 25 per cent of special schools and 70 to 80 per cent of normal schools were lacking infrastructure facilities for the education of children

with disabilities. As such, the special and normal schools must be provided with adequate equipment and materials needed for the education of the disabled in segregated setting or in inclusive setup. While planning integrated or inclusive education, provision of basic facilities in every school at primary level particularly is the key for success of such programmes.

10. The study also revealed that out of 84 special schools, 35 schools were with good, 48 with moderate and one with poor infrastructure facilities. Out of 76 normal schools, 26 were with poor, 49 moderate and one school with good infrastructure facilities for the education of disabled children. It also indicated better the facilities, less will be the percentage of dropouts both in normal and special schools, and less the infrastructure facilities more will be the dropouts. This result once again, highlighted the need for providing better infrastructure facilities both in special and normal schools.

11. Around 70 per cent of the non-disabled children possessed positive attitude on more than 85 per cent of attitudinal statements. It means, still there are 30 per cent of children without proper attitudes on all the aspects and all the children on 15 per cent of the attitudinal aspects. This raised the need for better attitudinal activities in the form of taking non-disabled children to the disabled children schools for better interaction and encouraging the disabled to enter to the normal schools. As we know teachers are the agents for development of proper attitudes in children, first the primary school teachers in normal schools must have proper attitude towards children with disabilities. Thereby, they will pass on the same to the normal children. This result once again, ascertained the need for awareness and attitudinal building programmes especially to the normal school teachers.

Limitations of the Study

1. Awareness, attitude and competencies of special and normal school teachers have been assessed based on the self-ratings of the teachers.

2. The study is confined to Madurai and Chennai districts of Tamilnadu and Chittoor and Hyderabad districts of Andhra pradesh states only.
3. Rating scale is the only tool used to assess the awareness, attitude and the existing competencies of special and normal school teachers in dealing children with disabilities.
4. Required competencies of special and normal school teachers in dealing children with disabilities are assessed based on the questionnaire in the form of checklist.
5. The research tools used in the study are teacher made tests having reliability and validity.

Suggestions for Further Research

1. Similar studies can be conducted covering the states in north, west and eastern parts of India.
2. In this study awareness, attitude and competencies are assessed based on self-ratings. Studies can be made to assess these aspects, based on classroom observations and observation of behavioural activities of the teachers in practical situations.
3. The study has not made attempts to identify the problems of the teachers in performing their competencies. Such a study will give more insight to the policy planning and implementation.
4. Attempts should be made to assess the awareness attitude and competencies of parents of children with disabilities. Similarly attempts should be made to identify the awareness and attitude of community towards children with disabilities.
5. Scientific investigations are needed to identify the problems of parents and management strategies to deal their children with disabilities.
6. Indepth studies can be made to find out the reasons behind the better performance of teachers with less qualification in special education than their counterparts.

7. Indepth studies can be made about the factors associated with successful special schools and normal schools in the education of disabled children.
8. Studies can be made on personality factors of effective and ineffective teachers with special reference to the education of children with disabilities.
9. Scientific studies that integrate the different strategies that promote awareness, attitude and competencies in special and normal school teachers to deal children with disabilities can be done.
10. Studies can be made on innovative strategies/activities to promote better attitude in normal school children towards their disabled children.

Bibliography

Abel, G.L. (1967). Teacher Training Whence and Whiter Bound. *Blindness*, pp. 105-125.

Adams, Kimberly, S., Christerison, Sandra, L. (1998). Differences in Parent and Teacher Trust Levels: Implication for Creating Collaborative Family School Relationship. *Special Services in the Schools*, Vol. 14, No. 1-2, pp. 1-22.

Aker, G.F. (1962). The Identification of Criteria for Evaluation of Graduate Programmes in Adult Education. Unpublished Doctoral Thesis, University of Winsconsin, USA.

Akkammadevi, B. and Nagarani, V. (2003). Developing Improved Aids to English Tactual Discrimination Ability of Visually Impaired Children. *Journal of Research Highlights*, Vol. 13, No. 1.

Allen, R.E. (1990). *The Concise Oxford Dictionary of Current English*. Clarendon Press, Oxford.

Anita Jukla, (1998). Teacher Empowerment Successful Mainstreaming of Visually Impaired Children. *Journal of Disabilities and Impairments*, Vol. 12, No. 1, pp. 40-50.

Annakodi, R. and Kasiviswambal, P. (2003). Techniques of Teaching Self Help Skills to Intellectually Disabled Children. *Journal of Research Highlights*, Vol. 13, No. 1, pp. 42-46.

Barber, G.A. (1960). Teaching the Blind—the Resource Room Approach. *Education*, 80 (6), p. 334.

Bearn, Alison, Smith, Colin (1998). How Learning Support is Perceived by Mainstream Colleagues. *Support for Learning*, Vol. 13, No. 1, pp. 14-20.

Bessand-Byrd (1981). Competencies for Educating Culturally Different Exceptional Children. In J.N. Nazzaro (Ed.), *Cultural Different Exceptional Children in School.* Reston, VA : ERIC Clearing House in Handicapped and Gifted Children.

Bill, J., Reynolds, Joanne Martin-Reynolds and Frank D. Mark, (1982). Elementary Teachers' Towards Mainstreaming Educable Mentally Retarded Students. *Education and Training of the Mentally Retarded,* Vol. 17, No. 3.

Bindu Prasad, (1992). Problems of Hearing Impaired Children and Suggested Solutions. *ICCW News Bulletin,* Vol. XXXX, No. 2, pp. 11-17.

Blackhurst, A.E., Mc Loughlin, J.A. and Price, L.M. (1977). Issues in the Development of Programme to Prepare Teachers of Children with Learning and Behaviours Disorders. *Behaviour Disorders,* 2, 157-168.

Blanchett, Wanda, J. (1001). Importance of Teacher Transition Competencies Rated by Special Educators. *Teacher Education and Special Education,* Vol. 24, No. 1, p. 3-12.

Bourgeault, S.E. (1960). A Discussion of the Integrated or Resource Plan for Education of the Visually Handicapped. *The New Outlook for the Blind,* 54 (4), pp. 153-159.

Bowers, Tony, Dee, Lesley, West, Mel (1998). The Code in Action: Some School Perceptions of its User-friendliness. *Support for Learning,* Vol. 13, No. 3, pp. 99-104.

Brent, G. Richardson and Margery J. Shupe (2003). Importance of Teacher Self Awareness in Working with Students with Emotional and Behavioural Disorders. *Journal of Teaching Exceptional Children,* Vol. 36, No. 2, pp. 8-12.

Brownlee, Joanne and Carrington, Suzanne (2000). Opportunities for Authentic Experience and Reflection: A Teaching Programme Designed to Change Attitudes Towards Disability for Pre Service Teachers. *Support for Learning,* Vol. 15, No. 3, pp. 99-105.

Butera Gretchen., Klein, Holly, McMullen, Lynn, Wilson, Brenda (1998). A Statewise Study of FAPE and School Discipline Policies. *Journal of Special Education,* Vol. 32, No. 2, pp. 108-14.

Campbell, F.A. and Ramey, C.T. (1994). Effects of Early Intervention on Intellectual and Academic Achievement. *Child Development*, Vol. 65, No. 2, pp. 684-98.

Catherine Schwartz (1992). The Chamber Concise Dictionary. Anmol Publication Pvt. Ltd., New Delhi.

Cook, Bryan, G., Tankersley, Melody, Cook, Lysandra (2000). Teachers Attitudes Toward Their Included Students with Disabilities. *Exceptional Children*, Vol. 67, No. 1, pp. 115-35.

Cornoldi, Cesare, Terreni, Alessandra, Scruggs, Thomas E. (1998). Teachers Attitudes in Italy After Twenty Years of Inclusion. *Remedial and Special Education*, Vol. 19, No. 6, pp. 350-56.

Cowasji, (1983). A Study on the Effectiveness of the Orientation Programmes for Teachers Working in the Integrated Education for the Disabled Children. *Fourth Survey of Research in Education*, Vol. II, NCERT, New Delhi.

De Bettencourt, Laurie, U. (1999). General Educator's Attitude Toward Students with Mild Disabilities and Their Use of Instructional Strategies: Implications for Training. *Remedial and Special Education*, Vol. 20, No. 1, pp. 27-35.

Dharmaraj, P. (2000). Awareness of Primary School Teachers Towards Learning Disabilities in Mathematics at Primary Level. Unpublished M.Phil. Dissertation, Alagappa University, Karaikudi.

Divya Jindal, (1996). Development of Social Skills of Children with Visual Impairment for Rehabilitation. *Indian Journal of Disability and Rehabilitation*, Vol. 10, Issue : 1, pp. 39-46.

Drury, John (1994). A Survey to Investigate Teacher Awareness of Alternative Assessment of Students in Mathematics. Ph.D. Thesis, Dissertation Abstracts International, 55/06, p. 1497.

Enright, K.H. (1963). *Childhood and Society*. 2nd ed. New York, N.Y: W.W. Norton & Company.

Fortner, E.N. (1945). Oregon State Supervisory Program for the Visually Handicapped. *The New Outlook for the Blind*, 39, (1), p. 3.

Geetha, T. and Dash, A.K. (2003). Outcomes of Adopted Physical Education on the Physical Fitness of Hearing Impaired Children. *Journal of Research Highlights,* Vol. 13, No. 2.

Gilmore, F. (1956). One Public School's Experiment with Blind Children. *The New Outlook for the Blind,* 50 (2), pp. 45.

Gold Hammer, R., Rader, B.T. and Reuschelin, P. (1977). Mainstreaming: Teacher Competencies. East Lansing, MD : Michigan State University, College of Education.

Grant, I.L.C.(1966). The Challenge of Modern Day Education of Blind Children and Youth. *Braille Monitor,* pp. 35-40.

Guido, D.L. (1990). Educators' Attitude Towards the Inclusion of Severely Profoundly Disabled Students in Regular Classrooms. *Dissertation Abstract International,* Vol. 51, No. 10.

Hampson, P.J. and Duffy, C. (1984). Verbal and Spatial Interference Effect in Congenitally Blind and Sighted Subjects. *Canadian Journal of Psychology,* Vol. 38, pp. 411-420.

Harris, Mary B., Curran, Christina M. (1998). Knowledge, Attitudes and Concerns About Portfolio Assessment: An Explanatory Study. *Teacher Education and Special Education,* Vol. 21, No. 2, pp. 83-94.

Heimbuch, D. (1962). *The Blind Child in the Public School.* Ohio Schools, 40(2), pp. 12-13.

Heller, Kathryn, Wolff, Fredrick, Laura, D., Dykes, Mary Kay, Cohen, Elisabeth Tucker (1999). A National Perspective of Competencies for Teachers of Individuals with Physical and Health Disabilities. *Exceptional Children,* Vol. 65, No. 2, pp. 219-34.

Hoffman, Barbara, J. (1995). Teacher Awareness of Speech and Language Therapists' Roles and Services. *Dissertation Abstracts International,* 33/05, p. 1389.

Hoffman Marcia Ann Halle (1997). An Analysis of Inclusion in New Jersey School Districts (General Education Teachers). *Dissertation Abstracts International,* A 58/05, pp. 1658.

Hudson, P. J., Morsink, C.V., Branscum, G. and Boone, R. (1987). Competencies for Teacher of Students with Learning Disabilities. *Journal of Learning Disabilities*, 20, 232-236.

Irwin, R.B. (1961). *As I Saw it*. New York, N.Y.: American Foundation for the Blind, Inc.

Jairrels, Veda (1993). The Multicultural Competence of Special Education Teachers'. Ph.D. Thesis, The University of Alabama, Dissertation Abstracts International, Vol. 54, No. 9.

Jangira, N.K. (1992). Education of Children with Mental Retardation in Natural Settings. *ICCW New Bulletin*, Vol. XXXX, No. 1.

Jayaprabha, R. (2003). Metacognitive and Cognitive Strategies to Overcome Behaviour Difficulties in Children. Unpublished Ph.D. Thesis, Alagappa University, Karaikudi.

Jeevanantham, (2002). Competencies of Teachers. *HRD Times*, Vol. 4, No. 6, June.

Jena, S.P.K. (2000). Priorities of Training and Attitude of Special Educators Towards People with Mental Handicap. *Journal of Disabilities and Impairments*, Vol. 14, No. 2, pp. 87-92.

Johnson, Y. (1961). *A Blind Child Becomes a Member of Your Class*. New York, N.Y : American Foundation for the Blind, Inc.

Jonathan Crowther, (1996). *Oxford Adv ed Learner's Dictionary*. New Edition, Oxford University Press.

Knowlton, Marie, Berger, Karen (1999). Competencies required of braille teachers. *RE : View*, Vol. 30, No. 4, pp. 151-159.

Kool, V.K. (1981). Memory of Blind People. Project Report, Ministry of Social Welfare, Govt. of India, New Delhi.

Kool, V.K. and Pathak, K.C. (1985). Some Variables Related to Recall of Linear and Curvilinear Movements. *International Journal of Educational Science*, 2, 1-10.

Kronick, D. (1988). New Approaches to Learning Disabilities. *Journal of Learning Disabilities, II*. The Professional Press, Inc.

Kundu, R., Sanyal, N. and Kundu, M. (1985). Muscular Sensation of the Visually Impaired and Sighted Persons: A Comparative Study. *International Journal of Educational Science,* Vol. 2, pp. 77-80.

Kusuma Harinath, P. (2000). A Study of Certain Factors Related to Learning Disabilities in English Among School Students. Unpublished Ph.D. Thesis, Alagappa University, Karaikudi.

Laura and Ashman (1985). *Moral Issues in Mental Retardation*. London: Goom Helm.

Logo-Delello, Ellie (1998). Classroom Dynamics and the Development of Serious Emotional Disturbance. *Exceptional Children,* Vol. 164, No. 4, pp. 479-492.

Lombard, Richard C., Miller, Robert J., Hazelkorn, Michael, N. (1998). School to Work and Technical Preparation: Teacher Attitudes and Practices Regarding the Inclusion of Students with Disabilities. *Career Development for Exceptional Individuals,* Vol. 21, No. 2, pp. 161-72.

Luckner, John (1991). The Competencies Needed for Teaching Hearing-Impaired Students: A Comparison of Elementary and Secondary School Teacher Perceptions. *Dissertation Abstracts International, American Annals of the Day,* Vol. 136, No. 1, pp. 17-20.

Luckner, John, L., Carter, Kathy (2001). Essential Competencies for Teaching Students with Hearing Loss and Additional Disabilities. *American Annals of the Day,* Vol. 46, No. 1, pp. 7-15.

Madhuraj (1996). *Encyclopedic Dictionary of Psychology and Education,* Anmol Publications Pvt. Ltd., New Delhi.

Madry (1963). The Function and Training Needs of Adult Education Directors in Public School System. Columbus, Ohio, Ohio State University (ERIC Document Reproduction Service, No. ED 195587).

Mani, M.N.G. (1993). *Source Book for Teachers of Visually Disabled Children*. Bangkok: UNESCO.

Manju Pandey (1999). Identification and Intellectual Development of Learning Disabled Children. *Journal of Disabilities and Impairments,* Vol. 13, No. 1 & 2.

Mc Nicholas, Jim (2001). The Assessment of Pupils with Profound and Multiple Learning Difficulties. *British Journal of Special Education,* Vol. 27, No. 3, pp. 150-53.

Meltzer, Lynn, Roditi, Bethany and Houser, Robert, F. (1998). *Perceptions of Academic Strategies and Competence in Students with Learning Disabilities,* Vol. 31, No. 5, pp. 437-51.

Merry, R.V. (1933). *Problems in the Education of Visually Handicapped Children.* Cambridge Mass: Harward University Press.

Meyer, G.F. (1925). Public School Training for Children with Impaired Vision. *American Association of Workers for the Blind,* USA.

Mittal, S.R. (1985). A Comparative Study of Blind and Sighted Adolescents on Some Personality Factors. *International Journal of Educational Sciences,* Vol. 2, pp. 33-47.

Moore, William, G. (1991). Identification of Children with Learning Impairments: A Baseline Survey. *Dissertation Abstracts International, Votta Review,* Vol. 93, No. 4, pp. 184-96.

Nagaraja, Nipa Raval, Shivali Bhatt (1996). Speech Reading Abilities in Different Groups of Hearing Impaired (HI) Children. *Indian Journal of Disability and Rehabilitation,* Vol. 10, No. 2.

Nagomi Ruth, R. (2000). Awareness on Learning Disabilities Among Regular School Teachers. Unpublished M.Ed. Dissertation, Avinashilingam Deemed University, Coimbatore.

Norman Lewis, (1985). *The New Roget's Thesaurus in Dictionary,* Goyl Saab Publishers, Delhi.

Pandey, (1985). Affectional Deprivation, Ego Strength and Adjustment Pattern Among Visually Handicapped Children and their Rehabilitation. *Fourth Survey of Research in Education,* Vol. II, NCERT, New Delhi, 1983-88.

Paterson, J.O. (1913). Elements of Strengths and Weaknesses in Educating Blind Children in Schools for the Seeing and in Schools for the Blind. *The New Outlook for the Blind*, 7(4), pp. 117-122.

Peter Westwood (1998). *Commonsense Methods for Children with Special Needs Strategies for the Regular Classroom*. Routledge, London and New York.

Peter, M.B. Walker (1996). *Dictionary of Science and Technology*, Allied Chambers Limited, New Delhi.

Polloway, E.A. and Patton, J.R. (1993). *Strategies for Teaching Learners with Special Needs*. 5th Ed., New York: Merrill.

Poon-McBrayer and Kim Forg (1998). Integrating Students with Disabilities in Hong Kong: Classroom Teachers Attitudes and Beliefs. *Journal of International Special Needs Education*, Vol. 1, pp. 7-12.

Praisner C.L.. (2003). Attitudes of Elementary School Principals Towards the Inclusion of Students with Disabilities. *Exceptional Children*, Vol. 69, No. 2.

Prem Victor, (1992). Early Detection and Early Intervention of Hearing Handicapped Children. *ICCW, New Bulletin*, Vol. XXXX, No. 2.

Premavathy Vijayan and Akkamadevi, B. (2001). Assessment and Training of Functional Vision of the Low Vision Children at the Primary Level. *Journal of Research Highlights*, Vol. 11, No. 4.

Premila Balasundaram (1992). Dramatic Play for Mentally Handicapped Children. *ICCW News Bulletin*, Vol. XXXX, No. 1.

Priti Rana and Sheela Sangwan (2000). Assessment of Memory of Slow, Average Learner Children: A Comparative Study. *Journal of Disabilities and Impairments*, Vol. 14, No. 1.

Rajaguru, S. (1996). A Study on Divergent and Convergent Thinking of Visually Impaired Children in Secondary Schools. Unpublished Ph.D. Thesis, Alagappa University, Karaikudi.

Ramar, R. (1999). Effectiveness of Multimedia Based Modular Approach with Special Reference to Slow Learners. Unpublished Ph.D. Thesis, Alagappa University, Karaikudi.

Redden, M.R. and Blackhurst, A.E. (1978). Mainstreaming Competency Specifications for Elementary Teachers. *Exceptional Children*, 44, pp. 615-617.

Reddy N.Y. (1997). Personality Correlates of Coping Behaviour in the Physically Handicapped Students. *Journal of Disabilities and Impairments*, Vol. 11, No. 1, pp. 24-32.

Reddy G.L. (1997). *Role Performance of Adult Education Workers*. Discovery Publishing Hose, New Delhi.

Reddy, G.L. (2000). Role Performance for Special Education Teachers. *NCERT-ERIC Research Project Report*. Department of Education, Alagappa University, Karaikudi.

Reddy, G L. (2003). Technology for Special Education. *HRD Times*, Vol. 5, No. 12.

Reddy, G.L. and Kanchanamala, (2002). Effectiveness of Multimedia Based Modular Approach in Learning Botany by the Slow Learners. *Journal of Research Highlights*, Vol. 12, No. 3.

Reddy, G.L. and Kusuma, A. (1995). Mental Retardation in Children—Causes and prevention. *Balak*-The Quarterly Journal of the Indian Association for Pre School Education, Second Quarter.

Reddy, G.L. and Kusuma, A. (2000). *Role Performance of Continuing Education Workers*. Discovery Publishing House, New Delhi.

Reddy, G.L. and Kusuma, A. (2001). Visual Impairments: Educational Implications. *HRD Times*, Vol. 3, No. 4.

Reddy, G.L. and Rajaguru, S. (1995). An Investigation of the Self Concept of Blind and Visually Impaired Children in Tamilnadu. *Indian Journal of Disabilities and Rehabilitation*, Vol. 8(2) & Vol. 9 (1&2).

Reddy, G.L. and Rajaguru, S. (1998). Divergent Thinking, Convergent Thinking and Mental Ability of Congenital Blind Children in Secondary Schools. *Journal of Disabilities and Impairment*, Vol. 12, No. 1.

Reddy, G.L. and Ramar, R. (1994). Effectiveness of Multimedia Based Modular Approach in Teaching Social Science to Low Achievers. *Journal of Media and Technology for Human Resource Development*, Vol. 6, No. 3, pp. 309-316.

Reddy, G.L. and Ramar, R. (1995). Effectiveness of Multimedia Based Modular Approach in Teaching Science to Low Achievers. *Journal of Research in Educational Media*, Vol. 2, No. 2, pp. 41-52.

Reddy, G.L. and Ramar, R. (1995a). Effectiveness of Multimedia Based Modular Approach in Teaching Mathematics to Low Achievers. *Journal of Higher Education*, Vol. 18, No. 2, pp. 283-287.

Reddy, G.L. and Ramar, R. (1997). Effectiveness of Multimedia Based Modular Approach in Teaching English to Slow Learners. *Journal of Disabilities and Impairments*, Vol. 11, No. 1, pp. 33-44.

Reddy, G.L. and Ramar, R. (1998). Effects of Video Instruction on the Achievement of Slow Learners in Mathematics. *Journal of Educational Technology*, Vol. 10, No. 3 & 4, pp. 43-50.

Reddy, G.L. and Ramar, R. (1999). Effectiveness of Computer Assisted Instruction in Teaching Science to Slow Learners. *Journal of Educational Technology*, Vol. 12, No. 1, pp. 37-44.

Reddy, G.L. and Shyamala, V. (2003). Thinking and Constructivism: Approaches in Classroom. *University News*, Vol. 41, No. 17.

Reddy, G.L. and Shyamala, V. (2004). Thinking Errors and Antisocial Behaviour. *Journal of Research and Reflections in Education*, Vol. 2, No. 1.

Reddy, G.L. and Sivakami, R. (1999). The Learning Curve in Dyslexia. *HRD Times*, Vol. 1, No. 12.

Reddy, G.L. and Sujathamalini, J. (2000). Educational Issues Related to Pupils with Visual Disabilities. *Journal of Disabilities and Impairments*, Vol. 14, No. 2.

Reddy and Sujathamalini, J. (2003). Teacher Preparation Efficiency Parameters for Normal School Teachers to Handle Children with Special Needs. *Journal of Research and Reflections on Education*, Vol. 1, No. 1.

Reddy, G.L. and Sujathamalini, J. (2003). Strategies for Development of Social Competence Among Disabled Pupil. *Journal of Research and Reflections on Education,* Vol. 1, No. 4.

Reddy, G.L. and Sujathamalini, J. (2003). Instructional Paradigms to Enhance Learning in Students with Learning Disabilities. *Journal of International Educator,* Vol. 15: 1.

Reddy, G.L. and Sujathamalini, J (2004). Rehabilitation Psychology with Special Reference to Pupil with Mental Deficiencies. *EDU Tracks,* Vol. 3, No. 5.

Reddy, G.L., Kusuma, A. and Jayaprabha, R. (1998). Assistive Technology to Overcome Learning Difficulties in Children. *Journal of Disabilities and Impairments,* Vol. 13, No. 1.

Reddy, G.L., Kusuma, A. and Jayaprabha, R. (1999). Developmental Disabilities in Children. *Journal of Indian Education,* Vol. XXV, No. 1.

Reddy, G.L., Kusuma, A. and Rajaguru, S. (2001). Relative Effectiveness of Tangible Materials (Braille) and Talking Books (Audio Cassettes) in Learning Social Science Concepts by the Visually Impaired Children in Secondary Schools. *Journal of Disabilities and Impairments,* Vol. 15, No. 1 and 2.

Reddy, G.L., Ramar, R. and Kusuma, A. (2000). *Education of Children with Special Needs.* Discovery Publishing House, New Delhi.

Reddy, G.L., Ramar, R. and Kusuma, A. (2000). Impact of Modular Approach on the Achievement of Slow Learners in Social Science. *Journal of Indian Education,* Vol. XXVI, No. 1, pp. 61-69.

Reddy, G.L., Ramar, R. and Kusuma, A. (2004). *Hearing Impairment: An Educational Considerations.* Discovery Publishing House, New Delhi.

Reddy, G.L., Sujathamalini, J. and Kusuma, A. (2004a). *Mental retardation: Education and Rehabilitation Services.* Discovery Publishing House, New Delhi.

Reiter and Shunit., Schanin., Michel., Tirosh, Emanuel (1998). Isreli Elementary School Students and Teachers Attitudes Towards Mainstreaming Children with Disabilities. *Special Services in the Schools,* Vol. 13, No. 1 & 2, pp. 33-46.

Rita, M. (1994). Attitudes of Case Managers Toward the Employability of Persons with Severe Disabilities. *Dissertation Abstracts International*, Vol. 55, No. 4.

Root, F. (1960). The Elementary School Meets the Blind Child. In V.J. Glennon (Ed.), *Frontiers of Elementary Education.* VI. Syracuse, N.Y.: Syracuse University Press.

Roush and Jackson (1991). Family-Centred Early Intervention. *The Perceptions of Professional. Dissertation Abstracts International, American Annals of the Deaf.* Vol. 136, No. 4, pp. 360-66.

Sangeetha, (1996). A Comparative Study of Learning Attitude of the Congenitally and Adventitiously Visually Impaired Pupils. *Journal of Disabilities and Impairments,* Vol. 10, No. 2, pp. 65-72.

Santhakumari (2003). Effectiveness of Metacognitive Strategies to Overcome Language Learning Difficulties Among Higher Secondary Students. Unpublished Ph.D. Thesis, Alagappa University, Karaikudi.

Sarojini, R. (2000). Awareness of Primary School Teachers Towards Learning Disabilities in English at Primary Stage. Unpublished M.Phil. Dissertation, Alagappa University, Karaikudi.

Sass-Lehrer and Marilyn (1986). Competencies for Effective Teaching of Hearing Impaired Students. *Exceptional Children,* Vol. 53. No. 3, pp. 230-34.

Sass-Lehrer and Marilyn (1986a). Competencies Critical to Teachers of Hearing Impaired Students in Two Settings: Supervisor's Views. *Dissertation Abstracts International, American Annals of the Deaf,* Vol. 131, No. 1, pp. 9-12.

Schumn, J.S and Vaghun, S. (1992). Planning for Mainstreamed Special Education Students: Perceptions of General Classroom Teachers. *Exceptionality,* 3, pp. 81-98.

Selvakani, S. (2000). Creating Awareness on Integrated Education of the Disabled Children to the Regular Teacher. Unpublished M.Ed. Dissertation, Avinashilingam Deemed University, Coimbatore.

Sharma, Premlatha, Pandey, Savitha (1992). An Experimental Study to Assess the Effectiveness of Adopted Instructional Material in Science on Hearing Impaired from IED and Special Schools. *Fifth Survey of Educational Research,* Vol. II, NCERT, New Delhi.

Sheela Sangwan, Nitasha and Krishna Duhan (2002). A Comparative Study of Perceptual and Conceptual Abilities of 4-6 Year Old Slow and Average Learner Children. *Journal of Disabilities and Impairments,* Vol. 16, No. 1.

Shyamala, V. (2004). Effectiveness of Certain Strategies in Overcoming Antisocial Behaviour Among High School Students. Unpublished Ph.D. Thesis, Alagappa University, Karaikudi.

Sibnath Deb, Chetna Duggal and Abhisek Sarkar (2002). Problems Encouraged by Sightless Children in Their Daily School Life and in the Educational Institution. *Journal of Disabilities and Impairments,* Vol. 16, No. 2, pp. 93-104.

Sivakami, (2000). Effectiveness of Certain Instructional Strategies to Overcome Learning Disabilities in English at Primary Stage. Unpublished Ph.D. Thesis, Alagappa University, Karaikudi.

Spungin, (1977). Competency Based Curriculum for Teachers of Visually Handicapped: A National Study. *American Publication for the Blind Inc.,* New York.

Sujatha Satapathy and Singhal (2002). Academic Performance of Visually Impaired and Hearing Impaired. *Journal of Disabilities and Impairments,* Vol. 16, No. 1, pp. 19-28.

Sujathamalini, J. (1997). Developing Daily Living Skills Among Intellectually Disabled. Unpublished M.Ed. Dissertation, Avinashilingam Deemed University, Coimbatore.

Sujathamalini, J. (2002). Competencies Required for Primary School Teachers to Handle Learning Difficulties in Children. Unpublished Ph.D. Thesis, Alagappa University, Karaikudi.

Susan Stainback and William Stainback (1982). Influencing the Attitudes of Regular Class Teachers About the Education of Severely Retarded Students. *Education and Training of the Mentally Retarded,* Vol. 17, No. 2.

Swartz, Diana Denise (1995). Teachers' Awareness of and Willingness to Report Suspected Child Abuse. Ph.D. Indiana University, *Dissertation Abstracts International*, 56/07, p. 2618.

Taplin, Margaret and White, Marian (1998). Parent's and Teacher's Perception of Gifted Provision. *Australian Journal of Gifted Education*, Vol. 7, No. 1, pp. 42-45.

The Hutchinson Encyclopedic Dictionary (1994). Hetecon Publishing Ltd., Oxford University Press.

MHRD, Government of India (1986). The National Policy on Education, MHRD, Government of India, New Delhi.

Tobin (1972). Conservation of Substance in the Blind and Partially Sighted. *British Journal of Educational Psychology*, Vol. 42, pp. 192-197.

Treder, David, W., Morse, William C., Ferron, John, M. (2000). The Relationship Between Teacher Effectiveness and Teacher Attitudes Toward Issues Related to Inclusion. *Teacher Education and Special Education*, Vol. 23, No. 3, pp. 202-10.

Trzcinka and Sheila Marie (1996). Curriculum and Teachers' Attitudes: The Impact of the Change Process in Special Education. *Dissertation Abstracts International*, 57/06, p. 2314.

Vasuki, N. and Mahima, B. (2001). Behaviour Problems in Intellectually Disabled Children. *Journal of Research Highlights*, Vol. 11, No. 2.

Venkatesan, S. and Hanumantha Rao, P. (1996). Significance of Some Birth Factors in Mental Retardation. *Journal of Disabilities and Impairments*, Vol. 10, No. 2, pp. 53-63.

Veri (1968). The Design of a Doctoral Programme in Adult Education Based on the Expressed Needs of Professional Practitioners. Unpublished Doctoral Dissertation, University of Nebraska, USA.

Vinitakrishna, (1992). Instructional Strategies for Teaching the Mentally Handicapped. *ICCW News Bulletin*, Vol. XXXX, No. 1.

Wallace, Teri, Shin, Jongho, Bartholomay, Tom, Stahl, Barrbara, J. (2001). Knowledge and Skills for Teachers Supervising the Work of Professional. *Exceptional Children*, Vol. 67., No. 4, pp. 520-33.

Wasik, B.A. and Kaeweit, N.L. (1994). Off to a Good Start: Effects of Birth to Three Interventions on Early School Success. In R.E. Slavn, N.L. Karweit and B.A. Wasik (Eds.), *Preventing Early School Failure*, Boston: Allyn and Bacon.

Westwood, P. and Graham, L. (2003). Inclusion of Students with Special Needs: Benefits and Obstacle Perceived by Teachers in New South Australia. *Australian Journal of Learning Disability*, Vol. 8(1), pp. 3-15.

White, T.J. (1950). Similarity of Training Interest Among Adult Education Leaders. Unpublished Doctoral Dissertation, University of Chicago.

Index

S

❑❑❑